Gothic Film

Edinburgh Companions to the Gothic

Series Editors
Andrew Smith, University of Sheffield
William Hughes, Bath Spa University

This series provides a comprehensive overview of the Gothic from the eighteenth century to the present day. Each volume takes either a period, place or theme and explores their diverse attributes, contexts and texts via completely original essays. The volumes provide an authoritative critical tool for both scholars and students of the Gothic.

Volumes in the series are edited by leading scholars in their field and make a cutting-edge contribution to the field of Gothic studies.

Each volume:
- Presents an innovative and critically challenging exploration of the historical, thematic and theoretical understandings of the Gothic from the eighteenth century to the present day
- Provides a critical forum in which ideas about Gothic history and established Gothic themes are challenged
- Supports the teaching of the Gothic at an advanced undergraduate level and at masters level
- Helps readers to rethink ideas concerning periodisation and to question the critical approaches which have been taken to the Gothic

Published Titles
The Victorian Gothic: An Edinburgh Companion
  Andrew Smith and William Hughes
Romantic Gothic: An Edinburgh Companion
  Angela Wright and Dale Townshend
American Gothic Culture: An Edinburgh Companion
  Joel Faflak and Jason Haslam
Women and the Gothic: An Edinburgh Companion
  Avril Horner and Sue Zlosnik
Scottish Gothic: An Edinburgh Companion
  Carol Margaret Davison and Monica Germanà
The Gothic and Theory: An Edinburgh Companion
  Jerrold E. Hogle and Robert Miles
Twenty-First-Century Gothic: An Edinburgh Companion
  Maisha Wester and Xavier Aldana Reyes
Gothic Film: An Edinburgh Companion
  Richard J. Hand and Jay McRoy

Visit the Edinburgh Companions to the Gothic website at:
www.edinburghuniversitypress.com/series/EDCG

Gothic Film

An Edinburgh Companion

Edited by
Richard J. Hand and
Jay McRoy

EDINBURGH
University Press

Edinburgh University Press is one of the leading university presses in the UK. We publish academic books and journals in our selected subject areas across the humanities and social sciences, combining cutting-edge scholarship with high editorial and production values to produce academic works of lasting importance. For more information visit our website: edinburghuniversitypress.com

Edinburgh University Press Ltd
The Tun – Holyrood Road
12(2f) Jackson's Entry
Edinburgh EH8 8PJ

First published in hardback by Edinburgh University Press 2020

Typeset in 10.5/13 Sabon by
Servis Filmsetting Ltd, Stockport, Cheshire
and printed and bound by CPI Group (UK) Ltd,
Croydon, CR0 4YY

A CIP record for this book is available from the British Library

ISBN 978 1 4744 4804 8 (hardback)
ISBN 978 1 4744 4807 9 (paperback)
ISBN 978 1 4744 4805 5 (webready PDF)
ISBN 978 1 4744 4806 2 (epub)

Contents

Acknowledgements

Richard J. Hand would like to thank his School colleagues at the University of East Anglia.

He would also like to thank his family: Sadiyah, Shara, Dan and Jim for their patience and support.

Jay McRoy would like to thank his family, friends and colleagues for their generous moral and intellectual support. In particular, he would like to thank the late Colleen McRoy for encouraging her eldest son's cinephilia and for kindly suffering his more esoteric preoccupations.

Figures

Introduction
Richard J. Hand and Jay McRoy

In *Gothic: Four Hundred Years of Excess, Horror, Evil and Ruin* (2000), his expansive introduction to the Gothic as a perpetually shifting aesthetic and socio-historical phenomenon, Richard Davenport-Hines notes that it is often difficult to ascertain precisely what people mean when they describe a text as informed by 'Gothic' sensibilities. Much of this confusion stems from the myriad ways that popular and academic discourses have deployed the term throughout the centuries following the destruction and pillaging of Rome by a combination of Scandinavian and Eastern European warriors (aka the Goths). From its earliest associations with destruction, violence, darkness and despair (connotations that persist to this day), 'Gothic' has been a very flexible term imbued with multiple connotations. While for many the term Gothic implies melancholic decay and decadence, for others it connotes a subcultural sartorial style grounded in dark colours (black, red), theatrical accents (French cuffs, lace trimming) and pallid complexions enhanced by dark eyeliner and lipstick.

More to the purposes of this volume, the term 'Gothic' is also frequently used to describe a particularly stylised approach to depicting location, desire and action in literature and film. For many contemporary film viewers, the term evokes images of derelict castles atop craggy hills or sprawling, labyrinthine ancestral mansions in various stages of ruin or disrepair. This association can, of course, be traced back to the influence of prominent eighteenth- and nineteenth-century Gothic novels like Horace Walpole's *The Castle of Otranto* (1764), Mary Shelley's *Frankenstein; or, The Modern Prometheus* (1818) and Bram Stoker's *Dracula* (1897); each of these works features action set in similarly imposing locales. Indeed, the connection between the Gothic and architectural design is profound. In the sixteenth century, 'Gothic' was a pejorative descriptor for an architectural style that, emerging in Northern Europe between the twelfth and sixteenth centuries (or from the late Middle Ages to the early modern period), posed a radical – and, for some Renaissance critics, 'barbaric' – response to classical Greco-Roman design. Gothic architecture integrates Romanesque elements into its propensity towards verticality, while its inclusion of copious and, in the case of gargoyles, grotesque ornamentations departs more radically from classical conceits. The most conspicuous 'Gothic' edifices, namely churches and cathedrals, integrated architectural elements like ribbed vaults, multiple arches, and flying buttresses to support impressive and ornately designed walls replete with stained glass windows and topped by towering spires. In the eighteenth and early nineteenth centuries, as a renewed interest in Gothic aesthetics gripped the popular imagination, it is from these towering structures that novelists drew inspiration for the decaying citadels that housed their ruthless patriarchs, incestuous families and victimised governesses.

Nature in Gothic novels and film is likewise extreme. Mountains are treacherously jagged at their cloud-bedecked peaks. Arboreal realms are dark, riotous and rarely hospitable. Characters that venture into such discordant vistas enter environments where the natural and the supernatural seemingly commingle, and where human intervention in the form of Enlightenment methodologies like science or reason is no guarantee of survival. In this sense, wild Gothic nature threatens notions of cultural and corporeal integrity, displacing humanity from its perceived perch at the top of the food chain and exposing us for the frail, clever and frequently hubristic animals we are. As Victor Frankenstein, the eponymous hero of Mary Shelley's iconic novel, pursues his pitiful creation across the merciless frozen wastes, there is a fatalistic tenor to the chase. In the face of nature's sublime and indifferent power, Victor Frankenstein's maniacal pursuit could have only ended tragically.

Verbal exchanges and paradigm-shifting revelations in Gothic narratives likewise tend towards extremity. In this way the Gothic is never far from melodrama and dialogues are frequently pitched for maximum emotional intensity. Conflicts assume near mythic proportions and social 'order' is regularly threatened, if not deliberately overturned. In this sense the Gothic is transformational and revolutionary, and Gothic narratives frequently capitalise upon their audience's simultaneous fear of, and attraction to, social change and rebellion. This association, which Eve Kosofsky Sedgwick describes as 'an aesthetic of pleasurable fear' (11), is especially compelling when one considers the durability of one of Gothic art's most popular figures: the monster. As Judith Halberstam reminds us in *Skin Shows: Gothic Horror and the Technology of Monsters* (1995), monsters are heterogeneous figures capable of not only representing 'any horrible trait that the reader feeds into the narrative' (21), but also, because of their radical irreducibility, of allowing for new ways of imagining 'social resistance' (23).

This commingling of threat and promise within the body of the monster is, of course, merely one facet of a constellation of aesthetic and narrative elements that many have come to associate with the Gothic. Nevertheless, given their status as hybrid entities, they are perhaps the ideal analogues for the Gothic's rich aesthetic and narratological approach to storytelling. At the very least, the hybridity that many Gothic monsters possess mirrors the complex of potential meanings and connotations that lead critics like Davenport-Hines to remark upon the Gothic's evasiveness as a literary and cinematic 'genre' (7). Similar to film noir, the 'Gothic' in Gothic film does not merely designate a *kind* of cinematic entertainment, like 'Western', 'Horror' or 'Science Fiction'. The Gothic, in other words, is not a genre per se, although an argument can be made for 'Gothic' as a very loose subgenre of horror. Rather, 'Gothic' is a *style*. It is a way of arranging literary and cinematic elements to create a particular affect. Whether an author or film-maker sets their tale's action in candle-lit mansions or populates their dark worlds with brooding or 'fallen' anti-heroic characters, Gothic motifs in cinema conjure a variety of variably foreboding tonalities. As such, it is understandably temping to reduce the Gothic to a classificatory function and, consequently, posit it as something resembling a genre. Such a perspective, however, should never neglect the extent to which the Gothic as aesthetic approach or style regularly traverses multiple established film genres.

Gothic Film explores the Gothic's resilience as a stylistic and aesthetic strategy that has permeated cinema from pioneering forays like Georges Méliès's *The Haunted Castle* (1896) and Edison Studio's *Frankenstein* (1910) to more technically and socially complex iterations like Park Chan-wook's *Stoker* (2013) and Jordan Peele's *Get Out* (2017). The articles that comprise this volume, each written by a prominent scholar in the field of Gothic and Film Studies, examine the ways that film-makers throughout history and across cultures have mobilised (and continue to mobilise) Gothic conceits in seemingly disparate and discrete genres, like 'Science Fiction' and 'Westerns', and in conjunction with other prominent film styles like film noir and aesthetic frameworks like surrealism. In the process, *Gothic Film* not only contributes exciting new readings of canonical works of Gothic cinema, including key German Expressionist texts and 1930s Universal horror films, but also explores important intersections between the Gothic and established film traditions, from the Italian *giallo* to the horror cinemas of South East Asia.

We have structured this volume into three sections: 'Gothic Film

History', 'Gothic Film Adaptations' and 'Gothic Film Traditions'. The chapters in the first section take a broadly historiographical approach from early cinema to the present day. The second section looks at examples of Gothic Film that feature aspects of adaptation, appropriation or parody. The third section looks at Gothic film in national contexts as well as identifying subgenres and hybridising techniques. Opening 'Gothic Film History', James L. Neibaur's 'Gothic Cinema during the Silent Era' is an exploration of the earliest articulations of the Gothic on screen, investigating in depth the work of George Méliès as well as the key achievements of German Expressionism and the Universal films of Lon Chaney. But Neibaur extends his remit further with accounts of the Charlie Chaplin comedy *Cruel Love* (1914) and Buster Keaton's *The Haunted House* (1921). Through this detailed account, Neibaur argues that it is in silent cinema that we find Gothic visuals presented with the greatest depth and care. It is thus by turning to early cinema that we can better understand the longer development of Gothic cinema, its assimilation of various genres and the inauguration of concepts and motifs that eventually become standard expectations in the evolution of 'Gothic cinema'.

In '"So why shouldn't I write of monsters?": Defining Monstrosity in Universal's Horror Films', Andy W. Smith explores the Universal Studios series of horror films from the 1930s and 1940s. Carefully exploring the source texts of *Dracula* and *Frankenstein*, Smith explores the construction and significance of the Universal film adaptations, finding in these monsters the very apex of Horror's Golden Age, iconic figures who abide and haunt Gothic cinema just as their textual ancestors haunt Gothic literature. In 'Film Noir and the Gothic', Jay McRoy analyses film noir in the context of Gothic cinema. A hybrid style – informed by German Expressionism, crime fiction and existentialism – film noir's cynicism and paranoia regarding changes in a variety of social and political contexts is emphatically a 'cultural barometer'. Through an exploration of film noir's aesthetic hybridity and its shifting cultural terrain, McRoy examines 'traditional' and contemporary iterations of Gothic film noir, namely Alfred Hitchcock's *Shadow of a Doubt* (1943) and Park Chan-wook's *Stoker* (2013).

In 'Transitional Gothic: Hammer's Gothic Revival and New Horror', Adam Charles Hart looks at the significance of Hammer Films, demonstrating how *Curse of Frankenstein* (1957) instigated a hugely influential Gothic revival in global cinema that remains core to horror cinema until the New Horror revolution in the late 1960s with films such as *Rosemary's Baby* (1968) and *Night of the Living Dead* (1968). For Hart, *Curse of Frankenstein* is a transitional film, bridging older traditions of the Gothic while being transformational, not least in its redefinition of monstrosity as internal and psychological, especially in the characterisation of a sadistic Victor Frankenstein. We close the 'Gothic Film History' section with 'Gothic Cinema from the 1970s to Now' in which Xavier Aldana Reyes traces the post-Hammer mainstreaming of horror in the late twentieth and early twentieth-first centuries, surveying subgenres such as exorcism films, slasher films, found footage horror, body horror and torture porn. Through these popular sub-genres of Gothic horror, Aldana Reyes demonstrates how excess and transgression has become normalised in the mainstream horror film.

In the second section of the volume, our authors explore 'Gothic Film Adaptations'. In 'Danny's Endless Tricycle Ride: The Gothic and Adaptation', Richard J. Hand examines a traditional process of perennial significance throughout the history of Gothic cinema: adaptation. From family-friendly horror movies to Lenny Abrahamson's 2018 screen version of Sarah Waters's neo-Gothic novel *The Little Stranger* (2009), adaptation has infused the full spectrum of Gothic cinema. In the case of Stanley Kubrick's 1980 film version of Stephen King's *The Shining* (1977), we find a film that has its own exceptional legacy as an adapted text. In *'Jekyll and Hyde* and Scopophilia', Martin Danahay uses the paradigmatic feminist lens of Laura Mulvey's scopophilia to explore the major screen adaptations of Stevenson's novel in the first half of the twentieth century and their performative progenitor: the Richard Mansfield stage version in the 1880s. Danahay reveals how these film versions implicitly raise subversive questions about masculinity and sexual violence and yet are ultimately conservative works, framed by patriarchy and heterosexuality. Ever since the Gothic literary form emerged there have been parodies of it. In 'Gothic Parodies on Film and Personal Transformation', Laurence Raw looks at Gothic film parodies by Mel Brooks, Gene Wilder and others through to the television series *Penny Dreadful* (2014–16). As well as exploring these screen versions' use of Gothic codes, conventions, intertextuality and nostalgia, Raw also explores the subgenre's themes regarding the therapeutic process of transformation.

In 'The Gothic Sensorium: Affect in Jan Švankmajer's Poe Films', Anna Powell uses Gilles Deleuze's work on film as a theoretical frame to analyse the Czech surrealist animator's *The Fall of the House of Usher* (1980) and *The Pendulum, the Pit and Hope* (1983). As Powell argues, Švankmajer's films reflect experiments in Tactilism (touch-based art) and were created within a culture of dissidence. In this regard, Švankmajer's imagination works not just to visualise the sense of touch but to bring out Gothic tropes and contradictions and the mobilisation of anti-totalitarian desire. We conclude 'Gothic Film Adaptations' with Andrew Hock Soon Ng's 'Dracula in Asian Cinema: Transnational Appropriation of a Cultural Symbol'. In this chapter, Ng examines the vampire in Asian cinema, but rather than looking at the many indigenous vampires of Asian cultures, he focuses on the appropriation of a Western icon inaugurated by Bram Stoker's creation of Dracula. Rather than being merely for commercial reasons, Dracula can be seen to fulfil a powerful symbolic and allegorical role in Asian horror films.

We open the third and final section of this volume – 'Gothic Film Traditions' – with Mikel J. Koven's 'The Italian Gothic Film'. Koven presents an exploration of the Italian Gothic horror movies produced in the early 1960s by Mario Bava and other directors, placing his analysis of this distinctive and influential genre into a nuanced context of the larger, cross-disciplinary, debates about the Gothic. In 'Gothic Science Fiction', Geraint D'Arcy gives an account of the complex relationship between the Gothic and Science Fiction in cinema (a somewhat ironic tension given the rich heritage of hybridising the Gothic and Science Fiction in literary fiction). Subsequently, D'Arcy examines and defines the presence of visual Gothic conceits in Ridley Scott's *Alien* (1979) and the appearance of Gothic themes in the visuals and narratives of Duncan Jones's *Moon* (2009) and Alex Garland's *Ex Machina* (2015).

In 'American Gothic Westerns: Tales of Racial Slavery and Genocide', Josef Benson argues that the American Western genre is particularly well suited for American Gothic narratives since the genre itself emanated from the legacy of racial slavery and the genocide of indigenous peoples. Benson finds this correlation reflected in the genre's tropes of aestheticised violence and dehumanisation and explores the progression of these elements in Western films such as Sam Peckinpah's *The Wild Bunch* (1969), Clint Eastwood's *High Plains Drifter* (1973), Jim Jarmusch's *Dead Man* (1995), *Django Unchained* (Tarantino, 2012) and others. Further exploring the context of American Gothic is Elaine Roth's 'This Is America: Race, Gender and the Gothic in *Get Out* (2017)'. Roth explores Jordan Peele's phenomenally successful *Get Out*, the most popularly acclaimed horror film since *The Exorcist* (1973). The author-director Peele describes the film as a 'social thriller' in the tradition of *Night of the Living Dead* (1968) and Roth reveals how richly *Get Out* evokes the themes and conventions of the Gothic tradition while being a thrilling revitalisation of the genre on screen.

We conclude 'Gothic Film Traditions' – and the volume as a whole – with Thomas Joseph Watson's '"Part of my soul did die when making this film": Gothic Corporeality, Extreme Cinema and Hardcore Horror in the Twenty-First Century'. In this chapter, Watson looks at films that have tested the boundaries between 'extreme pornography' and 'torture porn' with particular attention given to Adam Rehmeier's *The Bunny Game* (2011). For Watson, this notorious film's aspects of realism and authenticity associated with extreme violence hinge on more than what is represented on the screen. Although still banned by the British Board of Film Classification, *The Bunny Game* should perhaps be regarded as a film that 're-politicises' porn, horror and the nature of the Gothic.

We hope that *Gothic Film: An Edinburgh Companion* makes a timely and appropriate intervention in the fields of Gothic Studies and Film Studies. The essays in this volume reveal how the Gothic's relationship with the screen has produced works that can be conservative or radical, nostalgic or revolutionary, family-friendly or outlawed. It can span multiple genres, textual forms and national cultures, examining contemporary preoccupations as much as historical motifs. As the reader will see, Gothic Film has a rich heritage and a dynamic future.

References

Davenport-Hines, R. 2000. *Gothic: Four Hundred Years of Excess, Horror, Evil and Ruin*. New York: North Point Press.

Halberstam, J. 1995. *Skin Shows: Gothic Horror and the Technology of Monsters*. Durham, NC: Duke University Press.

Sedgwick, E. K. 1986. *The Coherence of Gothic Conventions*. New York: Methuen.

Part I

Gothic Film History

Chapter 1

Gothic Cinema during the Silent Era
James L. Neibaur

The moving picture was initially a novelty, really no more than a picture that moved. Perhaps the best way to appreciate the nineteenth-century's reaction to the very first moving pictures is to imagine being handed an old snapshot and seeing the images actually show movement. Moving pictures, running only a few minutes and featuring such activities as a man riding a horse, a train pulling into its station or a girl climbing a tree were exciting novelties that enthralled those that gathered in empty store fronts to see them projected.

Gothic cinema began during cinema's infancy, when French magician George Méliès sought to use the new medium's technology to expand the sort of illusions he'd performed on stage. Méliès investigated the possibilities allowed by multiple exposures, stop-action photography, hand-painted colour and using dissolves as transitions. While his enormous filmography of nearly 500 subjects ranged from the straight filming of actual events to movies that attempted to follow a narrative structure, his use of Gothic imagery is central to expanding the language of cinema.

Méliès is best known for his 1902 short *Le Voyage dans la lune* (*A Trip to the Moon*), where cinema moves past single-shot films and extends to presenting special visual effects to enhance the idea of space travel. Perhaps best known by the iconic image of the moon, with a face, being hit in the eye by a landing spacecraft, *Le Voyage dans la lune* combines its effects with set design, live action and animation, some of these ideas being used near to their first time.

While *Le Voyage dans la lune* is Méliès's best-known film, he had already produced several interesting subjects that explored the possibilities cinema had to offer. Even as far back as *Une Nuit terrible* (1896), Méliès presents the macabre scene of a sleeping man being attacked by a large bedbug which he kills with a broom. The effect is simply a large bug made of pasteboard and moved with a wire, but it is the portent for the film-maker's further investigations as to what ideas he could convey with film. *Une Nuit terrible* is certainly not that last time a movie featured giant insects attacking unsuspecting citizens, but it is very likely the first.

Later that year, Méliès made *Escamotage d'une dame chez Robert-Houdin* in which he performs the role of a magician, along with his assistant Jehanne d'Alcy. His assistant sits in a chair, the magician puts a blanket over her, and when he lifts the blanket she has gone. He performs this same process again and produces a skeleton. Many have concluded that Méliès simply stopped the camera to create this effect, but he actually employed something known as a substitution splice, the first special effect Méliès perfected and the most important in his body of work (Williams, 1992: 36). The effect was the result of Méliès's carefully matching frames while editing the film, creating a seamless cut from two separately staged shots (Lim, 2009: 279–80). Simple by current standards, it was an amazing leap in cinematic development as early as the nineteenth century.

Méliès films are most impressive for their visual imagery. The 1903 subject *Illusions funambulesques* is filled with superimposed images, moving objects, people disappearing and then reappearing as another person and other magical tricks (Neibaur, 2008: 66–8). There is a great deal of artistry evident in the 1908 subject, *La Cuisine de l'ogre (The Bogie Man's Cave)*, which features an impressively decorated set containing skeleton bones and shows what a 'bogie man' does in his leisure time at home.

While the Méliès films have a reasonably good survival rate, it is unnerving that his film, *Cléopâtre*, is among those that do not. Probably the first horror film, *Cléopâtre* depicts a man removing the mummified corpse of Cleopatra from its grave, chopping it up, and burning it until the smoke conjures up a living woman. Once again, Méliès himself plays the male role and his assistant d'Alcy plays the woman.

From 1896 to 1913, George Méliès made films with various running times, from one minute to about forty minutes. And while his filmography numbers in the hundreds and covers every conceivable genre, his work as cinema's earliest illusionist is his most significant contribution. Méliès understood cinema's visual process. He comprehended how using darkness to frame carefully lit images could convey an idea, an attitude that was unsettling and scary. His use of these ideas helped to inspire other film-makers who further explored film's ability to frighten its audience, including some of the earliest American cinematic pioneers.

Edwin Thanhouser founded the Thanhouser Film Corporation, one of the first movie studios, in 1909. Lucius Henderson joined the company as a director in 1910, and during his seven-year career as a film-maker, would direct over seventy movies. In 1912, Henderson directed a one-reel movie adaption of Robert Louis Stevenson's novella *Strange Case of Dr Jekyll and Mr Hyde* (1886), basing his film on the 1887 stage version by Thomas Russell Sullivan. Employing Méliès ground-breaking methods of cinematic presentation, Henderson shows actor James Cruz (later a noted director) as Jekyll, drinking his potion and reacting to its effects. He slumps into a chair, holds his face, and suddenly he turns into his evil alter ego Mr Hyde, heavily made up to present a beastly appearance. When he drinks the concoction again, he turns back into Jekyll.

The Méliès influence is quite evident as Henderson features actor Cruz in the centre of the frame and the picture seamlessly evolves from the Jekyll make-up to the Hyde make-up and back again without any jerky cuts jarring the visual's impact. However, this subject extends beyond Méliès' scope. Méliès did not develop or evolve much as a film-maker, despite his massive body of work. He honed his special effects over time, but his later films differed little in style from his earliest ones. With *Dr Jekyll and Mr Hyde*, Lucius Henderson is working with narrative cinema that had already been established earlier by the likes of Edwin S. Porter, whose *The Great Train Robbery* (1903) is one of the most noted early examples of film using editing to tell a story.

While the Méliès films also used garish make-up to create macabre-looking characters, the actors in these films (usually Méliès and his assistant) would employ the sort of florid gestures that display the transition from the broader gestures of stage acting to the more intimate motions of screen performance. Director Henderson and actor Cruz appear to understand the intimacy of the motion picture camera as the film-maker allows the performer to employ a great deal of subtle nuance. This is especially evident with Jekyll's struggle while getting up the courage to drink the potion. The Hyde character's actions are more blatant as befitting the character, while Jekyll's are more subtle. Therefore this film uses ideas established by the very first film-makers and, as early as 1912, combines these elements to create a subject that further defined Gothic cinema's development.

Gothic cinema is not a specific genre unto itself, but an idea that extends to different genres. In 1914, a Keystone comedy with Charlie Chaplin, *Cruel Cruel Love*, made during the iconic comedian's first year in movies, explored how Gothic elements could enhance a slapstick comedy. This one-reeler was made before Chaplin began directing his own films so he approaches it as an actor. Director George Nichols had a keen visual sense and was attracted to a script by Keystone screenwriter Craig Hutchinson, who usually penned typical slapstick comedies. This time Hutchinson created a screenplay in which the central character, played by Chaplin, is mistakenly believed, by his fiancée, to be flirting with the maid. When she gives back his engagement ring, he attempts suicide by taking poison, not realising what he consumed was harmless. His fiancée forgives him after being given an explanation by the gardener and she resumes their engagement. The man believes the poison he consumed will soon kill him so he frantically tries to find an antidote.

While much of *Cruel Cruel Love* features the sort of frenetic slapstick that continues to define Keystone comedies, it has a much more consistent narrative than the studio's usual productions, and it features a great Gothic sequence filled with macabre images. After taking the poison, Charlie imagines how his death and afterlife might be. Director Nichols offers a scene with Charlie in hell, pursued by devils with pitchforks. The imagery is unusual for a Keystone subject, especially when the notoriously budget-minded studio head, Mack Sennett, rarely allowed a setup that probably took longer to film than it took the scene to play out in the movie. But it is a good example of how Gothic imagery could be used effectively in the slapstick comedy genre.

By the time German Expressionism and Robert Wiene's film *Das Cabinet des Dr. Caligari* (1920) appeared, narrative cinema had extended to feature length productions, and an art form had begun to develop. While cinema had advanced, the ideas of pioneers like Méliès and Henderson were still clearly evident. *Caligari* stems from Méliès's approach to create a strong visual sense to the proceedings. Director Wiene used the talents of art directors Walter Reimann, Hermann Warm, Robert Herlth and Walter Röhrig to design the set, creating the expressionist background. According to Warm:

> We realized that a subject like this needed something out of the ordinary in the way of sets. Reimann, whose paintings in those days had expressionist tendencies, suggested doing the sets expressionistically. We immediately set to work roughing up designs in that style. (Ott, 1986: 50)

Expressionist film-makers frequently challenged the practice of depicting environments realistically. The film-makers assumed an artistic control over the use of light or shadow, straight lines or altered geographies, and how these aspects could affect the mood of a film. The distortions in *Caligari* helped to alter its thematic reality through artistic expression. To compliment the unorthodox set design, actors Conrad Veidt, Lil Dagover and Fredrick Feher added expressionistic touches to their make-up. The sets and make-up of the actors, as well as Wiene's slow, intense approach to presenting the narrative, caused *Caligari* to be an emotionally stirring experience the likes of which previous Gothic films had not achieved.

The film opens with a young man seated on a bench telling an older man that spirits have driven him from his home. A woman slowly walks past them. Francis identifies her as his 'fiancée', Jane. The film then shows, in flashback, their story. Francis and his friend Alan go to see an exhibit called 'The Cabinet of Dr Caligari', which presents a strange doctor's exhibit. The mysterious doctor's showcase presents Cesare, a somnambulist who has been asleep for more than two decades. Approaching the entranced Cesare, Alan asks about his own future and is told he will die that night. When Alan is found dead the following morning, a suspicious Francis starts spying on Cesare and Caligari. Cesare is ordered to murder Jane but is so taken with her beauty that he instead kidnaps her. Awakened by the noise, Jane's father pursues Cesare, who runs away until, eventually, he places Jane on the ground and escapes into the night. Francis and the police investigate the caravan of Dr Caligari, but the doctor succeeds in slipping away. Francis pursues the fleeing Dr Caligari and sees him disappear into an insane asylum. Francis enters the madhouse where he is sure he will find the truth behind all these mysterious events.

Das Cabinet des Dr. Caligari extends far beyond the parameters of Gothic cinema on virtually every conceivable level. There are the afore-mentioned performances, set design and the director's expressionistic visual approach to narrative cinema. However, as a technical achieve-ment, *Caligari* also employed, according to an analysis by C. Dennis Pegge, over 378 cuts in the completed film. Pegge states:

> There is an intricate interweaving both of shots and of sequences. *Caligari* must be recognized as a pioneering effort in editing, but also as a demonstra-tion of that affinity between filmic expression and the thought process. The result is an emotional experience that is both intense and, at times, highly subjective. (Ott, 1986: 50)

Caligari, however, owes much more to George Méliès than, say, D. W. Griffith, who had advanced cinema in the wake of Méliès, using varying shot distances and compositions to create a more cinematic and less overtly theatrical *mise-en-scène*. Robert Wiene keeps the camera sta-tionary, while the sets frame the characters. And yet without the use of unorthodox camera angles to enhance the visual presentation, *Caligari* still manages to convey its psychological theme, its ambiguous thoughts and its emotional impact.

That same year, Germany produced *Der Golem, wie er in die Welt kam* the third in a series of films directed by Paul Wegener and Carl

Boese, and the only one of the three that is not lost. Usually referred to as *Der Golem* (or *The Golem*), this film, like *Caligari*, has made a similarly lasting impact on the presentation of Gothic cinema. Hans Poelzig designed the film's sets, which reproduced a Jewish ghetto in Prague. Cinematographer Karl Freund's approach to the sets and performances is what is most responsible for the visual impact of *Der Golem*. Freund, who would later act as cinematographer on F. W. Murnau's *Der Letze Mann* (1924) and Fritz Lang's *Metropolis* (1927), worked closely with the film-makers on the look of the film, integrating the physical performances of the actors with a creative approach to the lighting and camera angles, causing the viewer to feel the central characters' dread. Freund would continue to work as a cinematographer well into the television era, including the *I Love Lucy* series (1951–7). He would also direct ten films, including *The Mummy* (1932).

In Kevin Hagopian's film notes for the New York Writer's Institute, Paul Wegender's performance in the title role is called out as a most significant factor in the film's success:

> But it is Wegener the actor, in his role as the Golem, who marks the film indelibly. Wegener's Golem, with his monstrous appearance and his trance-like obedience to the command of a legendary megalomaniac, is one of the most significant ancestors of the cinematic Frankenstein of James Whale and Boris Karloff. Huge, avenging and violent, Wegener's Golem terrorizes the enemies of the Hebrews. Yet, however superhuman his attributes, Wegener's creature is undeniably Romantic. Having tasted eternal life, he nonetheless yearns for the fragile mortality of the people he observes. As a timeless invention of Rabbi Loew's supernatural abilities and Nietzschean conscience, the Golem's existence allows him neither pleasure nor pain. Ironically, the Golem envies the uncertainty and finite life of the humans who stand in terror of him. They fear his immortal powers, and he desires a short, passionate, unpredictable life like theirs. The grasping toward humanity by Wegener's beast is one of the most affecting transformations in all of cinema.[1]

Der Golem had a significant impact on James Whale's quintessential screen version of Mary Shelley's *Frankenstein* (1931). The impact this pioneering film had on subsequent examples of Gothic cinema is at the same level as *Caligari*.

Gothic cinema once again extended to the comedy genre with Buster Keaton's *The Haunted House* (1921). Keaton was a master at redefining comedy within whatever plot structure he chose. That is why *The Haunted House* is more than a simple slapstick comedy with a series of scare gags. It is an insightful blend of comedy and horror elements, stemming from the established visual styles already discussed. The premise is typical – Buster Keaton must spend time in a house that is said to be haunted. But to allow any plot contrivance to be at least reasonably acceptable, he structures the narrative by having a theatre troupe playing *Faust* seeking refuge in the same house, while still in costume. Keaton's encounters with Faustian spirits and demons are the basis for the comedy derived from Gothic symbolism. Comedy continued to visit Gothic themes with Harold Lloyd's *Haunted Spooks*, Laurel and Hardy's *Habeas Corpus* and other, less insightful, more mechanical examples.

One particular scene in *The Haunted House* features two men dressed as skeletons putting body parts together to create a fully formed person. The legs are set up, followed by a torso stacked upon them, and then arms, and a head. Once these are in place, the image comes to life and reaches out his hand to greet Buster. It is a scene of visual brilliance that might have dazzled George Méliès. The scene, as explained, utilises the cinematic medium to create a visual effect. This is what Méliès would do. However, by the time this Keaton short was produced, cinema's ability had become slightly more sophisticated, thus allowing for a more intricate visual illusion than the innovative French film-maker could have accomplished.

If *Caligari* and *Der Golem* bolstered the cinematic syntax provided by Méliès, it was F. W. Murnau's *Nosferatu* (1922) that provided the artistic culmination. Perhaps the finest example of aesthetically rewarding Gothic cinema during the silent era, this German version of Bram Stoker's *Dracula* (1897) draws from all of the aforementioned influences, even Buster Keaton's penchant for fleshing out Méliès's technical achievements. The emptiness of the long shots frames the actors in dark negative space, the reflective close-ups, the slow-moving tracking shots, the cuts between a still life setting on a table, a long shot of an actor in a corridor and the close-up of a positive gleeful reaction are just some of the establishing ideas.

Murnau could not obtain the rights to the Stoker novel so he used it as a basis and changed names; this alteration, however, did not present Stoker's widow from launching a successful lawsuit.[2] *Nosferatu* follows the Stoker novel pretty closely, taking only enough liberties to avoid copyright infringement. For instance, unlike Dracula, the vampire here does not make other vampires when he attacks them. He kills them outright. The imaginative prose that the novel provides is effectively translated to cinematic images. *Nosferatu* may not seem as superficially 'scary' in the more sophisticated twenty-first century. However, as a film created before the sudden jump cuts, splattering blood and other, more boisterous concepts in contemporary horror movies, its artistry continues to be remarkable.

Along with Murnau's direction, there is Max Schreck in the title role. According to Felicia Feaster of Turner Classic Movies:

> An actor whose own name is German for 'terror,' Schreck is certainly a nightmarish apparition with his bulbous head, pointed bat like ears and long, talon-like fingers and fangs. His rat-like facial features also associate him with the rodents who spread the plague across Europe. And Schreck's eerie, stammering, zombielike walk has since become a feature of numerous screen monsters, from the stammering gait of the Frankenstein monster to the deliberate, determined pace of the killer Michael in *Halloween* (1978). Schreck's vampire was a thoroughly original creation, a monster far from the bloodsucking playboys of later Draculas.[3]

While it is in some ways a culmination of the original ideas set down by earlier cinematic pioneers, *Nosferatu* is also the foundation of so many future Gothic films that feature a monster character as the central figure, even if it is not a vampire. *Nosferatu* also offers a balance of lighter scenes along with the more frightening imagery; scenes of characters frolicking with a game of croquet are offset by depictions of bleak scenes or of another character sitting alone on a desolate beach as waves crash onto the shore. Murnau did not rely on studio sets but actually went on location, which was something of a rarity for UFA, the company that produced *Nosferatu*. His locations are a series of dark skies, towering mountains and restless seas.

As with *Caligari* or *Der Golem*, Murnau's *Nosferatu* also creates an emotional mood that permeates every scene. Even when the director is briefly offering a more light-hearted sequence as a respite, the overwhelming emotional structure of the film is very tense, frightening and absorbing. German Expressionism has already presented, with its earlier films, an emotionally unsettling series of distortions and abstractions, twisted visuals and sets. The basis was more in fantasy than realism. Murnau's imagery, his use of darkness and light, his distorted views, double exposures, and hypnotic mood all combine to present what many consider to be the greatest vampire film of all time.

Lon Chaney became one of the truly great actors of the silent era, mostly due to his penchant for artistic make-up effects that transformed him into different characters. After applying the make-up, Chaney *became* these characters. At the silent era's conclusion, Chaney's films stand out as the most striking examples of Gothic cinema. Chaney only lived to make one sound film, dying in 1930 (he was set to play the title role in *Dracula* at Universal but his death allowed Bela Lugosi to take the role).

Perhaps the most noted Chaney film that investigated Gothic ideas is *The Phantom of the Opera* (1925). Chaney was already a noted star by the time he did *Phantom*, having famously played the title role in *The Hunchback of Notre Dame* a couple years earlier. Being allowed to create his own make-up, Chaney created a face for the Phantom role that has itself become iconic and is also said to be the closest in concept to Gaston Leroux's 1910 novel *Le Fantôme de l'Opéra*. Chaney painted his eye sockets black to make them more skull-like. The tip of his nose up was pulled up and pinned with wire. Finally, false teeth were placed into his mouth. During the revealing scene where the woman pulls the Phantom's mask away and reveals his face, audiences screamed, ran out of the theatre and fainted.

Chaney followed up *The Phantom of the Opera* with *The Unholy Three* in which he plays a circus ventriloquist who dresses as an old lady and commits crimes with his girlfriend, and a midget performer from the circus who pretends to be his grandson. Tod Browning's direction was clever enough to make an ordinary chimpanzee seem like a large, imposing beast with some basic camera tricks and carefully angled shots. According to Bret Wood at the TCM website:

> The ape was nothing more than a large yet docile chimpanzee, which was made to appear bigger than life through the use of miniature sets and optical effects. To accomplish the illusion in one scene, a child was costumed as (the chimpanzee) so that the ape would loom large in comparison.[4]

As the silent era concluded at the end of the 1920s, cinema's reliance on brilliant visuals gave way to sound. And while it had evolved into an art form unto itself, silent cinema was considered archaic as soon as 1930. Exhibitor H. E. Hoag stated in *Film Daily* that year: 'A silent comedy is very flat now. In fact, for the past two years, my audiences seldom laughed out loud at a silent' (*Film Daily*, 6 April 1930). The bigger studios hastily transformed recently shot silent features into talkies by dubbing in voices and sound effects. The smaller studios did not have the funds to accomplish this, and thus their late silents of late 1929 and early 1930 received very little distribution, save for small town theatres that were not yet equipped for sound. By the 1930s, though, sound was so firmly established in the cinema only someone with the status of Charlie Chaplin was able to pull off making a silent picture.

While sound movies did attempt to retain the visuals of Gothic silents, silent cinema, by necessity, presented these elements with more depth and greater care. Also, it is the silent movies that allow us to better understand the history and development of Gothic cinema, its extension over several genres and its creation of the concepts that eventually became commonplace as the motion picture continued to advance its scope.

Notes

1. https://www.albany.edu/ writers-inst/webpages4/filmnotes/fns05n1.html
2. Despite the filmmaker's careful attempts to separate his movie from the novel, Bram Stoker's widow sued the production for damages and won. It was ordered that all prints of *Nosferatu* be destroyed.
3. http://www.tcm.com/this-month/article/437%7C0/Nosferatu.html
4. http://www.tcm.com/this-month/article/59975%7C0/The-Unholy-Three.html

References

Lim, B. C. 2009. *Translating Time: Cinema, the Fantastic, and Temporal Critique*. Durham, NC: Duke University Press, pp. 279–80.
Neibaur, J. L. 2008. 'George Méliès: First Wizard of Cinema', *Cineaste*, XXXIII: 4, Fall, pp. 66–8.
Ott, F. W. 1986. *The Great German Films*. Secaucus, NJ: Citadel.
Williams, A. L. 1992. *Republic of Images: A History of French Filmmaking*. Cambridge, MA: Harvard University Press, p. 36.

Chapter 2

'So why shouldn't I write of monsters?': Defining Monstrosity in Universal's Horror Films

Andy W. Smith

The transition from silent cinema to sound coincided with one of the most influential series of films to be produced by a major Hollywood studio. Universal Studios' series of Horror films from the 1930s and 1940s can be traced back to the most significant moment in the history of Gothic literature, a June evening on the shores of Lake Geneva, when Lord Byron, Percy Shelley, Mary Wollstonecraft Godwin and Dr John Polidori amused, shocked and frightened each other with stories of the supernatural. As Christopher Frayling writes:

> The modern vampire story was born – in suitably oral circumstances – inside a villa overlooking Lake Geneva rented for the holidays on the night of 17 June 1816, when the weather was unusually wet and the atmosphere unusually tense. The birth coincided with that of *Frankenstein*, and their paths were destined to cross over the next two hundred years many, many times. (Frayling, 2016: 13)

Mary Shelley, in her introduction to the 1831 edition of *Frankenstein, or the Modern Prometheus*, recounts a terrible nightmare vision that came to her after listening to Byron and Shelley:

> 'We will each write a ghost story,' said Lord Byron; and his proposition was acceded to. There were four of us . . . I busied myself to *think of a story* – a story to rival those which had excited us to this task. One which would speak to the mysterious fears of our nature, and awaken thrilling horror – one to make the reader dread to look round, to curdle the blood, and quicken the beatings of the heart . . . Many and long were the conversations between Lord Byron and Shelley, to which I was a devout but nearly silent listener. During one of these, various philosophical doctrines were discussed, and among others the nature of the principle of life, and whether there was any probability of its ever being discovered and communicated . . . Perhaps a corpse would be re-animated . . . perhaps the component parts of a creature might be manufactured, brought together, and endued with vital warmth. (Shelley, 1968: 9–11)

Over one hundred years on from Shelley's nightmare that birthed a monster, James Whale opened his sequel *Bride of Frankenstein* (1935) with a prologue depicting Percy Shelley, Lord Byron and Mary Shelley discussing the events of her hitherto unpublished story. Byron and Shelley wonder at how this 'delicate creature' could conceive of such monsters. Mary explains that she has written her story not out of a prurient desire to shock but as 'a moral lesson' about the 'punishment that befell a mortal man who dared to emulate God'. Byron teases Mary Shelley about her creation:

> *Lord Byron*: Look at her Shelley. Can you believe that bland and lovely brow conceived of Frankenstein, a monster created from cadavers out of rifled graves? Isn't it astonishing?
> *Mary*: I don't know why you should think so. What do you expect? Such an audience needs something stronger than a pretty little love story. So why shouldn't I write of monsters?
> (James Whale, *Bride of Frankenstein*, 1935)

This opening scene acts as a coda to *Frankenstein* (James Whale, 1931), as Lord Byron, 'England's greatest sinner', takes the spectator through the events of the first film in a series of edited flashbacks that concludes with the death of the monster in the mill fire. Mary surprises the two men by telling them that the story did not end that way and the camera tracks back from the three of them sitting on the couch and cross fades into a shot of the burning mill. This prologue attempts to instil literary authenticity to the sequel, partly in the hope that it will prevent the censorship that almost ruined the first *Frankenstein* film, as the cultural angsts of the Great Depression found expression in the sublimated monsters of Universal Studios. The social context of Whale's *Frankenstein* films, and of the Universal production output during the 1930s in general, cannot be underestimated. David J. Skal writes that Frankenstein's monster was 'like a battered hood ornament for a wrecked economy' (Skal, 1992: 132). Elizabeth Young also uses *Bride of Frankenstein* as a way of analysing social attitudes to race and gender in 1930s America in her essay 'Here Comes the Bride: Wedding, Gender and Race in *Bride of Frankenstein*', a text I shall be returning to later as it offers cogent arguments in the way systems of repression are encoded, subverted and reinforced in Whale's films.

Tod Browning's *Dracula* opened in February 1931, quickly followed by *Frankenstein* in December 1931. The box office success of these two films (*Dracula* alone brought in receipts of half a million dollars) set the demand for Universal Studios' series of 'monster movies' that were to frighten the cinema-going public of North America and Europe in the

1930s and 1940s. The authority of Gothic tropes in defining the context and thematic significance of the 'monster' brings into question the relationship between the original source material and the films, with the cinematic depictions of both titular characters at odds with their representations in Bram Stoker and Mary Shelley's novels. Following on from *Dracula* and *Frankenstein* were films such as *The Mummy* (Karl Freund, 1932), *The Invisible Man* (James Whale, 1933), *Bride of Frankenstein* (James Whale, 1935) and *The Wolf Man* (George Waggner, 1941). These 'monsters', derived from either Gothic or Science Fiction novels (H. G. Wells, *The Invisible Man*, 1897), or original depictions in the case of *The Mummy* and *The Wolf Man*, have themselves become indexical signifiers of monstrosity, foreignness and the 'Other'. Robin Wood, in his pivotal essay 'The American Nightmare', defines the concept of 'Otherness' in relation to the Horror genre: 'Otherness represents that which bourgeois ideology cannot recognize or accept but must deal with in one of two ways: either by rejecting it and if possible annihilating it, or by rendering it safe and assimilating it, converting it as far as possible into a replica of itself' (Wood, 2002: 27). Wood's Marxist-Freudian critique frames the horror film from the perspective of repression and class: while Whale's Frankenstein's monster is costumed in the clothes of the plebeian working class, his creator Dr Henry Frankenstein is signified through his patrician status, education and nobility as the heir to Baron Frankenstein's estate.

Similarly, twentieth-century popular depictions of Count Dracula owe their origin not to Stoker's description of the Count but to Browning's 1931 film and, more specifically, to Bela Lugosi's performance, costume and make-up. David J. Skal notes how Stoker's description of the Count differs from the usual 'Byronic image of vampirism that had already been popularized on the stage and in penny dreadfuls like James Malcolm Rymer's *Varney The Vampyre* (1847). Dracula spends little time on social niceties and is physically repellent, a cadaverous old man who grows younger as he drinks blood but who never becomes attractive' (Skal, 1993: 83). Stoker describes Jonathan Harker's first encounter with Count Dracula thus: 'Within, stood a tall old man, clean-shaven save for a long white moustache, and clad in black from head to foot, without a single speck of colour about him anywhere' (Stoker, 1994: 25). Universal's depiction of Count Dracula owed much to Hamilton Deane's 1927 London stage play, approved by Stoker's widow Florence, who held a firm grip on the rights of the work, going so far as to legally suppress the distribution of F. W. Murnau's silent classic adaptation of Stoker's novel *Nosferatu, Eine Symphonie des Graunes* (1922). The rights and subsequently the play were brought to the New York stage by the producer Horace Livewright and the playwright John L. Balderstone, who had rewritten much of Deane's dialogue. The casting of Bela Lugosi, a Hungarian émigré who barely spoke a word of English, in the New York production proved highly prescient for the future direction of the character's depiction in popular culture. Lugosi's cultivation of a foreign 'otherness' in the role of Dracula due to his inability to speak English fluently contributed to the financial, if not critical, success of the stage play. As Skal writes, 'he acted in a language he didn't know through titanic willpower. Almost anyone else would have just taken English lessons' (Skal, 1993: 89).

The establishment of Lugosi as Dracula in the middle-class theatre-going public consciousness was not enough to convince Carl Laemmle Junior of his casting once Universal Studios had acquired the rights from Florence Stoker to make the first sound version of the Dracula story. Laemmle's father Carl Senior had co-founded Universal Studios in 1912. Although Universal had one of the largest studio lots in Los Angeles, relocating there from New York in 1915, in the early days most of its film productions tended to be low-budget Westerns and melodramas, before branching out into more prestige film-making with directors such as John Ford and Erich von Stroheim. Despite this talent Universal was not in the same financial position as larger studios such as MGM and Paramount, not owning the large number of theatres that the major studios did and thus not exerting the significant amount of control over screenings and profit that the major studios had. The option of purchasing the rights to a Broadway success such as *Dracula* was too good to turn down for Laemmle Junior, and he saw this as an opportunity to increase the profile of the studio, much against the wishes of his father. Using the Deane/Balderstone adaptation of *Dracula* as the basis for the film, the script was rewritten by Louis Bromfield, Tod Browning was to direct and after much debate about casting, Lugosi was chosen to revive his stage performance as Dracula.

While the film was a success financially, technically and aesthetically it lacks both the eeriness and horror of Murnau's *Nosferatu*, nor the playful camp Gothic of Whale's later *Frankenstein* films. It is a film that relies on the screen presence of Lugosi to cover up its origins as a melodramatic stage play; the first half of the film, set in Transylvania and the boat crossing to England, is reliant on German cinematographer Karl Freund's evocative use of lighting and is a portent of what was to follow in subsequent versions of the Vampire genre, using high-contrast lighting that created a *chiaroscuro* effect of shadows and light. Renfield's arrival at the castle (significantly changed from that of Jonathan Harker in the novel) is preceded by scenes populated with superstitious local villagers dressed in what looks like Hollywood's idea of a Hungarian national costume. The film thus sets up this dichotomy between an atavistic folklore – 'It is Walpurgis Night, the night of evil – Nosferatu!' – and the rational, practical science of Dr Seward's medical Sanatorium near London, mirroring the contrast between a modern, civilised world of nights at the opera, telephones and automobiles and the devoutly religious, superstitious culture of the villagers that Dracula holds in thrall. The midnight coach journey to Dracula's castle is at once both suspenseful and, in hindsight, unintentionally amusing: as Renfield looks out of the black coach to ask the driver a question (the coach driver being Dracula himself), he sees the horses being driven on by a jangling, rubber bat, which makes several reappearances in the film at key moments, none of them entirely believable. As Wood writes, 'The monstrous figures from our dreams are our images of our repressed selves, and thus Transylvania, by extension, becomes the land of the unconscious . . .' (Wood, 1996: 369). This 'unconscious dreamscape' is where we first meet Dracula and his vampire brides: the camera pans slowly across a crypt, cross cutting to close ups of scurrying insects and rats (later on in the scene armadillos even make an appearance, not a species native to Eastern Europe), before unveiling our first look at Lugosi as Dracula. Lugosi here defines the iconic image that Dracula morphs into in twentieth-century popular culture: swept back jet-black hair, a hint of white foundation make-up, slightly coloured lips and the formal dress dinner suit with a long black cape. Most importantly there is a close-up of Lugosi's face with a key light thrown across the eyes, emphasising his 'hypnotic' stare. This device of the key light close up on Lugosi's eyes is used extensively throughout, especially in the latter half of the film, which is hampered by clumsy expository scenes of dialogue in brightly lit and tastefully furnished drawing rooms. In all there are seventeen close-ups of Lugosi in the film, including an extreme close up of his face moving towards and then underneath the camera frame in the scene where he attacks Mina Seward in her bedroom. According to David J. Skal, on Universal's insistence these close-ups were added after the main filming had been completed, which accounts for the fact that none of them actually match in the edit (Skal, 1993: 124).

Given its staging, framing, dialogue and characters, it is difficult to think of Browning's film as 'horrific' in a contemporary sense, and certainly there is an absence of gore on screen; all the deaths take place off camera, including Dracula's ritual staking by Van Helsing, in part due to the strict censorship mores of the time. The complete lack of any non-diegetic sound or music adds to the strangeness of the film and provides a link to the pre-sound horror films of Universal starring Lon

Chaney and directed by Browning (Skal, 1993: 126). James Craig Holte notes the technical problems the film presents, with gaps in the plotting and characters appearing after supposedly being killed (Holte, 1997: 39). Indeed, the 1931 Spanish language version of *Drácula*, directed by George Melford and shot on the same sets after Browning's filming had wrapped for the day, is much more imaginative in the way it uses *mise-en-scène*, sound effects, cinematography and editing, radically changing the context through which Dracula is presented as the 'monstrous lover'. For example, in the Spanish language *Drácula*, when the public autopsy is carried out on Lucy's body, there is a close-up of the vampire bite marks through a magnifying glass on her neck, something missing entirely from the Browning version. Dracula is filmed rising from his coffin at several points in the film, underlit to create a very powerful cinematic image, unlike in Browning's version where the camera cuts to Lugosi standing beside his coffin. The scene onboard the ship taking Dracula and Renfield to England is again very different in the Spanish version: there is no dialogue as in the more famous film, but instead we see Renfield maniacally laughing, framed by the ship's port window as Dracula rises from his coffin to slaughter the crew. The staking of Dracula again takes place off-camera but this time the drama is accentuated by the response of Eva Seward (played by Lupita Tovar) as she clutches her breast as the stake is driven into the vampire's heart. There are far fewer close ups of Carlos Villar as Dracula than of Lugosi, suggesting that the film's structure, pace and storytelling is far more accomplished and less in need of judicious editing and re-shooting then the English version.

The immediacy and textual playfulness of *Drácula* may have something to do with its 'Latin' context, as Lupita Tovar remarks in an interview: 'We Latins have a different way of expressing ourselves' (2012). It helps that the actors actually communicate with each other in a naturalistic style that works for the film medium rather than the mannered stage delivery of the English actors. Tovar's Eva Seward and Pablo Alvarez Rubio's Renfield are particularly convincing in their roles, with Tovar being aided by a costume design that emphasised her character's vulnerability and sexuality, and Rubio's crazed Renfield capable of moments of genuine pathos and terror. Still, the importance of *Dracula* as one of the first Horror films to be made in the sound era, along with Lugosi's eccentric performance, has established its legacy, as Holte writes:

> Despite the many problems with the Universal film, however, Tod Browning's *Dracula* has become a cultural icon, influencing every adaptation that has followed and establishing the character of Bela Lugosi in evening clothes and cape as the most widely known visual image of Dracula in the world. (Holte, 1997: 38)

Universal's *Dracula* sets up a structural template that the other Universal horror films would follow: the monster as outside of normative culture, seen as a threat to social/patriarchy/gender roles, and needing to be destroyed in order to disavow chaos and restore order to 'bourgeois/capitalist ideology' (Wood, 2002: 226). Usually, the monster in Universal's films threatens the heterosexual coupling of key characters (Jonathan Harker/Mina) and exists either as a supernatural entity (Dracula/The Mummy), a construction of 'bad' science (Frankenstein's monster/The Invisible Man) or as a folkloric hybrid of animal and human (the Wolf Man/the Creature from the Black Lagoon). The combination of Lugosi's highly stylised performance, where he elongates vowels to a ridiculous degree, coupled with his 'foreign' masculinity, sets a marker for future interpretations of the Dracula character.

Hammer Studios' *Dracula* (1958), directed by Terence Fisher and released in North America as *Horror of Dracula*, places the threat to bourgeois morality centre stage, in what Christopher Frayling describes as 'the Victorian household assailed by the demon lover' (Frayling, cited in Hearn, 2012). Hammer's *Dracula* frequently frames Christopher Lee in long shot, emphasising the actor's height and physicality, but also his maturity and virility. Lee's Dracula is all about penetration, an emphasis on his long, curved fangs (missing from Lugosi's make-up and costume) as a metaphor for sexual intercourse. Frayling further makes the point that each generation's Dracula draws upon a different version of the character: Max Schreck's Nosferatu is the vampire as folkloric myth, Lugosi's is the posturing vampire in the opera cloak and foreign accent, and Lee's is the highly masculine, sexually beguiling English aristocrat. James Sangster's script for the 1958 *Dracula* is recognised as a classic interpretation of Stoker's novel, paring the story down so that Dracula's castle and the Victorian household he terrorises are in adjoining countries, thus cutting out the need to film the expensive sea crossing and taking out the supernatural elements. By placing the idealised Victorian couple as the source of bourgeois morality, Fisher's *Dracula*, in Frayling's word's, for the first time 'becomes about sex' and the threat of adultery to Victorian family values. This is beautifully expressed in the final scene where Peter Cushing's Van Helsing, in the climactic final battle between good and evil, destroys Dracula by leaping across a table and ripping open the drapes in his castle, thus exposing Dracula to sunlight. As Dracula horrifically burns to ash, the crucifix imprint on Mina Holmwood's palm that is an indexical sign of her infidelity with the monster fades away to reveal her wedding ring as she clasps hands with her husband, just as Dracula's ring is all that is left of his ashes in the final shot of the film (Frayling, cited in Hearn, 2012).

In contrast, Francis Ford Coppola's *Bram Stoker's Dracula* (1992) reveals a very different image of the vampire myth, one that is not without its problems of representation. Gary Oldman's Dracula first appears as a handsome young man in the prime of his life, a medieval warrior warlord fighting against the Turkish 'infidels' and gains immortality through renouncing Christianity following the suicide of his wife. When Jonathan Harker first encounters him, however, he resembles a cadaverous, frail, almost alien being, 'an aged and very Orientalized figure with a kabuki bouffant, long scarlet gown, and Mandarin fingernails' (Sharrett, 1996: 266). After travelling to London in pursuit of Harker's fiancée Mina, a reincarnation of his long-deceased wife, Oldman again takes on the visage of a young man. Christopher Sharrett criticises the film as overly self-conscious in its 'romanticizing the Other': 'No single film has incarnated the Other so handily, nor with such unproblematic contempt and revulsion.' Sharrett writes that 'by returning to Stoker's novel, the film merely replicates rather than criticizes Victorian morality' (Sharrett, 1996: 265) and he categorises Coppola's version as deeply troubling in its depiction of female sexuality: 'There is little in the work of Murnau, of Tod Browning or James Whale, of Val Lewton or Terence Fisher, of any contract director working under the demands of the US or British production codes of the last century, as hackneyed or reactionary as this film' (Sharrett, 1996: 268).

Like the 1931 *Dracula*, Universal Studios' *Frankenstein* saw its origins in a 1920s stage play, this time by Peggy Webling, produced and performed by Hamilton Deane who also produced the English stage version of *Dracula*. This symbiosis between the vampire and the monster has a rich history: in 1826 a double bill appeared at the English Opera House in London featuring a play called *The Vampire: Or, The Bride Of The Isles* followed by *Presumption! Or The Fate Of Frankenstein!*, with both roles played by T. P. Cooke (Frayling, 2016: 127). This twinning of the vampire with Dr Frankenstein's unnatural creation reaches its apogee with the publication of *Dracula* in 1897; as Skal writes, 'After the publication of Stoker's novel, the word "Dracula" became a virtual synonym for "vampire", and the Shelley-Stoker creations became associated as two sides of a coin, complementary high points of scary entertainment' (Skal, 1993: 84). Webling's version of the story, titled *Frankenstein: An Adventure in the Macabre*, positioned the relationship between creator and monster as that of a doppelgänger, as Skal writes: 'Webling intentionally named her monster Frankenstein . . . and wore a costume identical to that of Henry Frankenstein' (98), thus providing a framing device that was to become crucial to the way the Universal films would portray the relationship between Henry Frankenstein and his monster. Producer Horace Liveright and writer John L. Balderstone, the same team that had brought the *Dracula* adaptation to New York theatres, were now involved in complex negotiations for Webling's play with an option for film rights as well as Broadway. Balderstone revised Webling's script and introduced elements that were to find their way into the films, notably bringing the monster to life using 'crackling electrical apparatus' (108), an event notably missing from Shelley's novel. Livewright fell out with Balderstone over his script and lost the chance to option the rights to Universal, being paid off for what would turn out to be the paltry sum of $4,500 considering how much *Frankenstein* finally made for the studio: from a budget of $291,000 it grossed the equivalent of $12 million dollars.[1]

Universal bought the rights to Balderstone and Webling's script in 1931 and handed the project firstly to Frenchman Robert Florey, who shot a test sequence on the sets of *Dracula* with Bela Lugosi heavily made up as the monster. The test sequence was not successful as Lugosi, fresh from his success as Count Dracula, felt the role of the illiterate, grunting monster beneath him. The project was handed over by Carl Laemmle Junior to James Whale, an English actor and director recently contracted by Universal who had emigrated from the UK in 1929 to work firstly on Broadway and then in Hollywood on R. C. Sherriff's First World War play *Journey's End* (1930).

Whale's *Frankenstein* films, along with *The Invisible Man* (1933) and *The Old Dark House* (1932), established him as one of the most influential horror film directors to come out of the Hollywood Studio system. Whale lived as an openly gay man in Hollywood with his partner David Lewis, a radical statement for the time period, and this sense of being an outlier, both culturally and sexually, affected much of his work. Whale's *Frankenstein* films share little in common with Shelley's novel, apart from the most basic plots lines and concepts of Faustian progeny; instead, Whale's vision of the monster as a deeply tormented and sympathetic antagonist offers a trenchant social commentary on the role of the outsider in a foreign culture.

As Mark Gatiss writes, Whale (like Florey in Paris) was experienced in working in the Grand Guignol theatre in London and would bring this experience of crafting horror and comedy to his interpretation of Shelley's novel, as Whale himself recounts:

> I chose Frankenstein out of about 30 available stories because it was the strongest meat and gave me a chance to dabble in the macabre . . . a director must be pretty bad if he can't get a thrill out of war, murder, robbery. Frankenstein was a sensational story and had the chance to become a sensational picture. (Gatiss, 1995: 71)

As part of his preparation, Whale revisited classic films from German Expressionism, including *The Cabinet of Dr Caligari* (Wiene, 1920), *The Golem* (Galeen and Wegener, 1920) and *Metropolis* (Lang, 1927) (Gatiss, 1995: 72). In terms of casting, Whale chose English actors he had worked with before for the roles of Dr Henry Frankenstein and his fiancée Elizabeth: Mae Clark had acted in Whale's first film for Universal, *Waterloo Road* (1930), and Colin Clive had worked with Whale on the stage and film versions of *Journey's End*. Gatiss quotes Whale on his astute casting of Clive: 'I chose Colin Clive for Frankenstein because he had exactly the right kind of tenacity to go through with anything, together with the kind of romantic quality which makes strong men leave civilization to shoot big game' (Gatiss, 1995: 73). The key casting was the monster and Whale chose Boris Karloff on the recommendation of his partner David Lewis, who had seen Karloff in the gangster film *The Criminal Code* (Hawks, 1931). Whale's intentions behind the film can be seen from his letter to Clive: 'There are none of Dracula's mania-cal cackles. I want the picture to be a very modern, materialistic treat-ment of this medieval story – something of Doctor Caligari, something of Edgar Allan Poe, and of course a good deal of us . . .' (74).

Casting Karloff as the Monster[2] was to have a profound effect on the way the character was subsequently perceived in popular culture. The construction of the Monster's image, a joint effort by Whale and the head of Universal's make-up department Jack Pierce, was to become the *tabula rasa* for all future depictions in Universal's films. The crea-ture's appearance has been remediated in popular culture in countless parodies and homages: a flat head, accentuated brow, electric bolts in the side of the neck, heavily lidded eyes, padded black jacket and trou-sers along with weighted workman's boots. Paul O'Flinn notes the effect of Karloff's Monster in different iterations in popular culture:

> There have been over a hundred film adaptations and there have been the Charles Addams cartoons in the *New Yorker*; Frankie Stein blunders about in the pages of *Whoopee* and *Monster Fun* comics, and approximate versions of the monster glare out from chewing gum wrappers and crisp bags . . . there is no such thing as *Frankenstein*, there are only *Frankensteins*, as the text is ceaselessly rewritten, reproduced, refilmed and redesigned. (O'Flinn, 2002: 105)

The only other previous film version of *Frankenstein* was the one-reel 1910 version made by Thomas Edison's studio, where the monster is made up to resemble 'an image of unkempt "savagery" . . . a primitive, missing link figure' with wild hair and 'talon tipped fingers' (Hand, 2007: 12). As Richard J. Hand notes, this image of the Monster was drawn from previous stage versions, notably O. Smith's from *Frankenstein or the Man and the Monster!* (1826), and had more in common with 'Calibans from the nineteenth century stage' (12). Karloff's Monster, 'caught, as it were, on the barbed wire between humanism and mechanism' (Skal, 1993: 135), is a creature for the Machine age. Whale brilliantly captures the Monster's first entrance as he backs into a doorway and turns around slowly in a series of three shots: firstly, a medium, then a medium close-up, then a close-up, all taken from different angles as jarring jump cuts that purposely do not match in the edit. Shortly after this entrance, another famous shot sees the Monster raise his face and hands up to the sky when he feels sunlight on his face for the first time, like an ancient sun worshipper genuflecting to the god of nature.[3] Karloff appeared in three Universal Frankenstein films, but the impact of his image, along with his performance, changed the way Horror was to be perceived in relation to the 'sympathetic' monster. Henry Frankenstein's hunchbacked laboratory assistant Fritz, played by Dwight Frye (who was the maniacal Renfield in Browning's *Dracula)*, is an important role in establishing this sympathy through antagonising and torturing the Monster until finally, with poetic justice, Fritz ends up hanged in the Monster's dungeon cell. Fritz is also responsible for the Monster's 'abnormal' personality, bungling the theft of a 'normal' brain from the medical school and bringing back the brain of a criminal, much to Henry Frankenstein's disgust.

Whale's film is troublingly anachronistic: the costume and art direction evoke modernity, particularly in the extraordinary set piece where the Monster is brought to life in a surge of electricity in Frankenstein's laboratory, but elsewhere the film struggles to convey a realistic sense of time and place. The bucolic villagers that dot the landscape are remnants of a romanticised past where social structures are unthreatened by popular revolution. Indeed, the conclusion of the film sees these villagers turn into a lynch mob, hunting down the Monster in the now clichéd trope of pitchforks and flaming torches, a reference not lost on a 1930s audience where the non-judicial lynching and murder of black men was a common sight in the American South, as O'Flinn notes: 'If Mary Shelley's monster alludes indirectly to working class insurrections, one answer to that canvassed in the 1930s was counter-revolutionary mob violence' (O'Flinn, 2002: 112). As Skal writes:

> The exact time period is vague – it *seems* to be the present; the women, for instance, wear 1931 fashions, and although the film is 'about' science, all of the trappings of technology and industrialization – cars, radio, telephones – are totally absent, as if their energy has been displaced totally into Frankenstein's laboratory equipment. (1993: 135)

Indeed, the reinforcement of class, patriarchy and social order at the conclusion of *Frankenstein* underpins the film's conservative values while subversively, outside that text, the Monster exists as Henry Frankenstein's unacknowledged and repressed homosexual double. As Wood writes of the relationship between normality and the monster:

> It is the third variable, the relationship between normality and the Monster, that constitutes the essential subject of the horror film . . . The relationship has one privileged form: the figure of the doppelgänger, alter ego, or double, a figure that has recurred constantly in western culture, especially during the past hundred years . . . But we should be alerted to the relationship's true significance from the moment in the James Whale original where Frankenstein's decision to create his monster is juxtaposed very precisely with his decision to become engaged. The doppelgänger motif reveals the Monster as normality's shadow. (Wood, 2002: 31)

This doubling is most effective in the scene where the Monster, after escaping from the laboratory and inadvertently drowning the child Maria, arrives at the Frankenstein mansion as preparations are underway for Henry and Elizabeth's nuptials. Hearing the Monster at large in the house, Henry locks Elizabeth in her bedroom, a gesture Whale emphasises with a close-up of the key entering the lock. While the men impotently search the rest of the house for the creature, the Monster enters the bedroom through the windows and confronts Elizabeth in her bridal gown. Whale cuts back to the men as they hear Elizabeth's screams and as they rush back into the room the inference is clear: her bridal veil is on the floor and she is lying on the bed, hair flowing, arms and neck exposed in a passing reference to Fuseli's 1781 painting *The Nightmare*. Henry rushes to Elizabeth's side, but the look of horror on her face and the tone of her words are suggestive of a subliminal force that exists outside of the realistic framework of the text: 'Don't let *it* come here' (emphasis mine). An analysis of this scene using Wood's doppelgänger motif would implicate 'it' as Henry's 'abnormal' sexual identity, a queer reading in keeping with both the 'otherness' of the narrative and Whale's public persona as a gay man in a social context when homosexual relations were both illegal and viewed as immoral. Whale is careful though to reinforce normative values with an epilogue filmed after the original ending where Henry, instead of being thrown to his death by the Monster, is reunited with Elizabeth and his father the Baron offers a toast to the continuance of the patriarchy: 'Here's to a son of the House of Frankenstein!' Gatiss muses that Whale's comment to Clive that the film will 'contain a good deal of us' may be a reference to their status as outsiders, 'flouting convention, wilfully detached from an all too straight laced society' (Gatiss, 1995: 82).

This reading of the Monster as a repressed doppelgänger is further complicated in Whale's follow-up *Bride of Frankenstein* (1935). Elizabeth Young puts forward an analysis of the film that 'refracts a series of social anxieties involving gender, sexuality and race' (Young, 1996: 309). Young elucidates:

> . . . the film's complex gender dynamics which consistently take the form of a triangle involving two men and a women, seem at first to enact the exchange and erasure of women . . . but the film also challenges the static parameters of such triangular models, both by transforming the competitive force of male rivalry into a subversive mode of male homoeroticism and by undermining its apparent demonization of women with a final, fleeting moment of female power. (310)

Young's 'male homoeroticism' is personified by the character of Dr Pretorius, played by Whale's theatrical mentor, Ernest Thesiger. Gatiss memorably describes Thesiger's performance as 'camp, shrill, frightening and oozing malevolent bitterness from every pore' (Gatiss, 1995: 112). Pretorius arrives at Henry's mansion and attempts to convince him to resume his work in creating life from the dead. Young's reading conforms to Gatiss's description of Thesiger's performance: 'The doctor appears in the visually coded form, here rendered campily, of the homosexual as decadent aristocrat' (Young, 1996: 315). Both through his role in the plot (Pretorius 'entices' Henry away from his bride-to-be Elizabeth and eventually blackmails him into creating a bride for the Monster) and performance style, the character exists outside of any heteronormative behaviour codes but also enforces the homosocial relationships that 'erase women'. As Young writes, 'Women serve, then, not merely as a medium of exchange in the homosocial system but also as a desperate cover-up, a means of channeling suspicion of homosexuality into heterosexual appearances' (Young, 1996: 315). Young notes that the opening prologue already sets up this threat with the isolation of Mary Shelley in relation to the framing of Percy Shelley and Lord Byron, and this triangle of erasure is duplicated with Elizabeth's 'disappearance' in the narrative. In this reading the Monster's threat as the abnormal sexual double is dissipated through Pretorius's Mephistophelian 'seduction' of Henry. The Monster accrues the rudiments of civilised behaviour, meeting a blind hermit who shows him compassion and in return the Monster learns to communicate his desires, perhaps not quite as eloquently as Shelley's monster in the novel, but a development nonetheless from the mute, grunting figure from the first film.

The creation scene that is the climax of the film is an extraordinary piece of film-making and editing, featuring multiple camera setups, Dutch camera angles and rapid-fire cutting to create a kinetic moment of cinematic power: 'Whale used 175 different shots, many uplit at bizarre angles, to convince the audience "that a miracle is going to take place"' (Gatiss, 1995: 119). Elsa Lanchester's iconic 'Nefertiti-like' (Gatiss, 1995: 112) Bride, a product not of a 'miracle' but a 'social construction of woman into an essentialist nightmare' (Young, 1996: 317), rejects the role defined for her as the Monster's mate and recoils in horror at the sight of Karloff's Monster. Gatiss reads this as Whale 'parodying heterosexual union' (Gatiss, 1995: 120), as the Monster destroys the laboratory, Pretorius and his reluctant bride, but not before saving Henry and Elizabeth: 'We belong dead!' Henry and Elizabeth escape the conflagration and the possibilities of an unholy matrimony for their own possibly loveless and sexless marriage.

So who exactly is the 'Bride of Frankenstein'? The doubling nature of the plot suggests it is both Elizabeth *and* the female Monster created by Pretorius and Henry. This is further exemplified by Elsa Lanchester playing both the role of Mary Shelley in the prologue and the Bride, a fascinating meta-text of embodiment as literary creator and monster that doubles as a reflection of Henry and his Monster. Young emphasises this doubling through the lens of female agency:

> After all, Shelley, who not only speaks but writes, sets the story in motion with a female signature. Reading backward, we can see Mary's opening words as forming the story that gives voice to the bride's scream; reading forward we can see the bride's scream as the most visceral and impassioned version of the 'angelic' Mary's story. (Young, 1996: 318)

Mary's line 'So why shouldn't I write of monsters?' in the prologue takes on a fresh significance when looked at through the doubling of roles by Lanchester. Instead of being 'a devout but nearly silent listener', Mary Shelley in *Bride of Frankenstein* articulates a 'monstrous power that informs the bride's shriek of refusal' (318). Vivian Sobchack writes of the power of representation, applicable to the way the figures of Dracula, the Monster and the Bride engage in complex negotiations of cultural identity:

> Figuration entails the figure actively engaged in transforming the text and being itself transformed through its work: adjusting the system of representation and the demands of the psyche and culture each to the other. The figure, then, is by nature and function unstable, problematic, and productive of new meanings and interpretations. (1996: 148)

Bride of Frankenstein is arguably the high point of Universal's horror output, 'extraordinarily carnivalesque, participatory, and resistant to closure' (Young, 1996: 332). By 1948 Universal was pairing up the Monster with their comedic duo Abbott and Costello in *Abbott and Costello Meet Frankenstein* (Charles Barton, 1948); whatever latent power the Monster embodied as an ambivalent signifier of sexual anxiety and 'insurrectionary violence' (O'Flinn, 2002: 112) had been dissipated, through the creature's constant remediation, into cliché and parody. However, like Dracula, Universal's Frankenstein's Monster still stands at the apex of Horror's Golden Age, lurking in the subconscious as the 'hideous phantasm of a man' (Shelley, 1968: 11) that once tormented the dreams of Mary Shelley.

Notes

1. www.imdb.com/title/tt0021884/business
2. From this point forward I shall capitalise Karloff's Monster to differentiate it from previous versions.
3. My personal copy of Mary Shelley's *Frankenstein*, a cheap paperback published in 1968, has on the front cover Karloff's Monster, lumbering out of the shadows, arms outstretched, a greenish hue covering his face and arms.

References

Frayling. C. 2016. *Vampyres: Genesis and Resurrection from Count Dracula to Vampirella*. London: Thames & Hudson.

Gatiss, M. 1995. *James Whale: A Biography or The Would-Be Gentleman*. London: Cassell.

Hand, R. J. 2007. 'Paridigms of metamorphosis and transmutation: Thomas Edison's *Frankenstein* and John Barrymore's *Dr Jekyll and Mr Hyde*', in Hand, R. J. and McRoy, J. (eds), *Monstrous Adaptations: Generic and Thematic Mutations in Horror Film*. Manchester: Manchester University Press, pp. 9–19.

Holte, J. C. 1997. *Dracula in the Dark: The Dracula Film Adaptations*. Westport, CT: Greenwood Press.

O'Flinn, P. 2002. 'Production and Reproduction: The Case of *Frankenstein*, in Jancovich, M. (ed.), *Horror: The Film Reader*. London: Routledge, pp. 105–14.

Sharrett, C. 1996. 'The Horror Film in Neoconservative Culture', in Grant, B. K. (ed.), *The Dread of Difference: Gender and the Horror Film*. Austin, TX: University of Texas Press, pp. 253–76.

Shelley, M. 1968. *Frankenstein*. London: Minster.

Skal, D. J. 1993. *The Monster Show: A Cultural History of Horror*. New York: Faber & Faber.

Sobchack, V. 1996. 'Bringing It All Back Home: Family Economy and Generic Exchange'. in Grant, B. K. (ed.), *The Dread of Difference: Gender and the Horror Film*. Austin, TX: University of Texas Press, pp. 143–63.

Stoker, B. 1994. *Dracula*. London: Penguin.

Wood, R. 1996. 'Burying the Undead: The Use and Obsolescence of Count Dracula', in Grant, B. K. (ed.), *The Dread of Difference: Gender and the Horror Film*. Austin, TX: University of Texas Press, pp. 364–78.

Wood, R. 2002. 'The American Nightmare: Horror in the 1970s', in Jancovich, M. (ed.), *Horror:, The Film Reader*. London: Routledge, pp. 25–32.

Young, E. 1996. 'Here Comes the Bride: Wedding, Gender and Race in *Bride of Frankenstein*', in Grant, B. K. (ed.), *The Dread of Difference: Gender and the Horror Film*. Austin, TX: University of Texas Press, pp. 309–37.

Chapter 3

Film Noir and the Gothic
Jay McRoy

Film noir as a style emerges at the intersection of multiple creative enterprises and social concerns. It is a hybrid style, informed visually by graphic conceits borrowed from German Expressionist cinema and, narratively, by elements familiar both to readers of detective and 'hard-boiled' crime fiction and to students of existentialism. As the critic/director Paul Schrader writes, film noir is defined not 'by conventions of setting and conflict, but rather by more subtle qualities of tone and mood' (1972: 8). What's more, like any aesthetic methodology, film noir provides audiences with a kind of cultural barometer. In its initial post-war Hollywood incarnation, for example, film noir captured a pervasive cynicism and emerging paranoia surrounding shifts in major socio-political arenas, from transforming sex and gender roles to new (and emerging) geopolitical conflicts that, at any moment, could transform the world into an atomic wasteland. Taking film noir's aesthetic hybridity and the shifting cultural terrain from which it emerged as a general starting point, this chapter examines the specifically Gothic pictorial and narrative trappings that inform film noir in its 'traditional' and contemporary iterations. By way of illustration, the chapter engages in a close reading of Alfred Hitchcock's *Shadow of a Doubt* (1943) as a Gothic noir, and culminates with an analysis of Park Chan-wook's *Stoker* (2013), a US-based production in which the acclaimed South Korean director deploys his trademark baroque style to advance a tale that combines many of the darker trappings of Gothic art with insightful homages to two of Alfred Hitchcock's most carefully modulated amalgams of Gothic and noir sensibilities: *Shadow of a Doubt* (1943) and *Psycho* (1960).

Film noir conventions inform visual and narrative approaches to films from genres as diverse as Science Fiction (*Kiss Me Deadly* (Robert Aldrich, 1955), *Alphaville* (Jean-Luc Godard, 1965), *Bladerunner* (Ridley Scott, 1982)), Westerns (*Pursued* (Raoul Walsh, 1947), *The*

Furies (Anthony Mann, 1950)) and Comedies (*Arsenic and Old Lace* (Frank Capra, 1944), *Dead Men Don't Wear Plaid* (Rob Reiner, 1982)). For over sixty years, film critics have enumerated and discussed film noir's most conspicuous features. These invariably include: the presence of a femme fatale – a beautiful, carnal and predatory woman who is every bit as deadly as she is seductive; complex plotting infused with fatalistic undercurrents, double crosses and sudden bursts of violence; morally and ethically ambiguous protagonists fatalistically swept up in events beyond their control; first-person voice-over narration designed to render suspect everything we see and hear; cynical – at times nihilistic – tonalities informed by pop-culture existentialism and a 'paranoid' mistrust of authority; and, lastly, a visual syntax comprised of exaggerated camera angles (e.g. extreme low- and high-angle shots, 'dutch tilts', etc.) and the frequent use of high-contrast, low-key lighting to produce rich, dark shadows. In fact, it is to these shadows that we must turn if we are to recognise the densely tangled webs of Gothic sensibilities that inform a substantial number of noir films, be they 'classic'/pre-1950 noir films or more contemporary, neo-noir productions.[1]

Strange Cousins: Film Noir and the Gothic

Since its emergence, film noir has coexisted with its partial progenitor, the Gothic, like a pair of ambiguously incestuous relations in a dark family melodrama. With enough illumination, however, the family resemblance between these cinematic styles becomes so uncanny that, as David Fine proposes, it may be possible to 'make the case that noir *is* a twentieth-century manifestation of . . . [the] Gothic' (2014: 475). Much of film noir's Gothic sensibility, after all, stems from the influence of German Expressionist cinema, a filmic tradition that, partly inspired by a popular revival of interest in Gothic art during the first decades of the twentieth century, is rife with Gothic sensibilities. The dark tone and shadow-draped urban milieus of films like Robert Wiene's *The Cabinet of Dr Caligari* (1920), Fritz Lang's *Metropolis* (1927) and *M* (1930), and G. W. Pabst's *Pandora's Box* (1930) have a direct influence upon film noir aesthetics, as do popular German Expressionist themes like fatalism, deception, entrapment, betrayal, alienation, the uncanny, and madness. These artistic, narrative and thematic preoccupations continued to inform the work of German film-makers who emigrated to the United States (and, often, Hollywood) to escape National Socialism. Thus, as directors like Fritz Lang (*Scarlet Street*, 1945; *Secret Beyond the Door*, 1948), Michael Curtiz (*Mildred Pierce*, 1945) and Robert

Siodmak (*The Killers*, 1946) crafted canonical noir films, they brought with them aesthetic sensibilities well steeped in the Gothic tradition as a result of their German Expressionist roots. This is particularly evident when considering film noir's dominant *mise-en-scène*. As Jack Morgan notes in *The Biology of Horror: Gothic Literature and Film*, '[f]ilm noir shared a complementary framing with the Gothic species all along – bleak, stylized landscapes and interior décor, investigation into uncharted territory, convoluted plot, aberrant psychology, claustrophobic spaces, disintegration, a sinister world viewed in nocturnal shadows, and so on' (2002: 130). This kinship, 'provides horror with a new and emerging frame, one as amenable to it as decadent aristocratic estates once were' (130) to readers of Gothic fictions.

In fact, one might argue that Gothic noir films retain Gothic literature and film's 'decadent aristocratic estates', but simply transform the exteriors to resemble urban apartments, suburban tract housing or once grand estates fallen into sullen disrepair. As we will soon see, Alfred Hitchcock's *Shadow of a Doubt* grimly refashions the suburban domestic sphere (aka 'the home') into a setting every bit as strange and treacherous as a rain-swept city street or empty waterfront warehouse. We can, however, find similarly dangerous domestic spaces in Gothic noir films like Alfred Hitchcock's *Rebecca* (1940) and *Notorious* (1946), George Cukor's *Gaslight* (1944), Robert Siodmak's *The Spiral Staircase* (1945), Charles Laughton's *The Night of the Hunter* (1955) and Robert Aldrich's *Whatever Happened to Baby Jane* (1963).

Perhaps the most archetypal Gothic locale in the history of film noir is Norma Desmond's decaying mansion in Billy Wilder's *Sunset Boulevard* (1950). In this sprawling, shadowy residence, the film's 'heroine' is 'haunted' by nostalgia, refusing to acknowledge that the film industry has left her behind. This behaviour renders Norma tragically abject, complicating our sympathies in a way similar to the catharsis desired by Greek tragedians. The architectural design of Norma's mansion and its dated interior decor render *Sunset Boulevard* 'as Gothic as any film can be, a perfect accompaniment to her fantasies, her ever present now; a decaying mansion filled with old photos of her as a screen star in a variety of costumes and crowded with every conceivable piece of memorabilia' (Fine, 2014: 486). At once the femme fatale responsible for the narrator's death and a victim both of her ex-husband's ill-advised manipulations and of Hollywood's veneration of youth and beauty, Norma Desmond is exemplary of the kind of female characters that populate Gothic noir films. Gothic noir films are, like so many female-authored Gothic novels, 'clear reactions to an acknowledged order, expressing feelings constrained and oppressed by social laws and practice, and addressing psychological, emotional and physical imperatives' (Wells, 2000: 39).

Film scholars have frequently interrogated the influence of a particularly 'female Gothic' on film noir. Adrian Martin, in his brief 2005 essay 'Lady Beware: Female Gothic Variations', advances one of the best rendered descriptions of the impact of the 'Female Gothic' on film noir this critic has ever encountered when he explains how '[t]he entire terrain of the Female Gothic is devoted to expressing, from the inside as it were, what it is like for women to live in a male dominated world' (para. 5):

> What is Gothic about such stories is precisely the fact that this experience is more likely to be characterized by a feeling of menace and threat – leading, inevitably, to states of catatonic fear or intense (and often quite justified) paranoia. Yet female Gothic is not only about victims. Just as significant, and driving, is the matter of women's desire. And hence the great, enabling, ever-fascinating paradox of this form: what a woman most desires is what may kill her . . . and in fact it may be this very frisson of on-the-edge, risky transgression that she most desires.

This 'paradox' Martin points out is exactly what makes the female characters in Gothic noir films so compelling. These female protagonists likewise illustrate the influence of both the 'female Gothic' and the 'woman's film' on noir style. Like their male counterparts, female protagonists in Gothic noir films long to make sense of their environments, and in their variable complexity resist simple classifications such as 'heroine' or femme fatale.

Given the historical moment during which film noir emerged, it is perhaps not surprising that many Gothic noir films with strong women characters are set within the home. These films transform the 'home' from a comforting and familiar locale into an environment every bit as strange and lethal as the mean streets of *The Naked City* (Jules Dassin, 1950) and *The Asphalt Jungle* (John Huston, 1950). This gesture of rendering the familiar strange recalls the Freudian uncanny that, as Jack Morgan points out in *The Biology of Horror: Gothic Literature and Film*, has a long tradition in Gothic narratives, from fairy tales to the Freudian psychoanalysis from which the idea emerges. Morgan writes: 'Our house defines our safe, familiar space; it is *heimlich*. Freud . . . makes much of this German word . . . and its opposite is *unheimlich*, that which is "unhomely [or uncanny]." The *unheimlich* falls outside the categories we are at home with, familiar with' (2002: 183). For Freud, the strange and estranging sensation we encounter in uncanny situations, like being unable to tell if a figure is a human being or a wax statue, or encountering familiar-looking figures that act in unexpected or oddly affected ways, ultimately reveals the extent to which we impose narratives upon our lives to comfort ourselves in the face of ambiguity. When traditionally safe spaces become sights of alienation and danger, we are firmly entrenched within the Gothic.

'The World's a Hell': Gothic Noir in Alfred Hitchcock's *Shadow of a Doubt*

Alfred Hitchcock's personal favourite of his own films,[2] *Shadow of a Doubt* was described/marketed upon its release as part of a 'bumper crop of blue-ribbon shivers and chills from a director who "can raise more goose pimples to the square inch of flesh than any other director of thrillers in Hollywood"' (Jancovich, 2014: 246). Although horror film as a genre had, by the early 1940s, waned significantly in terms of box office appeal, the use of words like 'shivers' and 'chills' position *Shadow of a Doubt* as possessing affective sequences analogous to those found in tales of terror and, by extension, as mobilising the Gothic stylistic and narrative conventions that inform them. As Mark Jancovich notes, 'since neither film noir nor the Gothic (or paranoid) women's film were categories that existed within the United States during the early to mid-1940s' (247), producers seeking descriptors to sell these amalgamations of Gothic and noir sensibilities adapted terminology usually set aside for marketing horror/Gothic films.

The relationship between Hitchcock's mode of suspense and horror cinema has long been a focus of film and media studies. An equally compelling, and yet less explored, kinship exists between Hitchcock's cinema and film noir. As Foster Hirsch notes, Hitchcock's films are rarely considered as film noir or even 'horror': '[a]s if his brand of suspense is *sui generis* above the sway and pull of genre, Alfred Hitchcock is usually placed outside noir. But at heart, no director is more deeply noir; and in the period right after the classic style ended, he created two symptomatic psychological thrillers located securely on noir grounds' (15). One of these, 1943's *Shadow of a Doubt*, is a Gothic noir film that, through its lead female protagonist's transformation, presents a subtle yet telling filmic critique of 1940s US culture and its ideological scaffolding.

Based on a screenplay by *Our Town* (1938) playwright Thornton Wilder, *Shadow of a Doubt* tells the story of two Charlies. The first is Charlotte (aka 'Charlie') Newton (Teresa Wright), a young woman still living at home with her seemingly idyllic family in beautiful Santa Rosa, California. The second Charlie is her serial killing uncle, Charles (aka

'Uncle Charlie') Oakley (Joseph Cotten), the 'Merry Widow Murderer'. We meet Uncle Charlie in the film's opening sequence, and we soon discover that federal agents are following/investigating him in regard to the deaths of several recently widowed women. Cunning and elusive, Uncle Charlie evades capture in urban Philadelphia and books a train to visit his sister Emma (Patricia Collinge), her husband, Joseph Newton (Henry Travers), and their children, Roger (Charles Bates), Ann (Edna May Wonacott), and, of course, Charlotte/Charlie, his namesake. Young Charlie, feeling unfulfilled and dreading the prospect of living an ordinary 'average' life, eagerly anticipates her uncle's arrival. At first, she overtly romanticises her uncle, seeing his charming demeanour and apparent erudition as the potential solution to the 'rut' she feels that she and her family are in. Life with Uncle Charlie proves exciting at first, and in an eerily incestuous gesture, Uncle Charlie offers his beloved niece a ring that, unbeknownst to him, contains initials matching those of one of the recent victims of the 'Merry Widow Murderer'. When young Charlie begins to tease her uncle by playing amateur sleuth, Uncle Charlie sets out to determine what, if anything, his naive niece knows about his murderous past.

Shadow of a Doubt's narrative shifts dramatically with the arrival in the Newton residence of two federal agents posing as a survey conductor and his accompanying photographer. They claim that they are chronicling 'typical American famil(ies)', but Uncle Charlie, suspicious of the newcomers' motives, refuses to cooperate. Jack Graham (Macdonald Carey), after spending the day with young Charlie, reveals that he is a federal agent investigating her uncle as one of two prime suspects in the 'Merry Widow Murderer' killings. Young Charlie promises to keep Jack's identity a secret from her family and subsequently commences her own investigation. When she confronts her uncle with her findings, he initially promises to leave town. These plans, however, are soon placed on hold when the other 'Merry Widow Murderer' suspect dies while fleeing the police, thus ending the federal search. Emboldened by this turn of events, Uncle Charlie attempts to kill his niece by, first, sabotaging the outside staircase to the house's second floor, and, second, attempting to trap her in a garage filling with carbon monoxide. When Young Charlie finally confronts her uncle with the emerald ring bearing the initials of one of his victims, he suddenly announces to family and friends that he must leave Santa Rosa, but he also promises to return one day. The two Charlies have one final confrontation on the train leaving Santa Rosa. Uncle Charlie traps his niece on the train and, once the engine has generated enough speed, attempts to throw her from it. After a brief struggle, it is Uncle Charlie who falls from the train and into the path of an oncoming locomotive. The film then cuts to its final sequence. Standing outside of the church where Uncle Charlie's funeral has just taken place. Charlie and Jack, now depicted as a romantic couple, agree to keep secret their knowledge of who her Uncle Charlie really was.

Hitchcock opens *Shadow of a Doubt* by introducing us to the film's two Charlies through a pair of complementary, dissolve-punctuated sequences that present the narrative's Charlies as 'doubles' whose perspectives we are compelled to compare. The first of these sequences immerses us unapologetically in a familiar noir cityscape, in this instance Philadelphia, Pennsylvania. We open with a horizontal left–right pan across a bleak waterfront which then dissolves to a shot of a discarded automobile near a sign that reads: 'NO DUMPING'. From here, Hitchcock dissolves to a new, secondary establishing shot: a city sidewalk filled with children at play. With the dissolve as the lone transitional effect, Hitchcock cuts to a canted angle of a boarding house, then to a close-up of a specific window and, finally, to the film's first interior shot. We find ourselves inside of a rented room with its boarder, Charles 'Uncle Charlie' Oakley, nervously puffing away at a cigar as he lies on his bed, money strewn carelessly about the nightstand and floor.

The second of these sequences introduces us to the seemingly idyllic West Coast community of Santa Rosa, California, where the remainder of the film's action transpires. As with the first sequence, we open with a wide, establishing shot. In this case, however, we see clear skies, clean white buildings and manicured streets. From here Hitchcock continues to establish the look and feel of this geographical space by dissolving to a low-angle shot of a smiling police officer confidently regulating traffic, and then to a quiet, suburban neighbourhood. In contrast to the boarding house in which we encounter Uncle Charlie, the Newton family home on 46 Burnham Street is framed in a conventional/straightforward manner, as is the bedroom window through which we dissolve to find Charlie on her bed, reclined and smiling despite the rut she perceives herself and her family to be in. The eventual entrance of the East Coast, urban(e) Uncle Charlie into this carefully maintained and regulated space (with its connotations of affluence, tranquillity and homogeneity) recalls Gothic 'invasion' narratives, with Bram Stoker's novel, *Dracula* (1897), and its narrative of resisting an intruding Eastern 'other', the most immediate example. Making the intruding (albeit initially welcomed) person a close relative with a mysterious and traumatic past further amplifies the film's Gothic sensibility.

Uncle Charlie is no vampire; however, a palpable blood lust certainly motivates him. He is, rather, a 'streetwise', fast-talking character who would be at home in virtually any film noir. What's more, like many

Gothic narratives, *Shadow of a Doubt* builds off of a self-conscious collision of two mythic US 'spaces': Philadelphia, PA, a once great city now a site of poverty and crime, and Santa Rosa, CA, with its lingering implications of Westward expansion and the hope of new frontiers. By setting this Gothic noir narrative in such an apparently tranquil (and white) suburban environment, Hitchcock capitalises upon audience presuppositions and prejudices surrounding the Gothic noir style more broadly; if at first glance Santa Rosa seems the 'incorrect' locale for a dark tale of deceit and serial murder, then Hitchcock has us right where he wants us.

Like many Gothic antagonists, Uncle Charlie uses his cunning and charm to 'pass' as a 'normal', if a tad 'eccentric', individual. His repressed urges surface sporadically, however, both through misogynist comments dismissed by others as dry humour and through physical tics, like hands grasping the air in front of them as if choking an absent throat. What's more, Uncle Charlie expresses his femicidal urges through language that, for audiences in 1943, would clearly resemble Nazi rhetoric. Consider the following remarks, delivered during a family dinner:

> The cities are full of women, middle-aged widows, husbands dead, husbands who've spent their lives making fortunes, working and working. And then they die and leave their money to their wives, their silly wives. And what do the wives do, these useless women? You see them in hotels, the best hotels, every day by the thousands, drinking the money, eating the money, losing the money at bridge, playing all day and all night, smelling of money, proud of their jewellery but of nothing else, horrible, faded, fat, greedy women . . . Are they human or are they fat wheezing animals, hmm? And what happens when they get too fat and old?

In *Sexual Politics and Narrative Film: Hollywood and Beyond*, Robin Wood reads Uncle Charlie's sinister discourse, punctuated by fascist comments ('[a]re they human or are they . . . animals'?), as part of what makes him the archetypal Hitchcock villain. Uncle Charlie 'characteristically dramatises fascist tendencies and is presented as at once fascinating, perverted, monstrous, and ultimately self-destructive, his seductive "potency" revealed as, at another level, impotence' (1998: 25). Despite his occasional outbursts, Uncle Charlie remains charismatic and alluring. He stands out in a crowd, his 'fashionable big city' swagger turning women's heads wherever he goes. Uncle Charlie's *carpe diem* attitude ('What's the use of looking ahead? Today's the thing!'), coupled with his cavalier attitude towards money and his cynical mistrust of social institutions, likewise conflicts with the values of the community into which he is attempting to assimilate. He literally leaves money 'lying around', and he openly admits that once he has earned money, he is 'not interested in it'.

These conspicuous statements and gestures position Uncle Charlie as a subject resistant to ideological interpolation. While in the bank where his brother-in-law works, Uncle Charlie jokes openly about embezzlement. '(It) looks alright on the outside', he says, 'but we all know what goes on when the doors are locked.' Uncle Charlie speaks the secret everyone knows but tries not to spill; he acknowledges the corruption beneath the United States' idealised edifice, reminding the community's residents of the very real underside of the 'American Dream' they consensually hallucinate. He eschews capitalist values and its institutions' illusion of legitimacy. In the Newton family at least, these attitudes and affectations are explained away/pathologised by Uncle Charlie's sister, Emma, as the result of an obscure childhood bicycle accident. In 'killing' her uncle, Charlie Newton not only rids her family, and Santa Rosa, of a Gothicised threat in the form of a misogynist serial murderer, but she also rids the town of a visible and vocal threat to the status quo and the illusions/ideologies supporting it. As the young Ann Newton reminds us, in Santa Rosa one does not 'talk against the government'.

Like Uncle Charlie, the character of Charlie Newton has long been the focus of analysis in Hitchcock studies. Some critics, like Tanya Modleski, see her as 'a typical Hitchcock female . . . because her close relationship to her mother arouses in her a longing for a different kind of life than the one her father offers them' (2011: 383). Furthermore, Charlie seems 'to possess special, incriminating knowledge about men. Charlie's attitude is representative of the two types of resistance to patriarchy . . . that which seeks to know men's "secrets" (patriarchy's "blind spots, gaps, and repressed areas") and that which knows the kinds of pleasures unique to women's relationships with other women' (383). Like many Gothic heroines, Charlie struggles against these 'secrets', ultimately electing to help keep some rather than reveal the 'blind spots, gaps, and repressed areas'. Also, in keeping with Gothic heroines, Charlie behaves in impulsive and, occasionally, uncanny ways; at one point in the film, she wonders if she might possess 'psychic powers'. Additionally, in keeping with the Gothic theme of a tension between the natural/scientific and the spiritual/alchemical, Charlie's professed 'telepathy' is met with suspicion and, at times, derision. 'She makes no allowance for science', her younger sister, Ann, observes; later, the same sibling mockingly reminds Charlie that '(s)uperstition has proven to be 100% wrong'.

Charlie's romantic naivety, coupled with an earnest desire to escape from the mundane routine of 'life as usual', places her at risk of becoming the focus of her uncle's murderous impulses. Although they share a disdain for money as a fetish and are, in their own separate ways, 'outsiders' within their immediate family, from the instant her Uncle presents her with an emerald ring that once belonged to one of his victims, they commence a dance of suspicion, danger and last-second escapes. In this sense, their conflicts recall the waltzing figures in black and white evening wear that comprise the film's opening credit sequence. By having Uncle Charlie place the emerald ring onto his niece's finger like a groom sliding a wedding band onto his bride's hand, Hitchcock capitalises upon the Gothic trope of implicit incest (Figure 3.1). At the very least, this gesture cements the importance of their relationship, leading us to consider carefully the myriad ways that their characters interact or are juxtaposed. Young Charlie's suggestions that she feels a deep connection to and knows 'secrets' about her uncle only further intensifies the danger she finds herself in, as it places her murderous uncle on the defensive. Later, from the moment that her own investigations convince her of her uncle's guilt, she is in constant peril.

As with Oedipus and other prototypical detective figures, Charlie Newton's quest for knowledge is a radically transformative and life-altering enterprise. It may even be possible, given Charlie's sheltered past and traumatic experiences, to consider *Shadow of a Doubt* as a kind of *Bildungsroman*. Over the course of the film, Charlie changes from a young, dissatisfied woman living at home with her family and

Uncle Charlie (Joseph Cotten) admires the ring on naive Young Charlie's (Theresa Wright's) finger in *Shadow of a Doubt* (Alfred Hitchcock, 1943). © 1943 Universal Pictures.

dreading the possibility of becoming 'average', to a melancholy young woman who, attracted to a federal representative of law and order, conspires to help conceal her uncle's crimes and, by extension, the patriarchal violence integral to, and sublimated by, the larger social system. Moreover, by learning the truth behind her once beloved uncle's murderous activities, and by surviving her uncle's repeated attempts upon her life, Charlie satiates her desire for 'something more' than the quiet domestic life on offer. At the same time, she finally, and self-consciously, reinforces the illusion of a life in which the American Dream for some does not result in an American nightmare for others.

The Kind of Family You Can't Bring Home: Park Chan-wook's *Stoker* (2013)

Gothic and noir sensibilities similarly commingle throughout Park Chan-wook's 2013 film, *Stoker*. In the acclaimed South Korean director's first English language feature, Gothic motifs abound. Much of the film's action transpires in isolated environments, characters function as doubles/doppelgängers, and troubled protagonists and antagonists vie for power within an abstrusely incestuous family that harbours deeply buried/repressed secrets. Even the film's title, derived from the surname of the disturbed protagonists at the centre of this dark chamber play, recalls the Victorian novelist Bram Stoker, author of the canonical Gothic vampire novel, *Dracula* (1897). However, if we also consider the film's title as a reference to a person who 'feeds' or 'strengthens'/'stokes' a smouldering fire into a larger blaze, it is possible to read *Stoker* as a sinister coming of age tale about eighteen-year-old India Stoker's repressed predatory and sexual urges exploding in a crescendo of liberating violence.

Park Chan-wook possesses a profound appreciation for the dark shadows and even darker souls that inform the history of both Gothic cinema and film noir. In his 2009 vampire film, *Thirst*, Park deploys an array of overtly Gothic conceits, and in his *Vengeance* trilogy – *Sympathy for Mr Vengeance* (2002), *Oldboy* (2003) and *Sympathy for Lady Vengeance* (2005) – Park blends an array of noir aesthetics with conventional thriller elements and digitally enhanced gore effects to revisit the theme of revenge, as well as the physical and psychological tolls that such rancour exacts. *Stoker*, however, is more than simply a creative melange of genre elements that both conform to, and confound, viewer expectations. At the film's core is a meta-cinematic engagement with two of Alfred Hitchcock's most celebrated and frequently 'cited' fusions of Gothic and noir conceits: *Shadow of a Doubt* (1943) and *Psycho* (1960).

Stoker's central narrative is a seemingly conventional Gothic melodrama. Following the mysterious death of the family patriarch, Richard Stoker (Dermot Mulroney), Richard's younger brother, Charles (Matthew Goode), arrives just in time for the funeral and is very soon invited to stay in the secluded Stoker home by his grieving sister-in-law, Evelyn/'Evie' (Nicole Kidman). Like his malevolent namesake in Hitchcock's *Shadow of a Doubt* (1943) Charles, or 'Uncle Charlie', has committed a series of murders (in this case, fratricides) and he exhibits a strange connection to his eighteen-year-old niece, India (Mia Wasikowska), despite his having never actually met her. Evelyn sees in Charlie a younger, more cosmopolitan version of her late husband, Richard, whose sudden absence creates what Phil Hoad describes as 'the void' at the story's 'heart' (2013: para. 4). Envious of the time Richard spent teaching India hunting and taxidermy, Evelyn channels her feelings of neglect into a virulent antipathy towards India, an open display of resentment that only intensifies when Charles seems less interested in Evelyn's blatantly romantic overtures than he is in showering vaguely incestuous attentions upon India. From the instant that India first sees her Uncle Charlie watching from afar as his brother's body is lowered into the earth, India is simultaneously intrigued by and wary of his motives. This dynamic intensifies until India finally realises her uncle's propensity for violence, as well as his obvious culpability in the sudden disappearances/murders of the family's housekeeper and a concerned aunt.

After Uncle Charlie saves India from a date rape by strangling the would-be lothario with a belt that once belonged to his brother/India's father, India helps her uncle bury the body. Mere hours later, India masturbates to the memory of her uncle breaking her date's neck as the choking boy lay on top of her, gasping for breath. Soon afterwards, as she is sorting through her father's affairs, India uses a key she received as a gift to open a locked desk drawer, where she discovers stacks of letters addressed to her from her uncle. Despite return addresses consistent with the journeys her uncle recounts throughout the film, the back of each letter bears the stamp of the Crawford Institute, a mental health facility in which Charlie has been housed since he murdered his younger brother many years ago. When India confronts her uncle, he confounds her further by explaining that he killed his brother/her father when it became clear that Richard had decided to set him up with an apartment and money in New York City rather than welcome him back into the family. Then, after presenting her with a pair of high-heel shoes to wear in place of the black-and-white saddle shoes she has worn virtually every day of her eighteen years, he lies to a police officer investigating the would-be date rapist's disappearance, and finally implores India to leave her hometown and live with him in New York. That evening, when an embittered Evelyn threatens to expose her brother-in-law's past in a desperate attempt to win him over, Uncle Charlie begins to strangle her with the same belt he used to kill India's attacker. He calls for India to witness her mother's death, but India saves her mother by shooting her uncle in the head and burying his body in the back yard. In the film's final sequence, a police officer in a pair of mirrored sunglasses pulls India over and asks her if she knows how fast she was travelling. She implies that she was trying to attract his attention and then, with alarming speed, stabs him in the throat. She watches as he stumbles into the tall grass on the side of the road before finally shooting him in the first in what will doubtlessly be a string murders that India will commit.

In his review of *Stoker*, Xan Brooks notes the obvious debt Park and his cinematographer, Chung Chung-hoon, owe to Hitchcock's cinematic approach. However, whereas Hitchcock injects 'a small drop of poison into picket-fence suburbia', *Stoker* 'stands poised as a full-blown Gothic nightmare, replete with cadavers in the freezer and sexual ecstasy in the shower' (2013: para. 2). While Brooks is ultimately hesitant to declare the film a success, he cites the work's overall visual and narrative style (its 'wild undulations' (para. 2)) as most effective when at its most exuberant. Though Brooks does not elaborate upon these remarks, several of these 'undulations' undoubtedly correspond with scenes in which Park masterfully integrates digital and practical effects. Digital effects have long been a staple of Park's cinema. Used sparingly, they infuse *Stoker* with an almost surreal, storybook quality. The tiny digitally generated spider that crawls throughout the Stoker residence, at one point disappearing beneath India's skirt, is a key example of this uncanny collision of the digital and the real. Rather than functioning as a plot point or antagonistic element, the digital arachnid assumes an almost extra-diegetic significance. The spider climbing towards the hem of India's charcoal blue skirt elicits dread and expectation, only to have that tension disrupted by a sudden cut to a medium shot of India sulking at a kitchen table, a hard-boiled egg's shell crumbling as she rolls it slowly back and forth. With this cut, the spider ceases to operate as a traditional point of conflict; indeed, it bears no immediate or consequential weight of the narrative action. Thematically, its recurrence graphically links vital moments or actions. The spider, in other words, operates simultaneously as an icon of predation and venom, as a portent of hidden dangers lurking beneath seemingly idyllic surfaces, and as a symbolic reminder of the webs of emotional and sexual traumas and tensions that infest virtually any – and most certainly *this* particular – family nest.

The spider's colouration is striking. Its legs are a dangerous mustard yellow, its head and abdomen an amalgam of brown, black and beige markings. This colour scheme is among *Stoker*'s most prominent, and Park links this associative combination of tones with potential danger as early as the film's opening sequence. Through this montage of variably balanced, lighted and angled framings, Park not only introduces India to the film's viewers, but also establishes the narrative to follow as a flash-back mediated from her perspective. India's clothing is dishevelled and seemingly discordant. As she states in the accompanying voice-over, the yellow-orange, blood-stained blouse is her mother's, the brown belt (her uncle's weapon of choice) once belonged to her father, and the black high-heel shoes are, she points out, 'from my uncle'.

Like *Shadow of a Doubt*'s Charlie Newton, India receives increasingly menacing and, at times, eerily incestuous attentions from her Uncle Charlie. However, while young Charlie Newton romanticises her uncle's arrival as a means of disrupting the monotony of daily life in a surreally idyllic Santa Rosa, India has no clue that she even has an Uncle Charlie until her mother introduces him to her after her father's death. Additionally, whereas Hitchcock creates suspense and fear for Young Charlie by ensuring from the outset that the audience knows more than she does about the lethal relative she mistakenly idolises, Park predominantly aligns the audience's perspective with India's point of view so that we are afforded the opportunity to 'think along with' and 'feel along with' our central protagonist. The film's opening voice-over further primes the spectator to identify with India, allowing us insight into how she experiences the world around her:

> My ears hear what others cannot hear; small faraway things people cannot normally see are visible to me. These senses are the fruits of a lifetime of longing, longing to be rescued, to be completed. Just as the skirt needs the wind to billow, I'm not formed by things that are of myself alone . . . This is me. Just as a flower does not choose its colour, we are not responsible for what we have come to be. Only once you realize this do you become free, and to become an adult is to become free.

Here, too, several compelling parallels exist between *Stoker*'s India and Hitchcock's Charlie. Both long to be rescued from an abiding sense of existential dissatisfaction. Both ultimately kill their murderous relations. However, despite occasionally viewing objects or actions through various characters' perspectives as we do in *Shadow of a Doubt*, India's voice-over narration, a trope common to noir films, frames and informs our very experience of *Stoker*'s action.

India, however, differs importantly from conventional Gothic heroines. Far from an endangered governess or vulnerable relation at the mercy of a powerful and sadistic patriarch, India is very much a predator in her own right. From the narrative's earliest moments, India is established as a skilled hunter with visual and auditory abilities that, if we take her at her word, are every bit as acute as those possessed by the birds of prey whose stuffed forms decorate the Stoker residence. These carefully poised birds at once fill the Stoker home with a tone of impending predation and deliberately evoke the similarly adorned main office of the Bates Motel in Alfred Hitchcock's *Psycho*. Bird imagery, in short, pervades *Stoker*'s *mise-en-scène*. India's headboard boasts chiselled wooden feathers; eggs, be they organic or artificial/decorative, constitute a conspicuous visual motif.

India's observation that her seemingly heightened senses are the result 'of a lifetime of longing . . . to be rescued, to be completed' introduces a familiar, almost clichéd, Gothic sentiment: a desire for deliverance or rescue. Given India's development from apprentice hunter to aspiring serial murderer, however, one cannot help but question exactly what India means by 'rescued' or 'completed'. As the film builds towards its climax and we find ourselves revisiting the action from the film's opening sequence, we realise that we have witnessed India grow increasingly more cunning and resourceful. We are aware of the propensity for violence India masks beneath a veneer of 'refined' civility. Uncle Charlie's homicidal impulses may awaken India sexually (she orgasms at the memory of her classmate's strangulation), but, more importantly, they 'stoke' the violent flames inside her, allowing her smouldering impulses and desires to burst forth in a climactic conflagration of violence. India, therefore, is not simply articulating consequentialist platitudes when she says: '[j]ust as the skirt needs the wind to billow, [she is not] formed by things that are of [herself] alone. Just as a flower does not choose its colour, we are not responsible for what we become'. India does not negate her agency. Rather, she acknowledges her participation and culpability in who/what she is becoming. However, she does so in a way that nevertheless locates her actions as part of a larger nexus of variables, the majority of which – as is the case with all humans – reside beyond her control. In one of the film's final images, as India raises her rifle and, in a medium close-up, aims it directly at the camera (Figure 3.2), she has 'come of age' as a cold-blooded killer, a woman every bit as deadly as the deadliest film noir femme fatale.

Much like the Newton house in *Shadow of a Doubt*, the Stoker residence serves as the locale for much of the film's action. In both films, these houses function as sites of seeming domesticity disrupted by the emergence of a mysterious relative who serves as a catalyst

India Stoker takes aim at her prey in *Stoker* (Park Chan-wook, 2013). © 2013 Fox Searchlight Pictures.

for our young female characters' entry into the duplicity and perils of adulthood. *Stoker*'s art design, however, amplifies the locale's Gothic elements. As the camera moves throughout the rooms of the Stoker residence, the interiors are at once expansive and labyrinthine, alienating and claustrophobic. Maroon walls evoke both feelings of passion and of danger; mysterious keys open locked spaces that lead to dark secrets. In an interview on the filming of *Stoker*, Park Chan-wook speaks about his aesthetic and narratological intentions regarding the Stoker house. He states that he 'wanted to give India and Evie this sense of a princess and queen trapped in a castle, literally' (2013). Consequently, when scouting locations for the Stoker residence, Park's emphasis was on finding a house that had the 'right amount of antiquity, right amount of grandeur' (2013). Unlike the multi-storey Newton house in *Shadow of a Doubt*, though, the Stoker residence is substantially removed from the community that surrounds it (Middlebend, Connecticut) by a long driveway flanked by trees and wide expanses of lawn. Sojourns into town are filled with hazards. India is harassed by her peers at school, and even the teenage boy that apparently stands up for her in front of his friends turns violent and attempts to sexually assault her when, while traipsing through a darkened playground, India fails to return his carnal advances.

Like many Gothic ancestral estates, from Jane Austen's Northanger Abbey (1803), to Charlotte Brontë's Thornfield Hall (1847), to Daphne du Maurier's Manderley (1938)), the Stoker residence proves an ideal environment for a twisted, darkly Freudian family drama to unfold. Resentful, lonely and jealous of the bond between her daughter and her late husband, Richard, Evelyn/Evie imagines Uncle Charlie's arrival as an opportunity for her to escape a life of solitude and seclusion. To India, however, Evie's affections towards Uncle Charlie seem precipitous. She accosts her mother with an attitude reminiscent of Hamlet's towards Gertrude. 'In Victorian times', India observes, 'a widow was expected to mourn her husband for two years – at least', to which Evie replies, 'Well we don't live in Victorian times . . . thank God!' When Uncle Charlie's attentions towards India disrupt Evie's desperate visions of a happier future filled with travel and companionship, Evie lashes out at India with a virulence that seems pointedly ironic, especially given her name's biblical/maternal implications:

> You know, I've often wondered why it is that we have children in the first place. And the conclusion I have come to is . . . at some point in our lives we realize things are screwed up beyond repair. So we decide to start again . . . And then we have children. Little carbon copies we can turn to and say, 'You will do what I could not. You will succeed where I have failed.' Because we want someone to get it right this time. But not me. Personally speaking I can't wait to watch life tear you apart.

Rather than conforming to traditional notions of gendered, maternal behaviour, Evie positions herself not as her daughter's champion, but as her daughter's rival. Evie and Uncle Charlie are indeed complementary characters, albeit – much to Evie's chagrin – not in a romantic sense. Instead, Evie and Uncle Charlie are linked by an almost pathological fear of abandonment, a terror of facing a world without at least the illusion of 'family'. 'Who are you?' Evie asks India, as she feels her world crumbling about her. 'You were supposed to love me, weren't you?' For Evie, India fails to perform her 'proper' function as a 'daughter' within the symbolic order to which Evie clings. India's bond, she believes, ultimately should have been with her and not Richard. Thus, the vaguely erotic tension surrounding India's exchanges with her uncle further violate Evie's understanding of a daughter's role: 'Take me not her', Evie says, clutching desperately to Uncle Charlie's sweater mere moments before he attempts to strangle her.

The Stoker residence likewise provides a kind of cinematic diorama within which Park Chan-wook stages action deliberately designed to recall iconic moments and techniques from Hitchcock's cinema. A flashback to a young uncle Charlie planning and executing his first fratricide features a doll's house-sized replica of the Stoker home. The basement containing the freezer in which Uncle Charlie hides the housekeeper's

corpse deliberately recalls the fruit cellar in Hitchcock's *Psycho*, an
homage that is made even more explicit when India – in a gesture
reminiscent of Lila Crane's (Vera Miles's) panicked arm flailing upon
the discovery of Mrs Bates corpse – pushes past a series of lights dangling from the ceiling, causing them to swing. There is even a shower
scene that, rather than ending in death, culminates in an orgasm. The
Stoker residence's main staircase, however, provides perhaps one of the
film's most overtly Hitchcockian spaces, as staircases have long been a
primary visual conceit in his films, including *Shadow of a Doubt*. These
locales provide dynamic arenas within which power shifts between characters transpire.

In *Stoker*, as in many of Hitchcock's films, staircases similarly function as sites of realisation and transformation. It is while descending the
Stoker residence's main staircase that India discovers that the hidden
letters from her Uncle Charlie were mailed from a mental hospital, and
it is Uncle Charlie's younger brother's obsession with stairs that partially
inspires Uncle Charlie's first fratricide. Crucially, two of the film's most
important scenes take place on, or near, the Stoker residence's main
staircase, and in each of these a consideration of the angle of the camera
to the action is essential.

The first of these sequences takes place relatively early in the film.
Uncle Charlie, having just received Evie's permission to stay for 'a
while', encounters India sitting below him on the staircase. In a series of
shot/reverse shots, they engage in a discussion that not only foreshadows
the shifting power relations between India and Uncle Charlie, but also
establishes India as an active subject who resists intimidation or victimisation. 'Do you know why you feel at a disadvantage right now?' Uncle
Charlie asks, standing at the top of the stairs and framed in a low-angle
shot. 'Because I didn't know you existed until today?' India asks, framed
from a high angle. 'Because you are standing below me', Uncle Charlie,
in a low-angle shot approximating India's perspective, replies. Park then
cuts to a medium close-up tracking shot of India in profile as she confidently ascends the stairs, pausing momentarily as she enters into a close-
up two-shot with her uncle. Park then breaks the 180 degree rule and
cuts to an image of India (screen left) and Uncle Charlie (screen right)
in a close-up two-shot, their eye-line (and its attendant negative space)
parallel with the top and bottom of the frame until, finally, Uncle Charlie
yields power to India by descending the staircase, pausing to ask India,
now looming above him, if he could have her permission to stay. In this
sequence, dialogue, cinematography and editing combine to simultaneously establish and subvert the visual logic behind this well-worn system
of establishing power relations through cinematic staging; the shifting

dispositions of Uncle Charlie and India's figures anticipate a power relationship that may very well prove changeable.

Stoker's second major stairway sequence deploys a comparable visual
logic. The scene transpires in a series of shot-reverse shots reminiscent of
the final staircase showdown between Young Charlie and Uncle Charlie
in *Shadow of a Doubt*. In *Stoker*, though, it is not a ring but a pair of
sunglasses that once belonged to her father with which the precocious
niece confronts her homicidal uncle. Wearing the very sunglasses that
link him to her father's demise, Uncle Charlie looks up at India, who
stands at the top of the staircase, framed from a low angle. He then
slowly ascends the stairs until he meets her at the top, the position of
their bodies once again suggestive of comparable power. It is here that
Uncle Charlie admits his murderous past, including his responsibility for
her father's death. He then presents India with her eighteenth birthday
present: a pair of high-heel shoes that stand in contrast to the mysterious
saddle shoes (gifts from her uncle) that India has received on every birthday. Donning these heels also suggests a passage into the insidious world
of adulthood. That Uncle Charlie drops to one knee to replace the saddle
shoe with this more 'adult' shoe is also crucial to note. His position in
the frame implies a willingness to subordinate himself to an emotionally
distraught India, but it also links him directly – in both India's mind
and the *mise-en-scène* – with India's final transformation from resistant
subject to active agent.

Stoker's final citation/reworking of Hitchcock's cinema takes place in
the film's closing sequence, in which the narrative finally catches up with
the atmospheric yet fragmented montage that opens the film. On her
way to New York City to live in the apartment – and off of the money
– that her father established for her Uncle Charlie, India is pulled over
by a sheriff whose appearance, especially his intimidatingly reflective
sunglasses, recalls that of the police officer who pulls over the fleeing
Marion Crane in Hitchcock's *Psycho*. In contrast to Marion Crane, who
fears that the officer will deduce that she has absconded with $40,000,
a smiling, seemingly friendly India admits to the sheriff that she was
not only intentionally speeding, but that she was doing so purposefully
to attract his attention. Ever the predator, India stabs the unsuspecting sheriff in the throat with a pair of gardening sheers, then follows
the wounded and fleeing lawman into a cornfield on the side of the
road before finally shooting him with her hunting rifle. Unlike *Psycho*'s
Marion Crane, India is no frightened, guilt ridden, soon-to-be-murder
victim. Nor is she, like *Shadow of a Doubt*'s Young Charlie, recuper-
ated into the patriarchal social order. Instead, India wields the phallic
hunting rifle, her eye digitally enhanced in the glass of the riffle's scope,

before Park cuts to the film's final image: tiny white blossoms dripping with blood.

Conclusion

Like the Gothic tradition that partially informs its visual and narrative iconography, film noir is 'first of all a matter of style' (Schrader, 1972: 13). However, as my discussions of Alfred Hitchcock's *Shadow of a Doubt* and Park Chan-wook's *Stoker* illustrate, when masterful direction complements and amplifies familiar subject matters in compelling ways, the results can be both artistically and critically rewarding. As Paul Schrader notes, 'because [film noir] as a style worked out its conflicts visually rather than thematically, because it was aware of its own identity, it was able to create artistic solutions to sociological problems' (13). In *Shadow of a Doubt* and *Stoker* respectively, Alfred Hitchcock and Park Chan-wook deploy distinctive visual and narrative strategies both to heighten the Gothic components inherent within noir's visual and narrative logics, and to allow for strong female characters to emerge within and against certain larger cultural logics. The result of this hybridity is a pair of Gothic noirs, the latter of which engages in an aesthetic and cultural dialogue with the former. Like female characters in nineteenth-century Gothic novels, Charlie Newton and India Stoker express 'feelings constrained and oppressed by social laws and practice' and, in the process, address an array of 'psychological, emotional and physical imperatives' (Wells, 2000: 39).

Notes

1. For more on the distinctions between 'classical noir' and 'neo-noir', see Foster Hirsch's *Detours and Lost Highways: A Map of Neo Noir* (1999), Mark T. Conrad's anthology *The Philosophy of Neo-Noir* (2009) and Alain Silver and James Ursini's *American Neo-Noir: The Movie Never Ends* (2015).
2. Hitchcock makes this admission in a 1964 television interview on film editing: https://www.youtube.com/watch?v=MJQE7Kv-9JU (accessed 6 July 2019).

References

Brooks, X. 2013. '*Stoker* – Review'. *The Guardian*, 28 February. Available at: https://www.theguardian.com/film/2013/feb/28/stoker-review.

Edmundson, M. 1997. *Nightmare on Main Street: Angels, Sadomasochism, and the Culture of the Gothic*. Cambridge, MA: Harvard University Press.

Fine, D. 2014. 'Film Noir and the Gothic', in Crow, C. L. (ed.), *A Companion to American Gothic*. New York & London: John Wiley & Sons, pp. 475–87.

Hirsch, F. 1999. *Detours and Lost Highways: A Map of Neo-Noir*. New York: Limelight Editions.

Hoad, P. 2013. '*Stoker* Director Park Chan-wook: "In Knowing Yourself, You Can Liberate Yourself", *The Guardian*, 28 February. Available at: https://www.theguardian.com/film2013/feb/28/stoker-review.

Jancovich, M. 2014. 'Horror in the 1940s', in Harry, M. B. (ed.), *A Companion to the Horror Film*. New York & London: John Wiley & Sons, pp. 237–54.

Martin, A. 2005. 'Lady Beware: Female Gothic Variations', *Film Critic: Adrian Martin*. March. Available at http://www.filmcritic.com.au/essays/female_gothic.html.

Modleski, T. 2011. 'Hitchcock, feminism, and the Patriarchal Unconscious', in Timothy, C., Patricia, W. and Meta, M. (eds), *Critical Visions in Film Theory: Classic and Contemporary Readings*. Boston & New York: Bedford/St. Martin's, pp. 377–85.

Morgan, J. 2002. *The Biology of Horror: Gothic Literature and Film*. Carbondale and Edwardsville IL: Southern Illinois University Press.

Park, Chan-wook. 2013. 'Stoker: A Filmmaker's Journey', *Stoker*. Fox Searchlight.

Schrader, P. 1972. 'Notes on Film Noir', *Film Comment*, Spring, pp. 8–13.

Scruggs, C. 2014. 'American Film Noir', in Jerrold, E. H. (ed.), *The Cambridge Companion to the Modern Gothic*. Cambridge: Cambridge University Press, pp. 123–37.

Wells, P. 2000. *The Horror Genre: From Beelzebub to Blair Witch*. London: Wallflower.

Wood, R. 1998. *Sexual Politics and Narrative Film: Hollywood and Beyond*. New York: Columbia University Press.

Chapter 4

Transitional Gothic: Hammer's Gothic Revival and New Horror[1]

Adam Charles Hart

The mid-1950s were eager for a Gothic revival. The cycle of Science Fiction creature features was petering out, increasingly the province of no-budget off-Hollywood productions. Audiences and critics were nostalgic not just for horror films, but for an older style of horror – and, crucially, the production values – that they associated with Universal in the 1930s. *Dracula* (Tod Browning, 1931), *Frankenstein* (James Whale, 1931) et al. had, after highly successful re-releases in the late 1930s, remained in semi-regular circulation and stayed at the forefront of the public imagination, but Universal had long since ceased producing monster classics, and Abbot and Costello were as prominent in the studio's monster productions of the 1950s as were any of the iconic creatures. Hammer Film Productions' *Curse of Frankenstein* (Terence Fisher, 1957) arrived at precisely the right moment to inaugurate what is often thought of as the last great Gothic horror revival, including a decade-plus of Hammer horror films and films by Roger Corman in the United States and by Mario Bava, Riccardo Fredo and Antonio Margheriti in Italy, but also the enormously successful 'Shock!' (and, then, in 1958, 'Son of Shock') packages of the 1970s that brought hundreds of horror films to American television audiences. This television revival also ensured that no critic or fan in the US could fail to compare *Curse* or *Horror of Dracula* (Terence Fisher, 1958) with their Universal forerunners. Hammer's films to an extent depended on those associations, beginning their horror output by re-imagining *Frankenstein* and *Dracula*, with an official collaboration with Universal – on a remake of *The Mummy* – not far behind.

Associated with this rosy look backwards, Hammer and its Gothic followers tend to be thought of as the last gasp of an older style of cinematic horror but infused with the vividly coloured blood and gore of an era-to-come: castles and monsters, foreign aristocrats and horse-drawn carriages, fog machine atmospherics, all the while boasting moments of

stomach-wrenching spectacle horror. This style was essentially old fash-
ioned but decorated with blood and scandalously deep cleavage to stand
out among 1950s genre cinema. According to this teleological narrative,
old horror, along with Classical Hollywood more broadly, was about to
be disrupted by Alfred Hitchcock's *Psycho* (1960), which, along with
a handful of art-house horror films like *Eyes without a Face* (Georges
Franju, 1960) and *Peeping Tom* (Michael Powell, 1960), inaugurated
a new mode of horror that would – eventually – revitalise the flagging
genre at the end of the decade with the massive successes of *Rosemary's
Baby* (Roman Polanski, 1968) and *Night of the Living Dead* (George
Romero, 1968). New horror, the history goes, was characterised not just
by contemporary, local settings but by very human, or at least familiar,
villains. New horror was closer to home; grittier and realistic rather than
fanciful; contemporary and urban or suburban rather than set among
Old World aristocracies. And though it had its monsters, new horror's
monstrosity was often internal – psychological, and perhaps moral,
rather than physical.[2]

Though this account is massively simplified, it is, broadly, very convincing. With the emphatic caveat that there are major exceptions on
both sides of the historical divide, horror in the cinema was largely associated with creatures and monsters before *Psycho*, and that association
would become decreasingly central to the genre as *Psycho*'s influence
took hold in the subsequent two decades. This has been explicitly understood as a turn away from the Gothic (or, perhaps, the 'Gothic') character of cinematic horror that we tend to align with the Universal horror
of the 1930s and, of course, Hammer, with its castles and barons and
lumbering monsters. But that version of the genre's history ignores the
post-*Psycho* stage of horror's return to central concerns of the Gothic
literary tradition, which certainly had its share of ghosts and vampires,
but was also largely marked by a concern for psychological monstrosity/
abjection: hallucination, sadism, madness. Even as horror cinema shed
much of its explicit Gothic signifiers, it did so with a renewed, post-
Freudian emphasis on shattered, dangerous, distorted psyches that took
its cues from the much older conventions of the Gothic novel. Horror
cinema, it seems, can never fully escape the Gothic.

In this respect, Hammer's 1950s films are transformational. They are
built on trappings that would have been immediately familiar to adher-
ents of the older Gothic cinema that still held some cachet in popular
culture, but they refocus the genre intently on the psychological. In
Curse of Frankenstein, for example, the creature made up of corpse-
parts – the one most cinema-goers would presumably be buying a ticket
to see – is strangely incidental to the plot. It's a device more than a

character, introduced surprisingly late in the film. The film's villain is the sadistic, murderous Baron rather than his shuffling, stumbling creation, a pained creature whose bodily coherence seems to be constantly in danger of disintegration. The Baron is ruthless in his pursuit of scientific knowledge, caring little for the well-being of others, but Peter Cushing's performance goes further than that. Far from simply being overly driven or uncaring, we see flashes of pure, vicious cruelty, of the Baron gleefully relishing the deaths of his/his monsters' victims. Other versions of the Frankenstein story implicate the doctor in his creation's crimes, but *Curse* was the first film adaptation to make the Baron an outright murderer, the unquestionable villain of the story. The monster, meanwhile, though it is dangerous, is an object of pity as much as it is horror. When it does lash out at innocents, its violence clearly comes from a place of inarticulate pain and suffering rather than malevolence. The little we actually see of the 'monster' shows us a creature mostly lacking self-awareness, a barely coherent collection of body parts that shows little intention of any kind, let alone malice.

And then there is its curious framing structure. Gothic literature is often distinguished by what Eve Kosofksy Sedgwick diagnoses as a claustrophobic adherence to embedded narration – which she likens to live burial (1986: 19–20). Much of the genre verges on the fantastic by virtue of its insistence on explicitly subjective and partial narration. Access to something like neutral reality seems difficult, if not impossible, when the narrative is filtered through an accumulation of narrational layers. *Curse* may eschew Mary Shelley's emphasis on the creature's psychology, but it follows the model of Shelley and the Gothic literary tradition in structuring the film around the Baron's death-row testimonial. The film's visuals, however, seem to wholly reject the Expressionism of earlier modes of horror that one might associate with an unreliably subjective narrator in the cinema. Terence Fisher's workmanlike, unfussy *mise-en-scène* is seemingly at odds with any sense of subjective distortion, but that's hardly the most notable thing about the flashback. The film is structured so as to imply that the main body of the film represents Victor's narration, but that presumption is undermined by the fact that, if that were true, Victor would be confessing to premeditated murder, among other crimes, and his gallows pleas would only ensure his execution.

Curse set the template for Hammer and for much of the Gothic revival to come. In these films – *Masque of the Read Death* (Roger Corman, 1964), *Black Sunday (La maschera del demonio)* (Bava, 1960), *The Pit and the Pendulum* (Roger Corman, 1961) and, later in the decade, *The Witchfinder General* (Michael Reeves, 1968) – monsters may stalk

- the castles of an earlier age, but the more pressing evil is psychopathy and sadism.[3] If the Universal cycle could be considered figuratively psychological in its Expressionism, Hammer and the Gothic revival would be far more concerned with the explicit study of damaged/damaging psyches. When the proto-New Horror films of Hitchcock, Powell and Franju debuted in 1960, they were largely following this template, their stories transported into less fantastic, more contemporary settings. And, of course, the need for creatures fell away. But, as I demonstrate in this article, monsters were already secondary in the Gothic revival, and so Hammer needs to be understood not as the last gasp of an older form of horror, but as the genre's first steps in a new direction. Hammer relocated monstrosity within the psyche, but did so alongside traditional creatures in old-world Gothic settings. The Gothic signifiers enabled a subtler generic transformation, but also anchor so-called New Horror in the much older thematic concerns of the literary Gothic – starting with a return to Mary Shelley that marries the psychological complexity of her version of Victor with the sadistic villainy of even older Gothic texts like Matthew Lewis's *The Monk*.

Ruptures

Horror scholars now take Hammer's historical importance for granted, but the precise valence of its innovations shifts from critic to critic. At the time of *Curse*'s (1957) and *Horror of Dracula*'s (1958) release, it was the novelty of colour that most impressed critics – apparently at the behest of the studio marketing department, hardly a review failed to observe the additive impact of colour for the horror genre. When *Curse* premiered, a *Boston Globe* critic observed that 'for the first time in Frankenstein films, colour has been used, and of course it serves to heighten the total effect' (1958: 8).[4] *Variety* noted that 'as this is the first time the subject has been depicted in colour, all the grim trappings are more vividly impressive' (Clem 1957: 22). In *The New York Times*, A. H. Weiler observes of *Dracula* that the 'vivid' colour 'makes its "undead" all the more lurid' (1958: 24). The nonplussed *New York Herald Tribune* critic, who called *Curse* 'tame stuff' compared to classic horror ('You probably won't get one good scream out of it . . .'), snarkily reveals how important the novelty of colour was for the studio's marketing: 'Finally, a press agent told us that this was the first Frankenstein film in color and that, consequently, the scenes involving blood were better than before' (Zinsser, 1957: 11). A *Los Angeles Times* critic loathed the film and all of its gimmicks and found its colour to detract from the horror: '[I]ts creamy tones fatally dissipate all the grimness vital to the genre. A new rule of thumb: black and white is *de rigueur* for horror films' (C. S., B11).

John McCarty, in his seminal fan-scholar work *Splatter Movies: Breaking the Last Taboo of the Screen*, notes the importance of *Curse* for introducing colour to the genre, but more specifically locates it as the starting point for what he would describe as the 'splatter' tradition – his term for a species of 'gory realism' in horror and exploitation cinema, for which colour was a key (if not compulsory) component (1984: 9–22). Indeed, if the novelty of colour horror would be crucial for the early 1960s, in which the Italian Gothics and Corman's Poe cycle followed in Hammer's richly saturated footsteps, the unflinching depiction of blood and viscera would set the tone for the 1970s, when gore films dominated the drive-in and exploitation circuits. Kevin Heffernan makes the link more explicit, claiming that colour gave *Curse* 'a high-end gloss in Hollywood's "color-optional" period of the late fifties and [added] an extra emphasis to the unprecedented levels of onscreen gore that the film offered as its main attraction' (2004: 44–8).

Heffernan, however, sees the film's importance as a transitional work in terms of its negotiations of old and new cinematic horror. (Those negotiations were literal, as the film required extensive and delicate arrangements with Universal-International.) But while the film grounds itself by explicitly recalling those old classics, it marries familiar subjects with gore, sensational publicity stunts and a 'refinement' of horror and Gothic traditions in the cinema. As Heffernan points out, its Gothic blend includes elements of the female Gothic – the melodrama – as well as the monster tradition more squarely within the realm of cinematic horror. In essence, Heffernan argues for Hammer's significance as a work of horror synthesis, combining various cinematic Gothic traditions with the rising sensationalism in 1950s horror cinema (48).

David Pirie makes a similar argument in *A New Heritage of Horror: The English Gothic Cinema* (2008).[5] Pirie catalogues the outraged responses of scandalised British critics to Hammer's initial horror offerings (a selective portrait of the morally scandalised UK critical consensus that would be somewhat tempered by Dennis Meikle's more rounded critical survey in his later *History of Horrors* (2009)), and seeks to recuperate Hammer's reputation by invoking a long British literary tradition, likening Terence Fisher's style to 'that of the nineteenth-century storyteller' (2008: 67) and characterising the Baron as 'a magnificently arrogant rebel, in the direct Byronic tradition' (82). For Pirie, Hammer is especially significant because, for the first time, it brings a specifically *British* Gothic style to the screen.

For all of these critics and scholars, the significance of *Curse of Frankenstein* and the other Hammer horrors comes from their importation of older forms into a new milieu. Hammer reached back not just to established, but older, archaic Gothic traditions, and invigorated them with novel cinematic sensationalism. For the critics in the 1950s, Boris Karloff and the Universal cycle were constant reference points, frequently used as a cudgel to pummel the newcomer. This was precisely Hammer's gambit, standing out from the horror class of 1957 by resurrecting the tropes of long-dead genre cycles while bringing eye-popping colour (not to mention sex and gore). In other words, Hammer's horror marks such a significant transitional work in the genre in part because it was explicitly *conceived and sold* as a transitional work, bridging two eras – or, rather, justifying entry into a new era by anchoring itself in the fondly remembered, comparatively distant past.

If *Curse of Frankenstein*'s style and story bridged two eras, so did its treatment of characters. Less noted by critics of its day, the decision to make Victor not just the central character, but the villain – a 'ruthless, sadistic, and odiously suave' villain (Heffernan, 2004: 48) – has emerged as the film's most lasting innovation. 'Nowhere', Heffernan observes, 'is *Curse of Frankenstein*'s refinement of the horror genre signaled more strongly than in this radical recentering of the story on the personality of the baron himself' (48). The Baron is

> a devious schemer who will tell any lie, contrive any situation, put anyone's life or livelihood at risk in order to get his own way. He contemplates and commits murder with unpalatable ease. He exercises his *droit de seigneur* with the chambermaid as to the manor born . . . He spends his nights in necrophilia, and his days plotting and indulging in illicit sex. (38–9)

He is, in the words of producer Anthony Hinds, 'a *shit*' (Heffernan, 2004: 37). McCarty notes that he is 'more a monster . . . than the mindless, feeble creature that he succeeds in giving life' (1984: 37). The sadistic aristocrat is, of course, a foundational figure in the literary Gothic. In other words, *Curse* points the genre forward by turning to the past. In the following section, I will explore the significance of the film's shift in character by analysing *Curse*'s Victor alongside his 1931 forerunner, Henry, in James Whale's *Frankenstein*.

Frankensteins

James Whale's 1931 *Frankenstein* tells the story of an obsessed scientist, Henry, who, at the beginning of the film, has rejected a proper aristocratic life (and his proper aristocratic fiancée) in favour of a very Gothic isolation in a very Gothic stone tower. His fiancée, Elizabeth, along with her friend Victor and Henry's former professor, Dr Waldman, intrude on his seclusion in an attempt to bring him back to sanity and civilisation. This comes too late, as they reach him at the moment he achieves his ambition to create life. The aftermath of the creation scene sees Henry's grasp on sanity break down, as he frantically declares that he now knows 'what it's like to be God' before devolving into hysterical laughter.

That is, Whale's *Frankenstein* begins with concerns over the mental (and, perhaps more pressingly, moral) 'monstrosity' of its titular scientist. But, after this moment of ecstatic triumph and the accompanying breakdown, Henry returns to his comfortable aristocratic life and a path towards marriage and baronhood. The monster remains a lingering, intrusive reminder of his time spent straying away from the prescribed path. It returns to derail his wedding plans, to delay that final step in Henry's return to heteronormative society. Once the monster is defeated, the film lingers on Henry's re-entry into the patriarchal aristocracy. The film ends not with Henry but with his father, the Baron. Spying on his convalescing son and daughter-in-law-to-be reconciled and together in Henry's bedroom, the Baron gathers his young, all-female servants (a sort of excess of heterosexuality to underscore the union in the background) and raises a toast: 'Here's to a son to the house of Frankenstein' (see Benshoff, 1997: 47–9).

Whale's *Frankenstein* sets up a tension and contrast between antisocial/antinormative behaviour and conforming heteronormativity. The monster, as the product of Henry's antisocial pursuits, acts as an obstacle between Henry and the 'normal' life he has suddenly taken to. But as much as the monster is an object of sympathy, he is also the threat.[6] Henry's momentary madness passes, and he is no longer an active danger to anyone; this was merely a passing deviation. He was possessed by an ecstatic obsession that he had now seemingly mastered and repressed. That final toast spells out the stakes of this contrast: the monster, whose defeat the Baron is celebrating, is the deviant son, while the implied consummation of the upcoming marriage (the brief glimpse of the couple shows Elizabeth at Henry's bed) will produce a proper, normal son. Through this purge of the monstrous son, evidence of his own deviant behaviour, Henry can rejoin his aristocratic path. The toast also, of course, implicitly refers to another son in the House of Frankenstein: Henry, who will now rejoin his proper place in the patriarchies of the house, the family and society.

The final words of the film being given to a relatively minor character – comic relief, in essence – is a curious decision. Because the Baron is a comic role, it ends the film on a note of levity, but also distances us from the primary conflict of the film. Victor may have returned to normative aristocratic life, but he is not the one who makes that final declaration. The film doesn't open up much room for uncertainty, but it does weaken the sense of affirmative choice on Henry's part. The result is an implied passivity and lack of agency. The aristocratic social structure reasserts itself upon Henry, with his silent affirmation. For a variety of reasons, the film cannot fully embrace or endorse Henry's 'deviant' aspirations, but it can mute its ultimate erasure. The patriarch has pronounced the son's return without vocal endorsement on the part of the son.

In *Curse*, by contrast, the madness and the deviance are ongoing. Victor is an orphan, on his own, with no House of Frankenstein to which he can return. There is no sense of a 'proper' normative path for him – even his marriage to Elizabeth is decided by an explicitly financial arrangement with her mother (made when both were children). And, far from saving him, *Curse*'s Elizabeth is unaware of Victor's transgressions, and she needs to be saved *from Victor* as much as she does from the monster. Indeed, Victor may be aiming for the monster, but his bullet hits Elizabeth – she is never directly harmed by the shambling creature, though she is by Victor.

There is, similarly, no loveable patriarch cajoling Victor into proper aristocratic life. He is himself the Baron, a character who has decided his own direction since his childhood. Whereas Henry's story starts with his manic pursuit of scientific accomplishment, Victor traces his own development as a scientist from the beginning of his education. And where Henry is saved not just by his fiancée and their friend (confusingly named Victor), but also by Dr Waldman, Victor has been educated and has operated outside mainstream science or education from the very beginning. In Hammer's telling, Victor never breaks from normalcy or from a prescribed aristocratic path: he was never part of polite society or the scientific establishment or even a close family unit. There is no sense of place for him in society, and his experiments do not represent a rejection of his official education but the logical culmination of his scientific and personal pursuits.

As such, *Curse*'s monster does not represent a lingering, deadly reminder of supposedly passing madness – a reminder that Henry tries hard to repress. Rather, it is a creature that Victor is constantly resuscitating, both literally as a scientist and figuratively through the story he tells. He spends the film not, as Henry does, disgusted at and fearful of the creature and his responsibility for its creation, but trying to prevent its destruction by his former tutor and colleague, Paul Krempe. Whereas the 1931 film ends with an effective erasure of the monster's existence from Henry's life and with Henry's return to normalcy, Victor ends *Curse* in hysterical insistence that the monster is real, with none of the other witnesses willing to confirm Victor's ravings. (Again, the idea that these ravings might be merely hysterical inventions is a tantalising suggestion, but one that runs counter to the implications of Fisher's declarative style.)

On the monster's first excursion outside the lab, it is quickly defeated by Paul, its only (offscreen) victim an elderly blind man. And after Victor resurrects him, the stumbling creature's only victims can be equally attributed to Victor. Justine, the maid with whom Victor is having an affair, is first the victim of Victor's cruel indifference and then his gleeful violence. After she reveals her pregnancy and threatens to expose him, Victor responds by locking her in with the creature, listening at the door as her horrified screams subside and we are left to imagine the specific details of her awful fate. The monster, here, is but a tool of Victor's own cruelty.

The other victim is more complicated. The climax of *Curse* sees Elizabeth, Victor's fiancée, stalked by the monster through the winding pathways of Castle Frankenstein. Victor's response to an apparently imminent attack is to recklessly fire his gun towards the two of them, hitting Elizabeth with what appears to be a fatal shot. The monster never actually touches Elizabeth – it's Victor who shoots her. The monster topples through the castle into a vat of acid, all evidence of his existence dissolving in a frothy pool. Elizabeth returns for the final framing sequence, alive but never speaking a word. She offers no testimony to confirm or deny Victor's incredible story and makes no effort to mitigate his guilt. We are, in fact, unaware if she had even witnessed the creature. The most grievously wronged of the surviving parties, she remains utterly silent, as if rendered mute by the revelation of Victor's violence.

If James Whale's creature is a mirror image of Henry, an expression of all that he represses in order to return to a heteronormative aristocratic existence, then Terence Fisher's monster is an extension of Victor – the two linked closely enough that responsibility for violence blurs between them. Both are responsible for the death of Justine and the near-fatal attack on Elizabeth. Furthermore, while Whale's monster appears near the beginning of the film, the creation scene instigating the narrative, Fisher's monster arrives relatively late and is a relatively minor presence onscreen. By the time the creature actually appears, Victor has been securely established as the film's true monster. Whale's monster arises in defiance of a restrictive social structure, but *Curse*'s creature enforces the violence of an even more cruelly repressive social order: unlike the 'deviant' tendencies of Henry, Victor is essentially normal in that he expresses the inherently cruel logic of a rigid class system.

Besides the monster's multiple demises, there is one onscreen death shown in *Curse*: Victor's murder of Professor Bernstein. We see Victor push the professor over the balcony in pursuit of a brain for his creature – the creature's death a clear echo of the murder that produced its brain. Victor is an athletic, sadistic villain whereas his monster is pitiful, a stumbling, cowering creature that occasionally expresses pained, inarticulate rage to bystanders. The creature may commit violence, but it carries none of the malevolence shown by its creator. Indeed, whereas Whale's film's lasting power largely comes from Karloff's exceedingly sympathetic portrayal, Lee's creature scarcely has what might be thought of as a complex psychology. It lashes out in pain, like a wounded animal. Karloff's creature, terrified of fire and tortured by Fritz, begins at that same point, but soon grows into a mature if inarticulate human psyche. The creature of *Curse* never grows, never matures, never becomes more human. The trajectory of growth plotted by Shelley and suggested by Whale and Karloff is wholly absent from *Curse*. Victor, however, grows increasingly cruel, and the cruelty Victor shows towards his victims is replicated in his cruel treatment of the creature. Late in the film, Victor reveals to Paul that he has 'trained' the creature. The spectacle of the monster fearfully responding to Victor's commands is its one moment of pathos, implicit evidence of ongoing abuse in their relationship. Whereas in Whale's film such cruelty is displaced onto the marginalised figure of Fritz, who taunts the creature and pays for it with his life, in *Curse* Victor torments and tames the creature himself.

Reliable Narration

If we are to assume that the flashback faithfully represents Victor's narration, his own confessed crimes equal those of the monster – arguably surpassing them, as the sinister plans behind his murder of a prominent scientist reveal a pre-meditation and cruelty of which the monster does not seem capable. This leaves us with a few options: either Victor is delusional, and/or he does not realise that he has incriminated himself, or there is a discrepancy between the story Victor tells the jailer and its presumed cinematic representation. As the former seems unlikely for the cold, calculating and highly intelligent Victor, we are left with the probability that there is a fundamental incoherency to the text: we do not know the precise relationship between Victor's version of events and the images we are shown. Framed narration, and frames within frames (within frames, etc.), are a hallmark of Gothic literature, with the reliability of the narrator almost always called into question. The specific valence of the narration in *Curse* is curiously positioned for a mid-century horror film: Are we presented with a 'true' account of events? And if so, what does Victor tell his captors?

Despite the film's sensational emphasis on brightly coloured gore and its illicit emphasis on sex, Fisher's direction is markedly different from the Expressionist style of James Whale and much of the 1930s horror cycle. Pirie, in his rather partisan, Hammer-centric history of Gothic cinema, opines that Fisher 'quite correctly . . . brings no expressionism to the piece at all', arguing that the precise and understated direction underscores the contrast between Victor's cold-blooded cruelty and the stateliness of the setting (2008: 83). As 'intricate (but economical)' as Fisher's *mise-en-scène* may be, it drastically changes the filmic language from Whale's version (Heffernan, 2004: 58). Fisher's matter-of-fact direction and what one might call workmanlike cinematography breaks, drastically, not just from the surreal Expressionism of the 1931 film, but also from the subjectivity and hallucinatory excitability of Gothic literature's unreliable narrators.

That is, even if there seems to be a fundamental incoherency, a disruptive lack of thematic and structural coherence, the film's presentation feels like it *should* fit together. Fisher's style feels authoritative and reliable. Without any signals of subjectivity, Expressionism or hallucination, the film seems to assert the 'authenticity' of everything it depicts. Even though it bears some of the structural outlines of a familiarly unreliable, claustrophobic framing narration, nothing within *Curse* invites you to question the images we see onscreen: as far as we know, we're given no reason to doubt the film's account of Victor and his creature. If the shift of emphasis from the physical, external monstrosity of the creature to the internal monstrosity of Victor is the most radical gesture of the film, the movement away from Expressionism is equally consequential for its impact on the genre. Where Expressionism externalises internal states through distorting sets and shadows and camera angles, *Curse* maintains their interiority. The locus of disturbance shifts from the *mise-en-scène* to the character; it has been internalised. And it is, therefore, never fully accessible. We see Victor's sadism emerge in words and actions, but we're never granted anything like privileged access into his psyche – even from a narration that is, supposedly, an attempt to exonerate himself.

Because *Curse* does not register its characters' disturbed emotional and psychological states through Expressionistic visuals, the film avoids associations with subjective, unreliable narration – it is stylistically distinct from film noir or the Gothic melodramas of the 1950s and other film genres whose narration signals unreliability. And yet it still necessarily encourages viewers to speculate on what Victor's narration may have left out. The narrative claustrophobia that Sedgwick ascribes to Gothic literature's multi-layered narrators is replaced with *Curse*'s careful distancing from its main character's internal states. We are not caught up in his distorted mind, or even in the minds of his victims and colleagues; instead, Fisher presents an exploration of psychopathy from the outside. Victor is at turns ecstatically sadistic and cold, maniacally driven but otherwise calmly indifferent. He narcissistically fails to recognise his shambling creation as a failure, seeing only evidence of his own glorious achievements.

This is why the lack of voice-over and Fisher's non-subjective, non-Expressionist style are so crucial for understanding *Curse*'s structure: Victor still remains a mystery. We are given no explanation or origin story for his moral failings besides his social status. The film solicits surprisingly little empathy for its main character, though it allows Peter Cushing to be a suavely charismatic villain. It invites no diagnosis, medical or otherwise – he was not in the grip of feverish madness à la Henry, nor does his intent appear to be *entirely* malicious. Victor is often more pragmatically villainous, killing to get what he wants, even if Cushing's performance elicits moments of cruel enjoyment. But is there anything to what he wants besides his will-to-knowledge/power?

Victor is a fascinating villain in horror's history because he is both outsider and, as a wealthy aristocrat, a fabulously privileged insider. In Robin Wood's influential formulation, a horror film's politics are expressed by the relationship between the monster and normalcy. Wood sees horror as not just dramatising a societal return of the repressed, but more or less enacting an allegorical attack on society's oppressive/repressive forces. In Whale's film, the monster is an eruption of Henry's own repressed self (as Harry Benshoff notes, with strong connotations of homosexuality (1997: 47–9)), attacking not just Elizabeth but marriage and the patriarchal system that perpetuates it. In *Curse*, the creature is a negligible enough presence that Victor seems necessarily to be the more appropriate object for Wood's rubric.

Thinking of Victor not in nineteenth-century terms but in those of 1950s Britain, he is a representative of an archaic, Old-World social structure. But his association there is tenuous, as his position has come unmoored from familial ties and obligations, save for his marriage to Elizabeth. His interest in Elizabeth might be the most puzzling thing about *Curse*, as Victor shows little genuine affection for her, yet seems perfectly happy to go through the motions of aristocratic life. As Paul insistently protests, Victor seems to care little that he has put her life in danger through his experiments. As in Whale's film, the monster does come for her, and yet that unseen confrontation results in Elizabeth recognising Victor as the true threat (again, *he* is the one who shoots her). Victor is as much a threat to the middle-class order as is his monster, or Whale's monster for that matter. But he comes not from the dispossessed lower classes (as Karloff's working-class clothes would imply) but from old money. He enacts a nightmarish return to aristocratic power, with the complacent Elizabeth as his unsuspecting victim. His violence, perpetrated in pursuit of personal gain, is essentially consistent with the fundamental violence of aristocratic reign. As a monster, he *represses* those marginal figures that Wood associates with monsters like the one played by Karloff.

Equally, Benshoff notes that *Curse* retains Whale's film's connotations of 'deviant' sexuality. The strong bond between Victor and Paul, with the creature the product of their 'union', is the central relationship of the film. More explicitly unorthodox – or at least socially unacceptable – is Victor's relationship with his maid, Justine, a callous abuse of power that ends in her humiliation and murder. However, Elizabeth's relationship with Victor is first and foremost a financial one. Because he supported her and her mother since she was young, she stays with him, as she explains to Paul, out of economic obligation. And if Victor is not as straightforwardly cruel to Elizabeth as he is to Justine, his indifference to her safety (and insinuations of her involvement in future experiments) indicates that social standing is all that distinguishes one romantic partner from another. The same, in fact, could be said of Paul, a friend and mentor but also an employee.

Per Wood, if horror films should be understood through their triangulation of monsters and normality, then Elizabeth and Paul might be the only representatives of normality as it was conceived of in 1950s Britain in *Curse*. Paul, a salaried employee, and Elizabeth, an aristocrat without money of her own, may belong to an aristocratic system but portend the societal shift to more solidly middle-class existences. In the final scene, the two are together, an implicit union. The film's resolution finds the monstrous Victor banished to the jail, allowing a more bourgeois, heteronormative, *modern* status quo to emerge. Crucially, this is not Victor's journey – he begins as a threat to middle-class values and never relinquishes that threatening status. He cannot be reconciled with the emerging middle-class order in which the heterosexual couple is the primary unit. It's not just that his implicit threat is both sexual and economic, but that economics enable his sexuality.

Pirie asserts the structural importance of contrast between Fisher's restrained style and the bloodiness of the narrative, but this contrast is also built into Victor's character at a fundamental level. His aristocratic gentility gives way to violence; it hides his monstrous nature. But in this film, you cannot have one without the other: the monster is Victor's painting in the attic, a manifestation of his internal ugliness without his socially redeeming manners: it has no psychology of its own because it is a visualisation of Victor's. Victor cannot maintain his position of power and cannot pursue his research without his immense aristocratic privilege. So too the stylistic contrast, which presents its gruesome imagery in a straightforward, non-sensationalising manner. Much of the horror comes not just from the imagery, but the film's flatly presentational manner. The film never takes on the tone of a dream or hallucination, but always asserts its factuality. Thus, when Paul claims ignorance of any creature in the film's final moments, it *feels* impossible to the viewer that the visibly distressed Victor may have simply imagined the events we just witnessed.

There is another contrast that needs to be considered, which is the drastic distinction between Victors within *Curse*. The miserable and desperate Victor in the framing story, especially in the final scene, is not simply the character stripped of the prestige and authority of his class but is rather a Victor that seems incompatible with the Victor of the main story. He shows so little recognisably human emotion in the main body of the film that these moments of abject emotional rawness do not seem reconcilable with the Victor we see in the body of the film. The film's structure wholly elides the journey from arrogant Victor to the miserable deject in his jail cell – though, as Heffernan points out, Fisher stages the jail cell scenes so as to directly echo a shot of the creature in chains (2004: 57–9). Once his creation plummets to its death and he is captured, in other words, Victor becomes his own monster. It's only then that he shows emotion, and it's of a base, animal kind: he may be pleading for mercy, but he's speaking out of pure fear. He has, in the unseen interim between his final confrontation with the creature and his jail cell confession, been reduced to inarticulate expressions of fear and pain. The film highlights those contrasts, in the beginning by jumping from the desperation of the jail cell to the jaunty tone of young Victor's first meeting with both Elizabeth and tutor-to-be Paul Krempe, and in the end by the harsh juxtaposition of the jail cell with the fiery final confrontation.

We do not see the full extent of Victor's comeuppance: it's a lacuna that is easy enough to infer, narratively, but the film leaves out that transformation. As a result, we see Victor in his moment of greatest hubris followed immediately by him at his abject lowest, without following the potentially humanising, sympathy-inviting descent. He remains a monster, his pleas for pity inconsistent with the Victor we have witnessed in the body of the film. These two Victors add up to a psychologically incoherent character to match the physiological incoherency of his creation.

Conclusion: New Gothic Cinema

Among the host of entries in the post-*Curse* Gothic revival, Roger Corman's Edgar Allan Poe adaptations hew to Hammer's template most faithfully. If anything, these lush colour adaptations only further emphasise the genuinely dark psychological nature of the horror found in Hammer's early monster movies – and which those movies took from much older, largely British, Gothic literary traditions. They mostly shed the monsters and often minimise or do away entirely with an analogue to the Krempe role. Their often-villainous main characters either teeter on the edge of sanity or have long since toppled into madness. They're gleeful sadists or stricken paranoiacs, obsessives and madmen fully in the mode of Cushing's Victor.

In what seems to be the consensus favourite of the Poe cycle among modern critics, *Masque of the Red Death*, Vincent Price plays Prince Prospero, a viciously cruel Satanist who delights at the suffering of his subjects, aristocrats and peasants alike. The Bergman-inspired Death figures who roam through the film are, as in *The Seventh Seal* (Ingmar Bergman, 1957), allegorically connected to the plague, but as with *Curse*, they play a minimal role in the story. Instead, the film is a study of the terrifying depths of darkness in Prospero's psyche and the similarly poisonous souls of the courtly figures who surround him. As in *Curse*, *Masque of the Red Death* climaxes with a sudden, violent reversal, here at the hands of the supernatural Red Death. The film literalises the connection between monster and apparent protagonist seen in *Curse* and countless other monster movies, as Death removes his veil to reveal Prospero's own face staring back at him. Whatever violence descends on Prospero is merely a replication of his own violence towards others.

Corman's gloss on Hammer is a Gothic cinema that's focused intently on dark psyches. And just as Shelley and the larger tradition of the British Gothic anchored Hammer's early horror productions in the genre, Poe signified an American Gothic tradition – even if it was set among the European aristocracy. But it also builds on Hammer, in the setting and the set design, the innovative use of often garish colours. If the hallucinatory dream sequences hatched by Corman and cinematographer Nicolas Roeg stray from the straightforward narrative presentation of Fisher and his Hammer cohorts, the film is grounded in a largely Fisher-esque *mise-en-scène* that prioritises staging and performance over camerawork or editing. And it alludes directly to the Hammer tradition, casting *Curse*'s Hazel Court as Prospero's wicked wife Juliana. What's clear from Corman's Poe cycle, and *Masque* in particular, is that Hammer had established a new cinematic horror tradition to which future productions must refer – even if that reference is a simple rejection.

In truth, the clearing away of horror's Gothic cobwebs at the end of the 1960s was also a step back from the intensity of the psychological explorations of Hammer and Corman – horror scholars endorse the teleological version of horror history at the expense of the subtleties within the Gothic revival. Hammer's – and Corman's – settings may have seemed distant and mannered, their medieval costumes cheesy, but *Curse* inaugurated a series of unprecedented cinematic examinations of damaged and damaging psyches. Horror's transition over the course of the 1960s is generally thought of as one from monsters to madmen, from the barons of faraway ancient lands to the neighbourhood boys-and-girls-next-door, from the airy realm of outdated fantasy to a gritty, documentary-inflected contemporary reality. But the Gothic revival made horror an insistently psychological genre, and if New Horror films eventually picked up that torch, few were as brutally clear-eyed in their dissections of the evil of their very human monsters. New Horror's monsters may be human, but the films tend to be more interested in victims.

Neither is it the case that New Horror films fully shed their Gothic elements. Like *Curse*, the first wave of late-1960s/early-1970s New Horror films often ground themselves in the genre through citation of those familiar Gothic tropes in order to signal to audiences that they were indeed horror movies. *Psycho* pairs the bland modernity of the motel with the imposingly Gothic old dark house that looms over it. *Night of the Living Dead* inaugurates its horrors with a Boris Karloff impression, before relocating to an isolated house in a treacherous landscape. The cavernous Bramford Building in *Rosemary's Baby* is the Manhattan equivalent of an ancient stone castle. These are not a rejection of the Gothic but an updating of its most durable tropes.

We might think, instead, of the 'New Horror' of the 1960s and 1970s as being part of a long transitional period initiated by *Curse*. In *Curse*, Fisher and Hammer create a film that has one foot explicitly and firmly planted in older cinematic traditions, but which inaugurates a modernised generic renewal through its engagements with an even older literary tradition. Through its insistence on Victor's sadism, the film serves a key role in redefining the nature of cinematic monstrosity away from the strictly physiological into something more internal, psychological. The negligible role played by the creature in the story – which confused critics who found Christopher Lee's creature particularly lamentable when compared with Karloff's soulful virtuosity – indicates a shift within *Frankenstein* adaptations to a brand-new emphasis on the monstrous psyche of its true villain, Victor.

Although *Curse*'s alignment with the British literary tradition is unmistakable, its break with the Gothic is equally instructive and key for the film's importance within the canon of horror cinema. Because it curiously disregards or counteracts the unreliability of its narrator, eschewing the Expressionist distortions of the Universal monster cycle, the film maintains Victor's moral, psychological monstrosity as a strictly internal phenomenon. It finds no aesthetic outlet, Fisher maintaining his cinematic propriety just as Victor contains his callous cruelty within a proper aristocratic exterior. But this transition away from the aesthetic innovations of Expressionism, from *The Cabinet of Dr. Caligari* (Robert Wiene, 1920) through *Frankenstein* through *Cat People* (Jacques Tourneur, 1942) and beyond, points the way forward for the style of New Horror. There seems, at first blush, little similarity between the shaky, newsreel-style cameras of *Night of the Living Dead* and Fisher's stagy presentations, but both approaches move cinematic horror away from the hyperstylised lighting, distorted sets and extreme angles of the Universal tradition. *Curse* conceives of horror as observational, as an examination of sick or traumatised psyches to which we have only limited access. That limitation, that mystery, is at the heart of horror after *Curse*. How do we understand, or even identify, the damage hidden within the brains of apparently normal men and women? *Curse* offers a traditional monstrous spectacle of Christopher Lee's creature, but hides the mental, moral rot of its true villain within a proper aristocratic, Gothic exterior. Its inquiries look past the decorative trappings that the next generation of horror would so forcefully reject to help establish a new phase in the horror genre.

Notes

1. A version of this article was originally published in *Studies in the Fantastic*. Adam Charles Hart, 'Transitional Gothic: Hammer's Gothic Revival and New Horror', *Studies in the Fantastic* 6 (Winter 2018/Spring 2019): 1–21.
2. The most succinct and insightful version of this history is by Andrew Tudor. Tudor argues convincingly for a shift in narrative resolution from the 'secure' narratives of the Classical era to the paranoid ones of post-*Psycho* horror.
3. Hammer's *Dracula* (1958) is interesting in this respect, as Van Helsing is here re-imagined as a ferociously, ruthlessly driven crusader, while Dracula himself is suave and pleasant. Dracula is assuredly the film's monster, but the film plays with the hero-villain dynamic in surprising ways. Later films

such as *Curse of the Werewolf* (1961) explore monstrosity as an extension or manifestation of psychological disturbance.

4. When the same paper reviewed *Horror of Dracula*, reviewer 'M. L. A.' asserted that:

> A vampire picture in color is far more exciting than one done in grays and blacks. The kids absent from school yesterday screamed with fearful delight when they saw bloodstained Dracula and his cohorts at the Keith Memorial. For the crime-hungry teenagers Christopher Lee, Valerie Gaunt and Carol Marsh, with their knife-like teeth and bright red gore running from their jaws, made the rainy afternoon a pleasant period. (24)

I have stuck to American reviews, as the British response has been well catalogued by others, those historical accounts focusing primarily on moral outrage. In the United States, Hammer horror was received as a continuation/revival of a horror genre that had never gone away but was languishing in the margins of popular culture. In the United Kingdom it was the beginning of a new generic tradition, to which several prominent critics objected. See Pirie (2008) and Meikle (2009).

5. Originally published in 1973 as *A Heritage of Horror: The English Gothic Cinema 1946–1972*. At the time of its initial writing, Hammer was in decline. Through its considerable success, the studio had earned substantial popular, and to some extent critical, respect in the United Kingdom. But by the late 1960s its franchises had been significantly overextended and it struggled to maintain relevance. Pirie is writing with the clear goal of not only rehabilitating Hammer's reputation, but in demonstrating its importance as an extraordinarily vital part of British cinema – not just genre cinema – during its initial entry into horror. All citations in this essay are from the revised edition, which retains the original text but with additional commentary.

6. Robert Spadoni (2006) demonstrates in his admirable study of horror and early sound cinema that, as much as subsequent audiences think of the monster as a pitiable victim, he terrified audiences in 1931.

References

Anon. 1957. 'Double Horror at Twins: Frankenstein Roams Again', *Boston Globe*, 15 July, p. 8.

Benshoff, H. 1997. *Monsters in the Closet: Homosexuality and the Horror Film*. Manchester: Manchester University Press.

C. S. 1957. '"Monster" Revived on Screens', *Los Angeles Times*, 18 July, B11.

Clem. 'Curse of Frankenstein', *Variety*, 15 May, p. 22.

Heffernan, K. 2004. *Ghouls, Gimmicks, and Gold: Horror Films and the American Movie Business 1953–1968*. Durham, NC: Duke University Press.

M. L. A. 1958. '"Dracula" at Memorial: Horror in English Style', *Boston Globe*, 29 May, p. 24.

McCarty, J. 1984. *Splatter Movies: Breaking the Last Taboo of the Screen*. London: St. Martin's Press.

Meikle, M. 2009. *A History of Horrors: The Rise and Fall of the House of Hammer*. Lanham, MD: Scarecrow Press.

Pirie, D. 2008. *A New Heritage of Horror: The English Gothic Cinema*. London: I.B. Tauris.

Sedgwick, E. K. 1986. *The Coherence of Gothic Conventions*. New York: Methuen.

Spadoni, R. 2006. *Uncanny Bodies: The Coming of Sound Film and the Origins of the Horror Genre*. Berkeley, CA: University of California Press.

Tudor, A. 1989. *Monsters and Mad Scientists: A Cultural History of the Horror Movie*. London: Basil Blackwell.

Weiler, A. H. 1958. '"Horror of Dracula" with Oxford Accent'. *New York Times*, 29 May, p. 24.

Wood, R. 2004. 'An Introduction to the American Horror Film', in Grant, B. K. and Sharrett, C. (eds), *Planks of Reason: Essays on the Horror Film*. Lanham, MD: Scarecrow Press, pp. 107–41.

Zinsser, W. K. 1957. 'The Curse of Frankenstein'. *New York Herald Tribune*, 8 August, p. 11.

Chapter 5

Gothic Cinema from the 1970s to Now

Xavier Aldana Reyes

Gothic cinema in the contemporary period is easily distinguished from its previous incarnations by its investment in increasingly explicit cinematic spectacles, the gradual relocation of events from medieval to Victorian, Edwardian or modern settings, the crystallisation of the supernatural monster as key villain, and the victory, more often than not, of evil over good. As a distinct aesthetic mode, one identifiable by a specific dark or baroque style, or else by given thematic leanings, Gothic cinema has also developed to embrace societal and technological changes: the late 1990s and 2000s saw the beginnings of what could be referred to as a digital Gothic, a cluster of films that explored the nightmarish side of new communication technologies. Although, for some, there is still a line between the Gothic (the subtle, the hinted at, the half-glimpsed, the uncanny, the atmospheric) and horror (the graphic, the explicit, the sadistic, the nihilistic), I would argue that the contemporary period has seen the steady commingling of both. As the Gothic fragments ever further and individual critical and artistic concepts (the sublime, the grotesque) and motifs (the double, hauntings) are themselves conceived as markers of Gothic indexicality, it becomes more and more difficult to extricate the two. While the Gothic is unlikely to overtake horror as a label to refer to frightening cinema because it is not a recognised genre, it is becoming increasingly popular following the widely publicised 'Gothic: The Dark Heart of Film' season (2013–14) organised by the British Film Institute.[1] If nothing else, its associations with the literary (via adaptation) and the socially repressed, alongside its high intertextuality and referentiality, will ensure that, at least at the academic level, the Gothic remains an area of debate and discussion in Film Studies.

From 1970 to the Turn of the Century

The early 1970s saw Hammer Horror's last attempts at rejuvenating its brand. Violence and sex had become more explicit in the late 1960s in films of the New Hollywood cinema like *Bonnie and Clyde* (Arthur Penn, 1967), *The Graduate* (Mike Nichols, 1968) and *The Wild Bunch* (Sam Peckinpah, 1969), and Herschell Gordon Lewis had created a more graphic horror subgenre, what would come to be known as 'gore', with his *Blood Feast* (1963) and *Two Thousand Maniacs!* (1964). These trends had an impact on films like *Scars of Dracula* (Roy Ward Baker, 1970), which featured a completely gratuitous scene of dismemberment, and on the new Karnstein trilogy, which included nudity. In particular, *The Vampire Lovers* (Roy Ward Baker, 1970), loosely based on Sheridan Le Fanu's 'Carmilla' (1872), dealt with lesbianism in as titillating a way as British cinema had ever done, making its two female leads take their respective tops off in a steamy bedroom scene.[2] In attempts to branch out from the Gothic period setting horrors that had once distinguished them but which were no longer in fashion, Hammer hybridised vampires with martial arts in *The Legend of the Seven Golden Vampires* (Roy Ward Baker and Chang Cheh, 1974) and returned to Dennis Wheatley's novels for inspiration in *To the Devil a Daughter* (Peter Sykes, 1976), having done so previously with success in *The Devil Rides Out* (Terence Fisher, 1968). Neither did particularly well, and Hammer would eventually disappear after the near-bankrupting flop of *The Lady Vanishes* (Anthony Page, 1979). It is perhaps not surprising that the company would only resurface in the twenty-first century, when the appetite for Gothic horror was renewed.

The 1970s were also marked by the success of one film, William Friedkin's *The Exorcist* (1973), which, despite troubled beginnings, became a major commercial success and ended up receiving nominations for Academy Awards, making it the first horror film to receive acclaim from the Academy of Motion Picture Arts and Sciences. The story, allegedly based on real events, of a teenage girl (Linda Blair) possessed by Pazuzu, a demon once defeated by Father Merrin (Max von Sydow) and who has returned for vengeance, was as simple as it was chilling. It also explored social taboos around female bodies and their sexuality, and the role of faith and religion in the twentieth century. The special effects for the film, including key scenes where the possessed girl, Regan, twists her neck 180 degrees and projectile vomits on Father Karras's (Jason Miller) face, are solidly ingrained in the history of horror cinema. Besides its technical accomplishments and record-breaking achievements, *The*

Exorcist is notable for its mainstreaming of supernatural horror, a genre which would gradually become profitable and a regular presence in major cinema theatres, and for its replacement of Hammer's Gothic period formula with a very contemporary one that brought horror closer to the everyday life of viewers. The most direct offspring of this turn to the modern supernatural Gothic, rich in telekinetic, energy-channelling or demonic individuals, were *The Omen* (Richard Donner, 1976), *Carrie* (Brian De Palma, 1976), *The Fury* (Brian De Palma and Frank Yablans, 1978), *Scanners* (David Cronenberg, 1981) and *Poltergeist* (Tobe Hooper, 1982). Horror also hybridised in its bid for mainstream popularity, with the eco-thriller in *Jaws* (Steven Spielberg, 1975) and with science fiction in *Alien* (Ridley Scott, 1979) – a haunted house narrative set in space – and *The Fly* (David Cronenberg, 1986).

The slasher cycle, started by John Carpenter's *Halloween* (1978) and crystallised by *Friday the 13th* (Sean S. Cunningham, 1980) and later by *A Nightmare on Elm Street* (Wes Craven, 1984) and *Hellraiser* (Clive Barker, 1986), has been more readily studied as part of horror history. This is understandable, given that the very contemporary suburban settings and heroes, the emphasis on sexuality (its exposure and subsequent punishment) and the films' increasing interest in what Cynthia Freeland has referred to as violent 'numbers', that is 'sequences of heightened spectacle and emotion' revolving around the reveal of the monstrous body and the histrionics of brutal death scenes (2000: 256), align them with the perceived excess of horror. It would be possible to argue, however, that the supernatural elements of the monsters involved, from mutilated cenobites summoned from alternative realms of pleasure and pain to the dream-active phantoms of burnt pederasts, draw from the Gothic tradition and expand the figure of the monster into new territories. In fact, as Peter Hutchings notes in a piece that neatly encapsulated the difficulty of pinning down the specific meaning of 'Gothic' within the context of modern cinema, films such as *Halloween* and *Nightmare* may be understood as cultural sites where 'Gothic themes and ideas' find an expression (Hutchings, 1996: 89–103). Hutchings argues that while 'these modern horrors might lack the more obviously Gothic trappings of the period horror film', they share with them the 'presentation of the past as a barbaric force which interrupts and threatens a mundane, everyday world' (94). For me, the focus on scares and thrills, as well as on the body as a site of entrapment and anxiety, both of which I read as a vital complement to the mode's aesthetics (Aldana Reyes, 2014, 2015a), also mark them out as relevant examples of Gothic cinema in the 1980s.

Another monstrous figure that deserves some attention is that of the serial killer. It, of course, does not grow out of the contemporary period – children serial killer Hans Beckert (Peter Lorre) in *M* (Fritz Lang, 1931), the hands of one Vasseur in *The Hands of Orlac/Orlacs Hände* (Robert Wiene, 1924) and somnambulist Cesare (Conrad Veidt) in *The Cabinet of Dr. Caligari/Das Cabinet des Dr. Caligari* (1920) are all a testament to the killer's appeal in early twentieth-century cinema – but it is reinvigorated in the 1980s and 1990s in the sordid films *Henry: Portrait of a Serial Killer* (John McNaughton, 1986) and *The Hitcher* (Robert Harmon, 1986) and, with a more obvious Gothic feel, in the many adaptations derived from Thomas Harris's Hannibal Lecter novels. The surprise recognition of *The Silence of the Lambs* (Jonathan Demme, 1991) in the form of Academy Awards for all the main cat-egories in 1992 helped solidify the psychologically complex serial killer as the realistic monster *du jour*. Later films, similarly Gothic in their dark aesthetics and often religious rationales, like *Seven* (David Fincher, 1995) and *Resurrection* (Russell Mulcahy, 1999), continued to prod the depths of the human soul and proposed fascinating murderers who, far from disposable or interchangeable, demanded to be taken seri-ously. The development of the sympathetic serial killer in the twenty-first century, albeit mostly in fiction and television, may be seen as the next evolutionary step for this monster (after the deconstructive postmodern games of *Scream* (Wes Craven, 1996) and other neo-slashers) and is very much in keeping with a cotemporaneous interest in complicating what, in the past, had been presented as evil characters. [3] As with slasher mon-sters, some critics may object that the intrinsic and gritty reality of the serial killer discounts it as a Gothic monster. While I would not want to suggest that all serial killer films are inherently Gothic – tone, cinema-tography and intent are decisive in this respect – it is worth pointing out that, for scholars like Philip L. Simpson, the history of the serial killer is actually steeped in the Gothic tradition (Simpson 2000: 26–69).

Ghosts would experience a strong revival in the twenty-first century, but two key films are responsible for creating an upsurge of interest in apparitions with a twist: *The Sixth Sense* (M. Night Shyamalan, 1999) and *The Blair Witch Project* (Eduardo Sánchez and Daniel Myrick, 1999). The former was responsible for the original figure of the unknowing spectre in child psychologist Dr Crowe (Bruce Willis) and for what is perhaps one of the most iconic phrases in horror cinema, 'I see dead people', uttered by medium child Cole (Haley Joel Osment). *Blair Witch* uses mood-enhancing atmospherics and uncanny occlu-sion and/or omission of its titular creature (if she exists at all) in ways that connect the actions to haunting experiences more typical of ghost films. Its reliance on handheld camera framing and on the cinematographic possibilities of the found footage motif – an echo of the found manuscript so prevalent in first-wave Gothic novels from *The Castle of Otranto* (1764) to *The Romance of the Forest* (1791) and *Melmoth the Wanderer* (1820) – eerily anticipated the rise of digital Gothic a few years later. If the 1990s were a slow-burning period for Gothic horror, the first two decades of the twenty-first century would see its strong resurgence among growing popular recognition of 'Gothic' as a term to define a certain type of cinema. In fact, the change in perception has been such that Gothic scholarship has gone from complaints that 'the Gothic does not "belong" to film, and the film medium must content itself with providing a home for that catch-all category of terror and spookiness, the horror genre' (Kavka, 2002: 209) to general acceptance that 'Gothic' is indeed a filmic and aesthetic category.[4]

Gothic Cinema in the Twenty-First Century

Despite its relatively short lifespan, the twenty-first century has seen a significant number of key Gothic films develop and gain notoriety. Although there have been no Gothic cycles like those that were popular in Europe during the mid-to-late twentieth century – Italy from the late 1950s to the late 1960s (Curti 2015), Spain from the late 1960s to the late 1970s (Aldana Reyes, 2018) – specific horror strands, such as the exorcism/possession film or the found footage horror film, have in places drawn from the Gothic tradition in their thematic focus on ghosts, hauntings and unruly demons. Ghosts, in particular, have been quite popular, especially after *The Others/Los otros* (Alejandro Amenábar, 2001) revived the haunted mansion story, a trope later expanded by compatriot J. A. Bayona in his *The Orphanage/El orfanato* (2008) and by Hammer Studios' comeback film, *The Woman in Black* (James Watkins, 2012).[5] Guillermo del Toro's *The Devil's Backbone/El espinazo del diablo* (2001) added a layer of social significance, or political allegory, to apparitions by connecting the silencing of the individual with the repression of national history.[6] Overall, however, the early twenty-first century is well-known for producing a number of unconnected Gothic films, such as Guillermo del Toro's love letter to the Female Gothic, *Crimson Peak* (2015), and *The Witch* (Robert Eggers, 2015), a period treatment of witchcraft in Puritan America. Altered or unhinged psychologies have also mixed with the Gothic in *The Babadook* (Jennifer Kent, 2014), which centres on an original children's picture book monster that may (or may not) be a projection of trauma and parental frustration; in *Black Swan* (Darren Aranofsky, 2011), where the motif of the dark double combines with body and metamorphic horror; and in the thriller *Shutter Island* (Martin Scorsese, 2010).

Other Gothic monsters have also thrived, their overfamiliarity clearly not a deterrent for audiences. Vampires, although largely co-opted by dark romance and the young adult trend kick-started by Stephenie Meyer's *Twilight* novels (2005–8) and its cinematic adaptations (2008–12), managed to keep their bite in films such as *30 Days of Night* (David Slade, 2007), adapted from the comic book mini-series of the same name (2002), *Daybreakers* (Michael and Peter Spierig, 2010) and *Stake Land* (Jim Mickle, 2011). As they did in the twentieth century, vampire films have continued to hybridise with other genres, such as the action film (*Blade II* (Guillermo del Toro, 2002), *Underworld* (Len Wiseman, 2003)), the faux documentary (*What We Do in the Shadows* (Taika Waititi and Jemaine Clement, 2014), *Vampires* (Vincent Lannoo, 2010)), melodrama (*Thirst* (Park Chan-wook, 2009), *Byzantium* (Neil Jordan, 2012)) and science fiction (*Dracula 3000* (Darrell Roodt, 2004)), among others. Perhaps as a response to the teenage vampire lover figure, or because the vampire no longer presents the type of threat it once did – surpassed, in its abjection, by the visceral zombie – it has been utilised to explore the 'othered' identities of social outsiders or subcultural communities. To Anne Rice's queer vampires, one must add those of *Let the Right One In/Låt den rätte komma in* (Tomas Alfredson, 2008), *Only Lovers Left Alive* (Jim Jarmusch, 2013) and *A Girl Walks Home Alone at Night* (Ana Lily Amirpour, 2014), the latter of which explores the plight of women in Iran.

As Stacey Abbott has noted (2016), the gap between the vampire and the zombie has shortened in the twenty-first century. Like vampires, zombies have cropped up in all number of genres, from rom coms, comedies and 'splatsticks' (*Warm Bodies* (Jonathan Levine, 2013), *Dead Snow/Død snø* (Tommy Wirkola, 2009), *Zombieland* (Ruben Fleischer, 2009), *Black Sheep* (Jonathan King, 2006), *Shaun of the Dead* (Edgar Wright, 2004)) to more sober, demanding and even political films (*Pontypool* (Bruce McDonald, 2009), *Land of the Dead* (George A. Romero, 2005)). Where zombies have truly blossomed, however, is in the apocalyptic horror film. Starting off in 2002 with *28 Days Later* (Danny Boyle) and the first in the *Resident Evil* series (Paul W. S. Anderson), and eventually influenced by the success of the comic series *The Walking Dead* (Robert Kirkman, 2003–19) and its television adaptation (2010–present), the zombie soon became a metonym for pandemic crises. Further films to expand on this notion include the Spanish *[•REC]* (Jaume Balagueró and Paco Plaza, 2007), whose zombies are revealed to be victims of possession in the second instalment (2009), and

World War Z (Marc Forster, 2013), where the zombie plague goes truly global. Although the zombie is more readily connected to the horror genre than to the Gothic mode, the case can be made that zombies are simply a modern Gothic monster (Ellis, 2000: 205–44). Since they have been as prevalent as, if not more than, vampires, it is perhaps time that we acknowledge that zombies are carrying out a lot of the critical and cultural work the Gothic is known for.

Apart from traditional monsters, the Gothic has also materialised in fragmented form in three distinctively post-millennial horror sub-genres: torture porn, found footage and the demonic possession film.[7] All of them have obvious precedents in twentieth-century Gothic and horror films. Torture porn most readily draws inspiration from exploitation and rape-revenge films from the 1970s – *The Texas Chain Saw Massacre* (Tobe Hooper, 1974), *I Spit on Your Grave* (Meir Zarchi, 1978), *The Hills Have Eyes* (Wes Craven, 1977) – so much so, in fact, that a number of torture porn features are remakes of these particular films. Found footage, as a filming technique in horror, has its beginnings in *Cannibal Holocaust* (Ruggero Deodato, 1980) and even in a proto-slasher like Michael Powell's *Peeping Tom* (1960), in which serial killer Mark (Carl Boehm) feels compelled to record his victims as they die in order to capture the essence of fear.[8] Demonic possession films are, naturally, intrinsically connected to Friedkin's *The Exorcist*, especially in their fixation with the female body. And yet, all these strands have gone beyond their predecessors and revived horror, sometimes developing a deliberately Gothic aesthetic and style or returning to traditional motifs or characters.

Torture porn's graphic scenarios, and its overwhelmingly contemporary settings, may lead viewers to think of them as the very embodiment of horror cinema and thus as directly opposed to the more subtle scares of the Gothic. Such an approach, however, only tells a partial story of the Gothic, and seems to forget that first-wave Gothic novels such as *Vathek* (1786), *The Monk* (1796), *Zofloya* (1806) and the aforementioned *Melmoth* could be every bit as perverse, gratuitous and excessive as the explicit nightmares of films like *Saw* (James Wan, 2004) and *Hostel* (Eli Roth, 2005). As I have argued elsewhere, it is, in fact, possible to find a number of similarities and shared preoccupations between early Gothic fiction and torture porn: the obsession with disproportionate and spectacular punishment, often a result of religious or moralistic overzealousness, the recurrence of torture chambers and similar chthonian and even Inquisitorial settings connected to captivity, and the emphasis on the cruelty of human nature (Aldana Reyes, 2014: 135–43). A film like *The Human Centipede* (Tom Six, 2010), perhaps the last noteworthy torture porn film, even incorporates traits from the mad science subgenre and invents a Dr Frankenstein for the twenty-first century in the figure of the demented surgeon protagonist (Dieter Laser). If Frankenstein's obsession was to create life, however, Josef Heiter's is to create the ultimate fetish, a centipede made out of living human bodies. *American Mary* (Soska Sisters, 2012), a feminist film that sees a woman taking vengeance on her rapist via bod mod, is representative of a minor surgical subgenre that also includes the Frankenstein-influenced *May* (Lucky McKee, 2002).

If *Ring/Ringu* (Hideo Nakata, 1998) put a ghost in the (video) machine and *Blair Witch* tried to record it, the rise of found footage, especially after the unexpected success of *Paranormal Activity* (Oren Peli, 2009), cemented the connection between the spiritual world and that of the digital camera. Linnie Blake and I have come up with the term 'digital horror' to refer to 'any type of horror that actively purports to explore the dark side of contemporary life in a digital age governed by informational flows, rhizomatic public networks, virtual simulation and visual hyper-stimulation' (Blake and Aldana Reyes, 2015: 3). Where this horror film takes on a decidedly Gothic or monstrous turn, for example in *Pulse/Kairo* (Kiyoshi Kurosawa, 2001), *Cloverfield* (Matt Reeves, 2008), *Grave Encounters* (The Vicious Brothers, 2011), *Apartment 143* (Carles Torrens, 2012) or *As Above, So Below* (John Erick Dowdle, 2014), one could equally speak of a digital Gothic. Films like *Megan Is Missing* (Michael Goi, 2011), *Paranormal Activity 4* (Ariel Schulman and Henry Joost, 2012) or *Unfriended* (Leo Gabriadze, 2015) have taken digital Gothic one step further by telling their stories via webcam. In them, computer screens either serve to tape ghostly visitations or else mediate nightmares. Horror is brought closer to home to become intimately connected to the profusion of recording devices, from phones to laptops, which now define human experience and interaction in the West. With the democratisation of information communications and digital technologies come the ghosts of surveillance, data control and social alienation.

Intimately connected to digital horror is the post-millennial exorcism film, although only by virtue of its preference for a found footage framing that may give individual titles a home tape feel. The demonic possessions of *The Last Exorcism* (Daniel Stamm, 2010) and *The Devil Inside* (William Brent Bell, 2012) or the son-of-the-devil shenanigans of *Devil's Due* (Matt Bettinelli-Olpin and Tyler Gillett, 2014) have thus attempted to give their otherwise fairly conventional occult fare a new and more immersive edge. Following the part-courtroom drama *The Exorcism of Emily Rose* (Scott Derrickson, 2005), other films, such as the blockbuster *The Conjuring* (James Wan, 2013) and *The Quiet Ones*

(John Pogue, 2014), have opted for more melodramatic treatments set in the 1970s featuring parapsychologists and demonologists. It is possible that this return to the supernatural is simply a response to the more realist horror of the torture porn phenomenon or motivated by profitable ventures – the enduring success of the *Paranormal Activity* series (2009–15) – but it certainly augurs an even more sustained Gothic focus for horror cinema in years to come.

Notes

1. My own *Gothic Cinema* (2020) traces the history of Gothic cinema as an aesthetic mode and discusses the implications of applying the term 'Gothic' to film.
2. Although there are no mentions of lesbianism in the film, women are seen clearly professing love for one another and, at one point, are seen in bed together.
3. I have in mind films like *Sweeney Todd: The Demon Barber of Fleet Street* (Tim Burton, 2007) and *Maleficent* (Robert Stromberg, 2014) or the planned *Wicked* (Stephen Daldry, 2021).
4. As the publication of the book that accompanied the first major film exhibition on the Gothic in Britain (Bell 2013) indicates, Gothic is now as solid a category as it could possibly be.
5. Hammer produced other films in the twenty-first century, but *The Woman in Black* was the first to command a significant audience and was one of the highest-grossing British films of all times, thus drawing attention to the studio's revival (Walker, 2016: 122).
6. Del Toro would go on to mine this vein with the Gothic fairytale *Pan's Labyrinth/El laberinto del fauno* (2006).
7. As I have argued elsewhere, found footage horror is technically a framing narrative and not a subgenre (Aldana Reyes, 2015b: 122–36).
8. The latter is, in some respects, also the grandfather of the snuff film, also popular in the twenty-first century. See Jackson et al. (2016).

References

Abbott, S. 2016. *Undead Apocalypse: Vampires and Zombies in the 21st Century*. Edinburgh: Edinburgh University Press.

Aldana Reyes, X. 2014. *Body Gothic: Corporeal Transgression in Contemporary Literature and Horror Film*. Cardiff: University of South Wales Press.

Aldana Reyes, X. 2015a. 'Gothic Affect: An Alternative Approach to Critical Models of the Contemporary Gothic', in Piatti-Farnell, L. and Lee, B. D. (eds), *New Directions in 21st-Century Gothic: The Gothic Compass*. Abingdon and New York: Routledge, pp. 11–23.

Aldana Reyes, X. 2015b. 'Reel Evil: A Critical Reassessment of Found Footage Horror', *Gothic Studies*, 17: 2, pp. 122–36.

Aldana Reyes, X. 2018. '"Fantaterror": Gothic Monsters in the Golden Age of Spanish B-Movie Horror, 1968–80', in Edwards, J. D. and Höglund, J. (eds), *B-Movie Gothic: International Perspectives*. Edinburgh: Edinburgh University Press, pp. 95–107.

Aldana Reyes, X. 2020. *Gothic Cinema*. Abingdon and New York: Routledge.

Bell, J. (ed.) 2013. *Gothic: The Dark Heart of Film*. London: BFI.

Blake, L. and Aldana Reyes, X. 2015. 'Introduction: Horror in the Digital Age', in Blake, L. and Aldana Reyes, X. (eds), *Digital Horror: Haunted Technologies, Network Panic and the Found Footage Phenomenon*. London and New York: I.B. Tauris, pp. 1–13.

Curti, R. 2015. *Italian Gothic Horror Films, 1957–1969*. Jefferson, NC: McFarland.

Ellis, M. 2000. *The History of Gothic Fiction*. Edinburgh: Edinburgh University Press.

Freeland, C. 2000. *The Naked and the Undead: Evil and the Appeal of Horror*. Oxford and Boulder, CO: Westview Press.

Hutchings, P. 1996. 'Tearing Your Soul Apart: Horror's New Monsters', in Sage, V. and Lloyd Smith, A. (eds) *Modern Gothic: A Reader*. Manchester: Manchester University Press.

Jackson, N., Kimber, S., Walker, J. and Watson, T. J. (eds) 2016. *Snuff: Real Death and Screen Media*. London and New York: Bloomsbury Academic.

Kavka, M. 2002. 'The Gothic on Screen', in Hogle, J. E. (ed.), *The Cambridge Companion to Gothic Fiction*. Cambridge: Cambridge University Press, pp. 209–28.

Simpson, P. L. 2000. *Psycho-Paths: Tracking the Serial Killer through Contemporary American Film and Fiction*. Carbondale, IL: Southern Illinois University Press.

Walker, J. 2016. *Contemporary British Horror Cinema*. Edinburgh: Edinburgh University Press.

Part II

Gothic Film Adaptations

Chapter 6

Danny's Endless Tricycle Ride: The Gothic and Adaptation

Richard J. Hand

The heritage of Gothic literature is evident in the way it continues to fascinate and haunt our contemporary culture. Whether it is atmospheric Victorian ghost stories, the exploits of mad scientists Frankenstein and Jekyll or the nightmare worlds in the fiction of Edgar Allan Poe and Bram Stoker, Gothic literature continues to be read, retold and contested, its themes, obsessions and worldview recurrently resonating into our own time. This is nowhere more evident than in the practice and industry of film adaptation. In its ceaseless search for source material, cinema has turned, time and again, to Gothic literature. Whether it is in examples of canonical masterpieces, literary obscurities or popular fictions, film-makers have found inspiration on the bookshelves of the Gothic. However, within the realm of Gothic screen adaptations, a wide variety of strategies have been used. In some cases, films have foregrounded their source: *Bram Stoker's Dracula* (Francis Ford Coppola, 1992) and *Mary Shelley's Frankenstein* (Kenneth Branagh, 1994) go so far as to include the authors' names in their titles. In other cases, strategies are more latent: the eldritch universe of H. P. Lovecraft has become a pre-eminent influence on contemporary horror and yet often remains a discreet source rather than a blatant one. Similarly, there are examples of film that are selective or allusive and borrow literary paradigms for their plots or archetypal figures. In so doing, we discover how literary tropes and themes have continued to manifest throughout the history of film: the philosophical anxieties and social tensions that were the impetus underpinning the literary Gothic have evidently continued to infuse twentieth- and twenty-first-century culture. Moreover, this infusion has an extraordinary breadth: as we shall see in this chapter, examples of Gothic adaptation have been centrally important in family-friendly horror films, as well as film versions of literary texts, from the popular novels of Stephen King to the neo-Gothic literary fiction of Sarah Waters.

The children's animation *Hotel Transylvania* (Genndy Tartakovsky, 2012) and its sequels (2015 and 2018) are a hectic bricolage of reference, constructing a vivid iconography of monsters and centrally foregrounding a classic pantheon of Gothic creatures instigated into popularity by Universal Pictures in the 1930s onwards, namely the protagonist Count Dracula and his friends Frankenstein ('Frank'), the Wolfman ('Wayne'), the Invisible Man ('Griffin', as in H. G. Wells's 1897 novel) and the Mummy ('Murray'). The series also features a wide panoply of other horror icons: animated suits of armour and skeletons; zombies and talking shrunken heads; the yeti and the chupacabra; and monsters allusive to the 'B Movie' era of *Creature from the Black Lagoon* (Jack Arnold, 1954), *The Blob* (Irvin Yeaworth, 1958) and *The Fly* (Kurt Neumann, 1958). The *Hotel Transylvania* films belong to a distinctive American tradition of family-friendly Gothic that goes back to the artwork of Edward Gorey (1925–2000) and Charles Addams (1912–88) and is embodied in popular television sitcoms such as *The Addams Family* (1964–6), *The Munsters* (1964–6) and their multiple transmedia manifestations. It is also a central impetus to much of Tim Burton's most successful work – family-friendly Gothic films such as *Beetlejuice* (1988), *Corpse Bride* (2005) and *Frankenweenie* (2012). As Aspasia Stephanou writes, Burton's 'films evoke the atmospheres of foggy, Gothic landscapes, mysterious, oneiric spaces, and ghostly presences' which feature the 'bittersweet melancholy of lonesome doppelgängers and outsiders' (Stephanou, 2013: 99). Ironically, Burton succeeds in creating a distinctive style – the 'Burtonesque' – through derivation and intertextuality, drawing his influences from the long tradition of popular Gothic culture, including the European cinema of German Expressionism and Hammer Films, but with a special place for Gothic Americana: the literature of Poe and Washington Irving; the artwork of Gorey, Addams and horror comic books; the image and voice of the actor Vincent Price; the gamut of Hollywood auteurs from Alfred Hitchcock to Ed Wood; television shows such as *The Twilight Zone* (1959–64) and even, in *Mars Attacks!* (1996), Science Fiction trading cards.

Some family-friendly horror adaptations, such as *The Witches* (Nicolas Roeg, 1990), based on Roald Dahl's 1983 novel, *Coraline* (Henry Selick, 2009), adapted from Neil Gaiman's 2002 novel, and *Goosebumps* (Rob Letterman, 2015) and *Goosebumps 2: Haunted Halloween* (Ari Sandel, 2018), adapted from the children's book, television and game franchise created by R. L. Stine, place resilient children at the heart of the narrative and chart their triumph over monstrous adversity and peril. In contrast, the *Hotel Transylvania* movies and the family films of Tim Burton make monstrosity their focus, frequently building empathy, humour and pity around its Gothic monsters. This can mean that the monstrous and abject is humanised while, conversely, the 'normal' humans are malevolent and destructive, such as the van Helsing family in *Hotel Transylvania 3* or the disapproving neighbours in *Edward Scissorhands* (Tim Burton, 1990), revealing uniquely human-specific traits of hypocrisy, mendacity and betrayal. Of course, there has long been a theme of 'sympathy for the devil' in Gothic culture, but this is consolidated into a key impetus in these examples of family-friendly Gothic cinema. As Catherine Lester observes:

> [Children's] horror films . . . draw heavily upon typical conventions of the genre, including the presence of monsters, the evocation of disgust, and narrative structures that hinge upon if and how the monstrous presence will be defeated. They are simultaneously able to deviate and become 'child-friendly' by excluding – or finding strategic ways to alleviate – horrific elements that might be thought to distress child viewers, such as the lessening of realism and violence through stylized animation or moments of humor. (Lester, 2016: 34)

Through the specific lens of adaptation, family-friendly and children's horror films can take the unsettling narratives, images and sequences of pre-existing Gothic texts and transform them: through strategies of empathy and subversion, the horrific can be made humorous and the perilous can be made safe. There is perhaps no limit to this as we shall see as we turn to the screen adaptation of Stephen King, especially in what has frequently been cited as the 'scariest horror movie of all time' in various populist polls, *The Shining* (Stanley Kubrick, 1980).

Published in 1977, Stephen King's *The Shining* has been perennially popular and has been interpreted as everything from a critique of corporate management – 'an "organizational structure" such as the Overlook brings loss of family, morality, and humanity' (Benevento, 2017: 723) – to a sustained exploration wherein the only true horror is the 'frightening and disturbing reality' of domestic violence (Hornbeck, 2016: 697). In a context of adaptation, the theme and techniques of textuality is particularly resonant. For John Sears, *The Shining*'s 'theme – the palimpsestic co-presence of the various moments of the hotel's history – is mimicked formally' (Sears, 2011: 173) through the novel's allusions to pre-existing texts of the Gothic and Modernism, above all Poe's 'The Masque of the Red Death' and T. S. Eliot's *The Waste Land*. To this we can add references as diverse as Lewis Carroll – '". . . I'm late," said the white rabbit' (King, 2018: 237) – and old-time radio superheroes – '*The Shadow knows*' (King, 2018, 50). In addition, Nick Freeman's interpretation sees King's construction of Jack Torrance as implying 'a Romantic conception of the artist as an asocial visionary'

(Freeman, 2018: 334), while the novel's narrative elements allude to haunted/haunting house stories such as Rudyard Kipling's 'They' (1904) and E. F. Benson's 'Pirates' (1928). *The Shining* therefore demonstrates, in Sears' words, 'its own self-reflexive textuality, its drawing on literary tradition, as a version of its own palimpsestic vision of Gothic place' (Sears, 2011: 173).

As a 'Gothic place' in cinema, there have been few sites that have been more analysed, contested or alluded to than the Overlook Hotel in Stanley Kubrick's adaptation of *The Shining* (1980). *The Shining* is a landmark of originality in horror cinema, with Kubrick employing bright lighting and vivid, even garish, colours where other filmmakers might have used a stereotypical Gothic vision of dark shadows and a gloomy *mise-en-scène* in the construction of the Overlook Hotel. There are certainly moments of intertextuality in the film, not least Jack Nicholson's line 'Here's Johnny!' (significantly adlibbed), which quotes the opening catchphrase in Johnny Carson's popular television talk show *The Tonight Show* (1962–92) but has now become more famous than the source itself. What is particularly interesting about Kubrick's *The Shining* is its place as a source for adaptation. Just as King draws on Romantic, Gothic and Modernist literature, quotes Poe, Eliot, Lewis Carroll and old-time adventure radio and echoes Kipling and Benson, creators of graphic novels to Hollywood blockbusters quote King as interpreted through the lens of Kubrick.

Brecht Evens' *Panther* (2016) is an ingeniously crafted graphic novel which looks, at first glance, like a children's book, but it tells a disturbing story of a girl, Christine, and her imaginary friend. In the tale, Christine lives alone with her taciturn father and her cat. When her pet dies, she descends into grief but is suddenly befriended by a colourful visitor, the feline of the title, who creeps out of a drawer in her bedroom. The panther is playful and comforting but becomes increasingly sinister, culminating in a nightmarish scene when he brings a group of 'friends' home to abuse the little girl. Many interpretations of the book are possible, but a subtle allusion to Kubrick's *The Shining* can provide a possible key to the horrific truth that lies at the heart of the story. In one image of Christine's home, a carpet repeats the pattern of the hallway floors in the Overlook Hotel, and we realise that the seemingly distant but gentle father is probably the perpetrator of child abuse, a predator who is undergoing a breakdown and descends into malice and paedophilia.

Ready Player One (Steven Spielberg, 2018) is a Science Fiction epic about virtual reality gaming and dystopia based on Ernest Cline's 2011 novel of the same title. The story is set in the 2040s and depicts a bleak, ecologically distraught world in which people disappear into escapist fantasy in a vast online world called OASIS. James Halliday, the creator of OASIS, dies and announces in his will that he has planted an Easter egg and that the first to solve the puzzle will inherit the creator's vast fortune. Thus far, the story may seem to allude to Roald Dahl's *Charlie and the Chocolate Factory* (1964) in its theme of a fantastical world and a contest to become heir to its eccentric creator. In attempting to solve the challenge, Wade Watts, the story's teenage protagonist, researches the 1980s films and games beloved by Halliday. In one sequence in the novel, Watts finds himself transformed: 'I was David Lightman, Matthew Broderick's character in the movie *WarGames*. And this was his first scene in the film. I was *in the movie*' (Cline, 2011: 108). In order to complete this task, Watts realises he has to re-enact the film, word for word and move for move. While Cline's novel uses *WarGames* (John Badham, 1983), Spielberg's film changes this for another classic 1980s film: *The Shining*. In an extraordinary and metatextual rendering, Parzival (i.e. the avatar of Watts) and his virtual teammates enter a cinema screening *The Shining* and find themselves in the Overlook Hotel. Rather than a sustained and immersed enacting of the film, the sequence is more allusive to a survival horror game experience: the team realise they have less than five minutes to locate the key. Through a mixture of CGI and physical reconstruction, an exceptional verisimilitude is created in the short sequence: core motifs and scenes from Kubrick's film are featured, as well as a concise use of its distinctive soundtrack (including the intense music of Béla Bartók and Krzysztof Penderecki).

As Parzival and the team enter the unmistakable setting of the Overlook Hotel, the typewriter churns out (to the rhythm of *The Shining*'s 'Dies Irae' title theme) 'All work and no play makes Jack a dull boy' albeit placed on the page as concrete text in the shape of a key. Humorously, one team member Aech admits to not having seen *The Shining*, so while the rest of the team recall and debate the many potential keys in *The Shining*, Aech makes poor decisions regarding defining moments in Kubrick's film: following the path of the rolling yellow ball; going after the ghostly twin sisters; trying to enter the elevator, only to be swept away in the deluge of blood which has a stronger impact on the surrounding furnishings than the torrent in *The Shining*. Grabbing and breaking the photograph of the 4 July 1921 party from the finale of Kubrick's film, albeit with James Halliday replacing Jack Torrance in the picture, Aech manages to cling onto the door to a room and escapes the sanguineous flood. The room is 237, location of the most famous scene of abject horror in Kubrick's film.

The young woman who emerges from the bath in *Ready Player One* is naked, although, in contrast to the original film, the point of view, camera angles and a deeper tub obscure anything too explicit. When the woman comes in for an embrace, Aech looks around and declares 'Am I being punk'd?', assuming this can only be a hidden-camera prank show. Going with the woman's invitation, Aech sees in the mirror the decomposing body of an old woman who begins to laugh manically but rapidly decays and collapses just as we are taken later into Kubrick's film and an axe smashes through the door (and, additionally, the wall). When Aech looks back the woman swipes with a knife. This addition to *The Shining* echoes the 'old lady' wielding a knife in perhaps the most famous bathroom scene in horror cinema, namely the shower scene in *Psycho* (Alfred Hitchcock, 1960), while Aech's evasive moves resemble the combination of moves executed in a videogame survival sequence. Eluding the knife, Aech topples into the bath and is flushed into the snowy maze at the climax of Kubrick's film. We see the hobbling silhouette of Jack Torrance while the old woman smashes an axe onto the miniature model of the maze from earlier in Kubrick's film, forcing Aech to survive the shadowy Jack and the gigantic axe wielded by the dead woman. Aech slips through the hedge which transforms into the storeroom door in the Overlook Hotel and, when he sees his teammates, complains of the 'crazy naked zombie lady' in room 237, only for Parzival to dismiss it with 'There are no zombies in *The Shining*!'

In many respects, the evil entity in room 237 (the ghost of Lorraine Massey) *is* like a zombie in King's novel (where the room number is 217). In King's novel, it is Danny's encounter with the undead Mrs Massey – left in ellipsis by Kubrick – that is described in depth, while his father's visit to the room is more obtuse and diffident, with the nervous Jack finding nothing in the room until he suddenly smells 'a lady's soap' (King, 2018: 277) and detects, 'ill defined and obscure through the plastic' (278), a dead woman in the bathtub. He flees the suite and detects the 'odd wet thumping sound' (279) as something approaches the closed door. To return to Danny's encounter, King writes: 'The woman in the tub had been dead for a long time. She was bloated and purple, her gas-filled belly rising out of the cold, ice-rimmed water like some fleshy island' (239). Suddenly this corpse sits up and Danny hears her dead palms making 'squittering sounds on the porcelain' as she crawls towards him, grinning and relentless but not breathing: 'She was corpse, and dead long years' (239). Danny closes his eyes to cancel out this uncanny vision, but 'the years-damp, bloat, fish-smelling hands closed softly around his throat' (240). The woman may be the ghost of Lorraine Massey haunting the room in the Overlook Hotel where she committed suicide, but she nonetheless can do physical harm. In Kubrick's film the encounter is refocused to be between Jack and the entity which, in a love-and-death sequence of Eros and Thanatos, shifts from a young woman who seduces Jack into the decomposing old woman who laughs and pursues him.

In *Ready Player One*, the slow burn and tension of Kubrick's adaptation is distilled into a quick-fire five minutes of key motifs, heightened peril and fluid movement. The laughing, staggering old woman in Kubrick's film swiftly morphs into a dynamic, fast-moving CGI zombie in Spielberg's movie. It is fascinating how scenes from an 18-certificate/R-rated horror film can become a central episode in a family adventure movie, but this can only be achieved by our *Schadenfreude* at the hapless exploits (but necessary survival) of Aech, a censorship of nudity and a heightening of the energetic and violent actions of the evidently animated 'crazy naked zombie lady'.

Whether in such dynamic episodes mediated through other film interpretations, or in wholesale adaptations of novels and short stories, the adaptation of Stephen King's fiction has become a subgenre in horror film as significant in its own right as King's contribution to horror fiction. Film adaptions such as *Carrie* (Brian De Palma, 1976) and *Misery* (Rob Reiner, 1990) have become classics of the horror genre, and their popularity shows no signs of abating in a culture where remakes, new adaptations and King's broad narrative influence continue to have enormous currency. Indeed, a short time before Spielberg's *Ready Player One*, *Gerald's Game* (Mike Flanagan, 2017) was released, a film based on King's 1992 novel. Very much an 'adult' story of a sex game that goes wrong, a husband handcuffs his wife, Jessie, to a bed in a remote cabin only to die of a heart attack. The subsequent narrative is dominated by Jessie's stream-of-consciousness and visions as she strives for freedom. As the director states, the 'book, as it's written, is really impossible to adapt' (Shepherd, 2017), and yet Flanagan succeeds in creating strategies through which the intense interiority of the source text is 'opened out' into a compelling filmic experience. Moreover, in the opening scenes of foreplay, the tale is convincingly updated for the Viagra generation. In the same year, *The Guardian* reported that *It* (Andy Muschietti, 2017) had 'broken the 44-year record set by *The Exorcist* (William Friedkin, 1973) to become the highest-grossing horror film of all time' (Mumford, 2017). However, as much as adaptation is important in popular horror fiction, it is just as significant in regard to contemporary neo-Gothic literary fiction.

Sarah Waters is an acclaimed contemporary novelist with a particular interest in historical fiction, especially the Victorian epoch but also, in *The Night Watch* (2006) and *The Little Stranger* (2009), 1940s Britain. Particularly rewarding as a postmodern take on the haunted house story,

The Little Stranger (2009), is set in rural England shortly after the Second World War. A local general practitioner, Dr Faraday – the narrator of the story – makes a house call to treat a maidservant at Hundreds Hall, a dilapidated Georgian mansion and home to the Ayres family, the siblings Caroline and Roderick and their mother. For Faraday, a local lad, the visit to Hundreds Hall is poignant. He had visited the house on one occasion, some thirty years before when he was ten and the Ayres family opened their grounds for an Empire Day fete soon after the end of the First World War. The ten-year old Faraday was able to slip inside the house and was entranced by its splendour and, in an uncharacteristic act of misbehaviour, snapped off a plaster acorn from an ornate border: 'I was like a man, I suppose, wanting a lock of hair from the head of a girl he had suddenly and blindingly become enamoured of' (Waters, 2009: 3). Despite the fond memory of his past enrapture, Faraday is appalled by the neglect and decay that has befallen the mansion. Assessing Betty, the fourteen-year old maid, it becomes evident that she is more depressed and homesick than feeling poorly. She confesses to a constant unease and recurrent nightmares in the rambling, creepy house where she does not know what is around its many dark corners and predicts 'I shall be dead of horror, I know I shall' (Waters, 2009: 13).

The doctor swiftly befriends the Ayres family, including Roderick, who was seriously injured and traumatised as an RAF pilot during the War. Faraday agrees to treat him for his physical (and, more discreetly, his psychological) wounds. Most significantly, Faraday befriends Caroline, seeming to find a rapport with the unmarried daughter. The Ayres are in torpor, unable to afford the necessary upkeep of Hundreds Hall and anxious about how the Labour government's socialist policies might impact on their life and inheritance. Once Faraday becomes a frequent visitor – principally in an ambiguous friendship/courtship of Caroline – we see things turn awry. During a party, the Ayres's normally placid dog mauls a child and that same night Roderick claims that some malevolent entity appeared in his room. After an act of arson in which Caroline and Roderick's bedrooms are set alight, Roderick is taken to a mental hospital. Increasingly, eerie phenomena occur, especially in the old nursery: childlike writing appears on the walls and the house's servant bells and communication tubes sound with no one at the other end. Mrs Ayres associates the supernatural occurrences with her first daughter, Susan, who died when she was eight years old (and who Faraday saw on the Empire Day celebration when she was six). As Beth Rodgers observes, in '*The Little Stranger*, each ghostly encounter causes an escalation in the emotional and psychological unravelling of the protagonists' (Rodgers, 2018: 345). The grand house and peacetime stability are eclipsed by the anxiety, instability and despair of those connected with Hundreds Hall, albeit inflected and manifested in diverse ways.

Waters's novel is a complex mesh of intertextual reference, while also being an original contribution to contemporary neo-Gothic fiction. The novel alludes to Edgar Allan Poe's 'The Fall of the House of Usher' in its depiction of a deteriorating house that almost seems to be sentient, reflecting the decline of the family who reside there (Roderick and Madeline Usher are paralleled by Roderick and Caroline Ayres). The first-person narrative likewise draws a parallel with Charlotte Brontë's *Jane Eyre* (1847), especially in the admission into a tarnished mansion – Thornfield Hall being a precursor to Hundreds Hall – where eerie incidents mix with dark secrets and repressed desires, the names of Eyre and Ayres an evident acknowledgement of this. Faraday shares his surname with Michael Faraday (1791–1867), the British scientist who pioneered work in the field of electromagnetism. The protagonist of *The Little Stranger* shares this interest in electrical technology and offers to treat Roderick's permanent leg pain with an electric induction coil. Faraday's confidence is counterbalanced with his patient's anxiety:

> I'd used the apparatus many times before, and it was simple enough, a combination of coil, dry-cell battery and metal plate electrodes; but it looked rather daunting with its terminals and wires, and when I raised my head again I saw that Roderick had left his desk and was gazing down at it in some dismay. 'Quite a little monster, isn't it,' he said, plucking at his lip. (Waters, 2009: 54)

When Roderick agrees to the treatment, he reveals his wounded, agonised leg and Faraday administers the device:

> . . . I went through the process of wiring him up: soaking squares of lint with salt solution, fixing these to the electric plates; putting the plates in position on his leg with elastic bindings. [. . .] I threw the switch. He yelped, his leg jumping forward in an involuntary twitch. (56)

In Waters's development of this scene, the protagonist of the story seems less like a GP than an experimental scientist evolving from his namesake Dr Faraday into a Dr Frankenstein. Even the 'yellow, bloodless' (55) skin of Roderick's leg calls to mind the 'yellow skin' (Shelley, 2010: 45) of the creature in *Frankenstein*.

The film adaptation of *The Little Stranger* (2018) was directed by Lenny Abrahamson, whose previous film, *Room* (2015), was an acclaimed adaptation of Emma Donoghue's 2010 novel, based on the Josef Fritzl case, about the incarceration of a woman and child. In his next film, Abrahamson abandons the claustrophobia and contemporary grime of *Room* but creates a film similarly characterised by a Gothic sense of oppressive environment and atmosphere. *The Little Stranger* draws on the tradition of heritage cinema (albeit in an emphatically twenty-first-century context), using apt rural locations and costume design to create a convincing 1940s 'Englishness', verdant yet fatigued. The story's themes of class division, pained nostalgia and social exhaustion are an apt reflection of the film's context of austerity and the tensions of 'Brexit Britain'. The film also draws on the genre of haunted houses in cinema, emphatically the 'high end' design and style of the Henry James *The Turn of the Screw* (1898) adaptation, *The Innocents* (Jack Clayton, 1961), the Shirley Jackson *The Haunting of Hill House* (1959) adaptation, *The Haunting* (Robert Wise, 1963), and the original, but highly intertextual, *The Others* (Alejandro Amenábar, 2001). As much as the adaptation of *The Little Stranger* constructs an evocative *mise-en-scène*, its actors chart carefully mapped journeys of characterisation. In particular, Domhnall Gleeson as Faraday locates a stiff upper lip post-war Britishness that seems to become sinister in its very neutrality: the more the story progresses, the more the latent desires beneath Faraday's inscrutable sangfroid become coldly unrelenting. The film follows the plot points of Waters's novel closely and its most radical departure from the source text is in its ending.

At the end of the novel, the Ayres have departed – Mrs Ayres has hanged herself, Caroline has fallen to her death down the stairwell and Roderick remains confined – and Faraday explores the house, pursuing the supernatural presence that its inhabitants claimed was there. In the final paragraph Faraday tells us:

> If Hundreds Hall is haunted, however, its ghost doesn't show itself to me. For I'll turn, and am disappointed – realising that what I am looking at is only a cracked window-pane, and that the face gazing distortedly from it, baffled and longing, is my own. (Waters, 2009: 499)

Obviously, this ending belongs to the rich tradition of using mirrors and the reflected self as motif, symbol and metaphor in Gothic literature. It also has enormous potential on screen and would hint at the memorable use of reflections in a variety of Gothic films, from the subtle to the extreme: 'The Haunted Mirror' episode within *Dead of Night* (Robert Hamer et al., 1945); Lila jumping when she sees her own reflection in *Psycho* (Alfred Hitchcock, 1960); Jack Torrance seeing what he is really embracing in the bathroom mirror in *The Shining*; and many more. However, the screen adaptation of *The Little Stranger* ends with Faraday as a child, standing alone and sobbing at the top of the stairwell from where Caroline fell to her death. The narrative puts time out of joint, with the chilling consequence that the little boy seems to have pushed Caroline to her death.

Faraday is, of course, the ghost of the house, the child whose yearning for the grandeur and glory of Hundreds Hall represents less aspiration than a frustrated desire that can never be fulfilled or, at least when it seems to be, is empty. It is a frustration compounded in adulthood when Caroline eventually rejects the chance to marry. When, in the novel, Faraday sees his own reflection distorted in the broken glass, he is indeed seeing a ghost: the ghost of himself, a confused and yearning ghost who – like the spectres in *The Sixth Sense* (M. Night Shyamalan, 1999) – does not realise he is a ghost. In the film version, Faraday sobbing at the end shows a frustration that became the force of malevolence in the house that killed Caroline. The 'little stranger' of the title is an odd little child, a working-class boy who wandered for a few minutes where he did not belong. The plaster acorn he snapped off and pocketed lays deep roots and grows into something huge and menacing, a malevolent force of destruction that Caroline beholds – calling out 'You' (Waters, 2009: 482) before she falls to her death.

Cinematic adaptation continues to be a key method by which Gothic narratives continue to be propagated, retold and appropriated. There is no limit to the potential audience. Children of the youngest age can recognise the slicked-back hair, cloak and 'blah blah blah' accented catchphrase of Dracula from *Hotel Transylvania*; Stephen King continues to be pervasive in blockbusters marketed to young and old, as well as abiding classics of horror cinema. Contemporary neo-Gothic fiction such as Sarah Waters's *The Little Stranger* is carefully adapted into a film that hybridises the genres of heritage and haunted house cinema to explore the psychological descent and angst of its characters. In one of the most enduring images from Stanley Kubrick's adaptation of *The Shining*, the little boy Danny rides his tricycle around and around the corridors of the Overlook Hotel. We hear the wheels thrumming over the bare floorboards, muffled when he rides over carpet, and coming to a halt when he encounters the ghostly twin sisters. In Gothic film adaptation, we find similarly different 'textures'. Sometimes narratives foreground their sources blatantly, sometimes a more muted and latent strategy is used. And sometimes, like the ghosts of the Grady girls, an allusion leaps out of nowhere to surprise us, stopping us in our tracks. While adaptors might find in their Gothic sources a deep textual palimpsest to uncover, the audience perhaps joins Danny on an endless tricycle ride, beholding never-ending but nonetheless thrilling cycles of adaptation.

References

Benevento, B. 2017. 'When Caretaking Goes Wrong: Maintenance, Management, and the Horrific Corporation in Stephen King's *The Shining*', *Journal of Popular Culture*, 50: 4, pp. 723–42.

Cline, E. 2011. *Ready Player One*. London: Penguin.

Freeman, N. 2018. 'Haunted Houses'. in Brewster, S. and Thurston, L. (eds), *The Routledge Handbook to the Ghosts Story*. London: Routledge, pp. 328–37.

Hornbeck, E. J. 2016. 'Who's Afraid of the Big Bad Wolf? Domestic Violence in *The Shining*', *Feminist Studies*, 42: 3, pp. 689–719.

King, S. 2018. *The Shining*. London: Hodder & Stoughton.

Lester, C. 2016. 'The Children's Horror Film: Characterizing an "Impossible" Subgenre', *Velvet Light Trap: A Critical Journal of Film and Television*, 78, pp. 22–37.

Mumford, G. 2017. 'Stephen King's *It* Scares Off *The Exorcist* to Become Highest-grossing Horror Ever', *The Guardian*, 29 September. https://www.theguardian.com/film/2017/sep/29/stephen-king-it-the-exorcist-highest-grossing-horror-film-ever (accessed 1 October 2018).

Rodgers, B. 2018. 'Haunted Houses', in Brewster, S. and Thurston, L. (eds), *The Routledge Handbook to the Ghosts Story*. London: Routledge, pp. 338–47.

Sears, J. 2011. *Stephen King's Gothic*. Cardiff: University of Wales Press.

Shelley, M. 2010. *Frankenstein*. London: Collins.

Shepherd, J. 2017. 'Gerald's Game: How Director Mike Flanagan Made Stephen King's "Unfilmable Book" into a film', *The Independent*, 28 September. https://www.independent.co.uk/arts-entertainment/films/features/geralds-game-mike-flanagan-stephen-king-unfilmable-book-movie-netflix-trevor-macy-director-producer-a7972651.html (accessed 1 October 2018).

Stephanou, A. 2013. 'Tim Burton', in Hughes, W., Punter, D. and Smith, A. (eds), *The Encyclopedia of the Gothic*. London: Wiley-Blackwell, pp. 99–100.

Waters, S. 2009. *The Little Stranger*. London: Virago.

Chapter 7

Jekyll and Hyde and Scopophilia
Martin Danahay

Laura Mulvey's article 'Visual Pleasure and Narrative Cinema' (1975) was widely influential and made the term 'scopophilia' central to feminist analyses of cinema. Mulvey argued that scopophilia 'arises from pleasure in using another person as an object of sexual stimulation through sight' (2004: 835) and that the cinema especially satisfied a primordial desire to look without being seen, or in other words that it satisfied a voyeuristic urge going back to early childhood. Furthermore, Hollywood films encoded a gendered way of looking at the screen in that 'the determining male gaze projects its phantasy on to the female figure which is styled accordingly' (837), so that the images of women satisfied male sexual desire exclusively. Mulvey presented a theoretical model in which the female is the passive object and the male the active bearer of the gaze, drawing on Freudian theory and a feminist critique of phallocentrism. Since the publication of the essay there have been modifications and expansions of Mulvey's original insights, such as those by Kaja Silverman and Jane Ussher, who have argued that women play a more active role in looking at images on the screen rather than being merely passive spectators. Ussher, in particular, has argued that the 'masculine gaze' is not monolithic and can be resisted and reformulated by female film-makers and viewers (1997: 85–6). In this article I will build on Ussher's argument for reformulation of the 'masculine gaze' to examine the way in which film versions of *The Strange Case of Dr Jekyll and Mr Hyde* complicate Mulvey's model of scopophilia through scenes that encode a 'feminine gaze' that gains pleasure from looking at a desirable image of masculinity in Dr Jekyll at one moment but that is threated by sexual violence from Mr Hyde at the next.

Dr Jekyll and Mr Hyde is a particularly apt vehicle for a discussion of scopophilia because the signature moment in any film adaptation of Robert Louis Stevenson's original story is the transformation scene. *Jekyll and Hyde* also exemplifies the definition of the Gothic genre in

Lisa Hopkins's *Screening the Gothic* in that it depicts a 'doubling' that reveals the hidden connections between apparent opposites (2005: xi). The transformation scenes foreground the male body as spectacle and encodes contradictory images of masculinity in the contrast between Dr Jekyll and his double Mr Hyde. Dr Jekyll represents the object of romantic interest while Mr Hyde is his violent and threatening antithesis who menaces women. In terms of scopophilia the transformation scenes combine pleasure in looking at the image of Dr Jekyll and fear of Mr Hyde in a double vision of masculinity as both attractive and sexually dangerous for women.

Jekyll and Hyde shows its Gothic lineage in this combination of pleasure and danger. Stevenson referred to Mr Hyde as a 'Gothic gnome' (Stevenson, 2004: 122) showing his awareness of how his tale aligned with others in the genre as he tapped into the deepest fears of his Victorian audience. His story featured women in only tangential roles and focused on a world of male professionals with no overt representation of sexuality. Indeed, Stevenson disliked readings of his story in erotic terms, saying that Mr Hyde was 'not, Great Gods! a mere voluptuary. There is no harm in a voluptuary; and none, with my hand on my heart and in the sight of God, none – no harm whatever – in what prurient fools call "immorality." The harm was in Jekyll, because he was a hypocrite – not because he was fond of women' (Maixner, 1971: 231). For Stevenson then, *Jekyll and Hyde* was foremost a cautionary tale of lies and hypocrisy in Victorian society rather than about unrestrained sexuality. While Dr Jekyll rents a flat in Soho to indulge desires incompatible with his social position, Stevenson does not specify the activities in which he indulged when in the body of Mr Hyde.

Mr Hyde is a 'meaning machine' (Halberstam, 1995: 21) in the text, a vessel that can be used in an adaptation to express a range of cultural anxieties. Stevenson's original drew on fears of degeneration and class-based anxieties about urban violence. Robert Mighall sees the text as a case study of transgression of boundaries in that 'it depicts . . . a disruption enacted in terms of class and urban geography' (1999: 151). The original text is an example of 'urban Gothic' (Mighall, 1999: 31; see also Alder, 2013) that depends upon a knowledge of the geography of London to understand how Mr Hyde crosses class boundaries, especially in the scene in which Dr Jekyll wakes up in his upper-class bedroom and realises that he is looking at a hairy, muscled hand; it's the hand of Mr Hyde, which is out of place in his upper-class surroundings.

The focus of Stevenson's text was changed in the first stage adaptation of the plot and in subsequent film versions by the addition of female characters who are notably absent from the original; William Patrick

Day reads this in terms of the need for Gothic masculine identity to deny and extirpate the feminine (1985: 93). Where Mr Hyde enacted violence in the streets of London against a child and a Member of Parliament, in adaptations of *Jekyll and Hyde* he also threatens women with sexual violence. In parallel with this Dr Jekyll is depicted not as a hypocrite as Stevenson intended, but as a tragic figure. The template for this shift in character in films was set by the first successful stage adaptation of Stevenson's *Strange Case of Dr Jekyll and Mr Hyde*. The 1887 stage version of *Jekyll and Hyde* written by Thomas Russell Sullivan and performed by Richard Mansfield was endorsed by Stevenson even though he did not see and despite the way in which it portrayed Dr Jekyll. In an early scene between Dr Jekyll and his fiancée Agnes Carew he is shown as having a saint-like devotion to his patients:

JEKYLL: You are an angel.
AGNES: (*In his arms*) Harry, do you remember where I met you first?
JEKYLL: In the ward of the hospital, yes.
AGNES: Where you watched by my poor old nurse who was dying. You were there night and day, with all that human skill could do, with more than human patience and devotion. I tried to thank you for your kind looks, your gentle words, I could not speak.
JEKYLL: But your eyes said it all. And then I loved you. It was a strange courtship.
AGNES: That is the man I know. There is no other. Drive away these morbid fancies – for my sake – for my sake.
JEKYLL: (*Kissing her*) For your sake, yes. You shall teach me to control myself. I will take courage.

(Danahay and Chisholm, 2005: 54)

This scene makes Dr Jekyll into a paragon and also introduces romance into the narrative. As a Victorian text it shows Agnes as an 'angel' who will help Dr Jekyll control his animal passions, drawing on the gendered stereotype of women as virtuous guardians of the domestic realm who provided a haven for excitable men. The romance plot and descriptions of his selflessness make Dr Jekyll into a desirable figure and encourages imaginative identification with him as a suitor. The drama then investigates the attempt of a divided masculinity to reconcile atavistic urges with the demands of civilisation, prefiguring a Freudian model of the id being channelled by the ego and controlled by the superego. In a later scene Mr Hyde threatens Agnes sexually and murders Sir Danvers Carew as the 'animal within' (Hendershot 1998: 107) once unleashed gains control. The narrative thus posits a conflict between romance and horror, and desire and fear, through the male body.

Mansfield's stage version was a popular hit on both sides of the

Atlantic and helped boost his career, but the role was a departure from his previous successes. In a later era, Mansfield might have had a career as a 'matinee idol' to rival that of Fredric March, who later won acclaim for his portrayal of Dr Jekyll and Mr Hyde in film in the 1930s as Mansfield did on stage in the 1880s. His biographer Wilstach records that when Mansfield achieved success in New York in 1886 with his performance of Prince Karl in the play of the same name 'young ladies began to wear Prince Karl finger rings, and the Prince's portrait became a photographic "best seller"' (Wilstach, 1908: 137). Later in his career Mansfield published *The Richard Mansfield Calendar for 1900*, which is the source for most of the photographs used in biographies and critical studies. The calendar was part of Mansfield's lifelong effort to achieve international fame as a serious actor, and it includes images of the roles of which he was most proud, such as Richard III; however, it is this photograph of him as Dr Jekyll and Mr Hyde (Figure 7.1) that has become the most enduring image from this calendar.

This double exposure photograph captures the signature moment of transformation for which Mansfield was famous. In contrast to the upright, kindly Dr Jekyll, shown looking heavenward, as Mr Hyde he would hunch over, change his voice and apparently become a different person. The image combines both the romance aspect of the drama and the horror of watching a man become a sexual threat in front of the audience. Wilstach relates the effect this had on spectators, especially women:

> One of Mansfield's purely theatric devices for horror was to convey the suggestion that Hyde was coming. This was effected with an empty stage, a gray, green-shot gloom and oppressive silence. The curiosity was fascinating and whetted every nerve. At such a stage as this . . . the prolonged anticipation . . . begot an hypnotic effect on the hushed, breathless spectators that held them in the fetters of invincible interest. Then with a wolfish howl, a panther's leap, and the leer of a fiend Hyde was miraculously in view. It was at such time as that that strong men shuddered and women fainted and were carried out of the theater. (1908: 146)

The description of fainting women underscores how Mr Hyde was perceived as a sexual threat in the Mansfield version of the plot. Interviews with Mansfield about his portrayal of Mr Hyde often dwelled upon his effect on women that attended his performances. Mansfield claimed that it was not his intention to inspire fear, saying that 'I do not delight to hear that just so many women have fainted of an evening in the theatre, but I, my art, and my nature, receive a fresh stimulus and inspiration from the breathless silence and the rapt attention of my auditors'

Richard Mansfield as Dr Jekyll and Mr Hyde, LC-USZ62-91528 (b&w film copy neg.)

(Danahay and Chisholm, 2005: 101). However, this ignores the way in which Mansfield deliberately reinforced *Jekyll and Hyde* as a horror story, in which the primary victims were women, and thus changed the focus of Stevenson's cautionary tale.

Not only did Mr Hyde threaten Agnes on stage, he also represented wider fears of violence against women. This was especially true when he took his production to London in August 1888. The city was in the midst of hysteria over the Jack the Ripper murders, to the point that Mansfield himself was denounced as a possible suspect by an audience member because of his compelling performance as Mr Hyde. Mansfield was forced to cancel his performance of *Jekyll and Hyde* because his fictional portrayal of a man murdering a woman on stage was too close to the horror of the Ripper murders. *The Daily Telegraph* noted that that 'there is quite sufficient to make us shudder out of doors' (Danahay, 2015: 16) and that Mansfield's 'creepy drama' was only adding to the fear provoked by the reports of a serial killer on the loose on the streets of London. The intersection of sexual violence on stage and in the streets of London underscores how the horror of Jekyll versus Hyde was identified with wider fears of male sexuality, especially of uncertainty over whether a man would be a loving suitor or a threat. This fear was obviously more acute for female audiences than male.

The plot of Mansfield's adaptation was carried over into film versions of *Jekyll and Hyde*. The earliest existing silent film version from 1912 by the Thanhouser Company has Dr Jekyll cast as the suitor of a clergyman's daughter, and a romantic scene between them is interrupted by Mr Hyde who then kills the clergyman. The slight change in dramatis personae in making his fiancée a clergyman's daughter seems more dictated by available costumes and scenery than by an attempt to make a comment on religion. The film therefore toggles rapidly between romance and violence in one scene. The film showcases one of the first uses of stop action photography to have Dr Jekyll transform into Mr Hyde before the audience's eyes, replacing Mansfield's onstage virtuosity with cinematic technology.

The 1920 Paramount version of *Jekyll and Hyde* featured John Barrymore, who starred in both plays and films and whose name was widely recognised due to his family's long association with the theatre. The film was a commercial and critical success, one reviewer noting Barrymore's 'natural beauty of form and feature' and then contrasting it with 'the beastiality in the transformed personality' of Mr Hyde (*Variety*). The review shows the combination of appeal in a leading man like Barrymore, who was known for his good looks, and the horrific contrast with the appearance of Mr Hyde. In Stevenson's original those who saw Mr Hyde could sense there was something wrong but could not name his 'deformity', but films show the contrast by making Mr Hyde appear as repellent as possible. Barrymore makes Mr Hyde's malevolence visible by hunching over his body, contorting his features and growing long fingernails. In an involuntary transformation scene a huge, ghostly spider is shown being absorbed into the body of Dr Jekyll as he assumes the persona of Mr Hyde. Overall the effect is designed to make Mr Hyde as repugnant as possible.

The adaptation follows the procedure of introducing a romantic interest with the character of Millicent Carew, but also adds an 'Italian exotic dancer' called Gina as a contrast to the virtuous fiancée. Mr Hyde lives briefly with Gina in a flat in Soho but then sends her away. The film also takes the rehabilitation of Dr Jekyll as a character even further than Mansfield's play by having numerous scenes at Dr Jekyll's 'human repair shop' as it is termed where he tenderly cares for an old woman and child. The film also has Sir George Carew as a licentious character who leads Dr Jekyll astray by telling him that he works too hard and should indulge his desires. All this exonerates Dr Jekyll from blame and makes him into a sympathetic character and appropriate love interest for the romantic scene when he proposes to Millicent.

In the climactic scene Dr Jekyll has an emotional conversation with Millicent through the locked door of the laboratory and then takes poison to avoid being arrested for the murder of Sir George Carew. However, he transforms into Mr Hyde and then unlocks the door and traps her in his laboratory. Mr Hyde then menaces Millicent but convulses and dies before he can harm her. In the final moments of the film he transforms back into Dr Jekyll before horrified onlookers, and the film closes with a lingering shot of his face in death. The horror of the moment lies in this transformation that visually shows what violence can lurk beneath the attractive exterior of a handsome man like Barrymore. However, where the only violence depicted in Stevenson's text was a murder committed in the street in an apparently random act, the focus on romance makes it clear that women are the primary possible victims of Mr Hyde's sexual violence. The film rescues Millicent from rape by having Mr Hyde die in the nick of time, but this does not solve the central problem that Mr Hyde is the inner desires of Dr Jekyll unleashed; having Mr Hyde transform back into Dr Jekyll restores the handsome face of John Barrymore to the screen but does not erase the potential threat of another Mr Hyde.

The most critically acclaimed adaptation of *Jekyll and Hyde* is the Rouben Mamoulian 1932 version. This adaptation is noteworthy for its use of a first-person viewpoint in the opening scenes as Dr Jekyll prepares to give a lecture, and for its self-conscious use of artistic references and symbols that chart how he increasingly loses control over his alter ego. The version also magnifies the romance between Dr Jekyll and his fiancée Muriel Carew by having an extended sequence in which the two profess their love for each other. The scene is shot with moonlight illuminating the couple to emphasise its idyllic nature, and gradually zooms in on their faces until they take up the entire screen. This is a moment of dual scopophilia in that two attractive actors are enlarged to more than human size by taking up the entire screen as they gaze lovingly into each other's eyes. The scene contrasts with Dr Jekyll's interactions with the lower-class prostitute Ivy Pearson, who tempts him to be unfaithful to his fiancée. The film thereby sets up a conflict within Dr Jekyll between his sexual desire for lower-class Ivy and his betrothal to the upper-class, respectable Muriel. When he transforms into Mr Hyde he sees an image of Ivy tempting him to come and see her again as she bares her leg seductively from under her bedclothes.

Rather than have Mr Hyde rent a flat in Soho for unexplained purposes, this version of the story has Ivy living there so that she is readily available for his sexual advances. Eventually Ivy comes to Dr Jekyll to ask him to protect her from Mr Hyde and shows him bruises caused by his violence. The film also underscores the connection between Mr Hyde and Jack the Ripper, especially when Mr Hyde murders Ivy in the flat. The transformation scene in this adaptation actively pits the charming and attractive Dr Jekyll against Mr Hyde as a sexual predator because Ivy has appealed to him directly to protect her. Of course, the audience knows that she is in fact asking Dr Jekyll to protect him from one aspect of himself in Mr Hyde.

As Virginia Wright Wexman points out, Paramount ran an advertising campaign for *Jekyll and Hyde* as a romance, drawing on the Hollywood discourse of beauty (1988: 300). While this may seem contradictory, it shows how the Jekyll/Hyde dichotomy in this and other retellings, such as the later and less successful 1941 Victor Fleming version starring Spencer Tracy, Ingrid Bergman and Lana Turner, convey a mixed message for both the male and female gaze. For men the transformation dramatises the 'double bind' of masculinity in which men must be simultaneously gentlemen and sexual 'animals' (Bordo 1999: 229). For women the transformation represents the contradictions between men as the objects of romance and as the potential source of sexual assault, made especially acute in *Jekyll and Hyde* in that they are the same man. Wexman quotes a *New York Times Review* remarking on the 'change from the sleek and handsome Dr Jekyll into the menacing and ugly Mr Hyde' (284), showing the attractiveness of Fredric March in playing the role and the horror of watching him transform into a sexual threat. In Stevenson's original Dr Jekyll and Mr Hyde had two distinct bodies, but in adaptations such as the Mamoulian the transformation scene makes it clear that Mr Hyde represents sexual violence that is unleashed from within by Dr Jekyll's potion. The transformation scene, as in when Barrymore played the roles, thus encodes both desire and fear as Dr Jekyll when played by Fredric March is presented as a worthy suitor but at the same time as having the potential to attack and even kill the object of his desire.

Every version of *Jekyll and Hyde* has a transformation scene that can be seen in terms of female scopophilia, even in the most unlikely of scenarios such as that in *Mary Reilly* (Stephen Frears, 1996) where a female servant is shown as having intimate talks with her employer and eventually falling in love with him. The film plays upon the danger that Mary Reilly might be sexually assaulted by Mr Hyde, but in the climactic scene where the violence could be played out her love for both characters saves the day. Mr Hyde in frustration finds that he cannot attack Mary. The conclusion thus aligns with the romance trope of the woman taming the unruly desires of a man through the power of love.

Because Mr Hyde is a 'meaning machine', this is not the only cultural anxiety that he can represent. Wexman has analysed Mr Hyde's hairiness in terms of racism and the Jim Crow laws of the 1930s, for instance (1988: 288–91). Later versions of the story such as the BBC *Jekyll* encode fears of surveillance and corporate power as Mr Hyde becomes a prototype super soldier unleashed by illicit experimentation. Other versions of the double story draw on the idea of a divided subjectivity without explicitly referencing Jekyll and Hyde. The 1999 film version of *Fight Club* is a story of a double that focuses on violence between men rather than on sexuality, and as such successfully reimagines the story in terms of a crisis of masculinity. The narrator, like Dr Jekyll, faces a crisis that he solves by creating a double who enacts his violent impulses and the story features a ruined house that is an echo of the haunted structures of Gothic fiction. Women play only a tangential role in the story and a subplot revolves around turning women's fat into soap in a strikingly misogynist rendering of men exploiting the beauty industry.

From the Jack the Ripper coverage in Victorian London onward when the story was invoked to explain violence against women, the reference to a 'Jekyll and Hyde' character has encapsulated the belief that one person could be comprised of two contradictory personalities. The reference can be as mundane as trying to explain why a sports team played badly for one half of a match and well for the next, or as extreme to explain why people living next door to a murderer had no idea that they were violent and saw them as a good neighbour. However, because of the transformation scene *Jekyll and Hyde*, unlike say *Dracula*, is a particularly suitable vehicle for expressing contradictions in masculinity. For women in particular the transformation scene can be seen in terms of both the pleasure of viewing an attractive man on screen and the horror of violence against women. As with any horror film, *Jekyll and Hyde* plays upon some of the deepest cultural anxieties of the period without offering a deeper analysis of the underlying problem. At the end of Stevenson's stories and adaptations like the Mamoulian version, Dr Jekyll dies, and his unleashing of Mr Hyde is seen as a result of experimentation carried too far that can presumably be avoided in the future.

Janice Radway in *Reading the Romance* (1991) analysed how women both accede to and resist the roles assigned to them by social convention. The plot of a woman reining in an unruly or even a potentially violent man was emotionally satisfying for the readers she interviewed, showing them to be actively reformulating the texts in the way that Ussher has suggested is possible in film as well. However, all of the adaptations discussed above are framed both by patriarchy and heterosexuality in the foregrounding of Dr Jekyll's relationship with his fiancée and his struggle with her father and represent a challenge to the romance plot in that women are killed by Mr Hyde who is, after all, a manifestation of Dr Jekyll's repressed desires. These adaptations of *Jekyll and Hyde* raise implicitly some subversive questions about masculinity and sexual violence but contain the scope of subversion by the death of Dr Jekyll in their final scenes. As in Stevenson's original the message is ultimately conservative in that the social order that produced both Dr Jekyll and Mr Hyde is restored, and it is left to the women watching the film to wonder how they can tell the difference between the two in real life once they leave the cinema.

References

Alder, E. 2013. 'Urban Gothic', in Hughes, W., Punter, D. and Smith, A. J. (eds), *The Encyclopedia of the Gothic, Volume 2*. Hoboken, NJ: Wiley, pp. 703–6.

Bordo, S. 1999. *The Male Body: A New Look at Men in Public and Private*. New York: Farrar, Straus & Giroux.

Danahay, M. A. 2015. 'Introduction', in Stevenson, R. L. *Strange Case of Dr Jekyll and Mr Hyde*, 3rd edn, pp. 11–26.

Danahay, M. A. and Chisholm, A. 2005. *Jekyll and Hyde Dramatized*. Jefferson, NC: McFarland.

Day, W. P. 1985. *In the Circles of Fear and Desire: A Study of Gothic Fantasy*. Chicago: University of Chicago Press.

Halberstam, J. 1995. *Skin Shows: Gothic Horror and the Technology of Monsters*. Durham, NC: Duke University Press.

Hendershot, C. 1998. *The Animal Within: Masculinity and the Gothic*. Ann Arbor, MI: University of Michigan Press.

Hopkins, L. 2005. *Screening the Gothic*. Austin, TX: University of Texas Press.

Maixner, P. 1971. *Robert Louis Stevenson: The Critical Heritage*. London: Routledge.

Mighall, R. 1999. *A Geography of Victorian Gothic Fiction: Mapping History's Nightmares*. Oxford: Oxford University Press.

Mulvey, L. 2004. 'Visual Pleasure and Narrative Cinema', in Braudy, L. and Cohen, M. (eds), *Film Theory and Criticism: Introductory Readings* Eds. New York: Oxford University Press, pp. 833–44.

Radway, J. A. 1981. *Reading the Romance: Women, Patriarchy and Popular Literature*. Chapel Hill, NC: University of North Carolina Press.

Silverman, K. 1992. *Male Subjectivity at the Margins*. New York: Routledge.

Stevenson, R. L. 2015. *Strange Case of Dr Jekyll and Mr Hyde*, 3rd edn, in Danahay, M. A. (ed.), Peterborough, ON: Broadview Press.

Ussher, Jane M. 1997. *Fantasies of Femininity: Reframing the Boundaries of Sex*. New Brunswick, NJ: Rutgers University Press.

Variety. 2 April 1920. 'Dr. Jekyll and Mr. Hyde', p. 93, col. 1. https://archive.org/details/variety58-1920-04/page/n91.

Wexman, V. W. 1988. *Dr. Jekyll and Mr. Hyde: After One Hundred Years*. Chicago: University of Chicago Press.

Wilstach, P. 1908. *Richard Mansfield: The Man and the Actor*. New York: Scribner's.

Chapter 8

Gothic Parodies on Film and Personal Transformation

Laurence Raw

The link between parody and the Gothic is a familiar one. In 1968 D. N. Gallon emphasised how Catherine Morland's exaggerated fantasies in *Northanger Abbey* (written in 1803 but not published until after Austen's death in 1817) contrast with the author's 'moral purpose' of appealing to readers 'for whom Gothic fiction of the Romantic era is dead. To give the burlesque side of the novel its relevance the critic almost has to resurrect a mode' (804). That process of resurrection, however well-intentioned, is ripe for parody. Janet Beer and Avril Horner offer a less stark vision of the Gothic parody through Edith Wharton's short stories which, 'while engaging with a target text or genre, exhibit . . . a keen sense of the comic, an acute awareness of intertextuality and an engagement with the idea of metafiction' (2003: 270). The art critic and television personality Andrew Graham-Dixon claims that Gothic remains perennially popular in all media whether in straight or parodic form. We reflect ontologically on what separates the human from the non-human, while giving full rein to the imagination. Through exposure to the genre we might experience a therapeutic process of transformation by viewing our lives in a new and more positive light.[1]

Writing with specific reference to parody Westerns but including the Gothic within his theoretical analysis, Matthew R. Turner argues that, while invoking familiar codes and conventions, we reflect critically on the artificiality of the films' construction – for example, the trope of the haunted house in the dead of night whose corridors echo to the roar of thunder and the flash of lightning (2003: 54). This chapter develops Turner's claim through a discussion of four well-known Gothic parodies – Mel Brooks's *Young Frankenstein* (1974) and *Dracula: Dead and Loving It* (1995); Stan Dragoti's *Love at First Bite* (1979) and Gene Wilder's *Haunted Honeymoon* (1986). All of them consciously reference the classical Hollywood era of studio production, when Universal, RKO and a host of smaller outfits churned out a production-line of adaptations, remakes and original work using specific repertory companies of actors and a raft of familiar stylistic conventions. The parodies appear interested in consistently making fun of an outdated genre through the exaggerated use of dialogue and gesture, thereby distancing viewers from the action taking place on screen. They introduce framing devices such as the radio play in *Haunted Honeymoon* or exterior shots looking from outside through the barred windows of an isolated castle (*Dracula: Dead and Loving It*) or introduce stand-alone sequences bearing little relationship to the plot (for example, the pastiche of Glenn Miller's 'Chattanooga Choo Choo' in *Young Frankenstein*).

There is more to this material than we might initially assume. *Love at First Bite* uses the parodic form to make some pointed criticisms of late 1970s New York, where an obsession with materialism has transformed the downtown region into a smog-ridden mass of freeways with sidewalks rife with potential hazards. Materialism runs riot – so much so that no one contemplates the presence of a vampire within their midst. *Haunted Honeymoon* uses the haunted house (reminiscent of James Whale's *The Old Dark House* (1932)) to warn viewers about the dangers of a world where no one is quite what they seem. The protagonists inhabit an amoral world where distinctions between good and evil seldom exist.

Nonetheless all four parodies include upbeat endings with the promise of emotional prosperity for all the protagonists – not in this world, perhaps, but in the more permanent spheres of the imagination or the after-life. We are reminded of the Gothic's potential to create worlds beyond worlds that fulfil an individual's potential. These worlds might be constructed, as Turner claims, but they have the power to negotiate between opposites – life and death, good and evil.

What really distinguishes these four films is their extensive use of intertexts. I saw all of them at the time of their initial release; I was fourteen when *Young Frankenstein* opened in London. I enjoyed the slapstick moments and the innuendoes such as the reference to the size of the Creature's (Peter Boyle's) manhood, but it was only after repeated viewings that I could identify the allusions to Brooks's earlier work – namely *The Producers* (1967) and *Blazing Saddles* (1974) – as well as classic horror films such as Whale's *Frankenstein* (1931) and the first *King Kong* (Schoedsack and Cooper, 1933). The range of references used by the respective directors is breathtaking, covering popular songs, Goethe's *Faust*, Orson Welles's *The Lady from Shanghai* (1947) and *Saturday Night Fever* (Badham, 1977). We take pleasure in recognising the source of these intertexts, while reminding ourselves that classics from the past have something to tell us about our futures. Described by

Nico Baumbach as a component of 'the new cinephilia', such creative encounters dissociate words and images from their source-texts (2012: 53) while creating new associations in our minds. Jacques Rancière believes that through this transformative process our 'knowledge of [the world] . . . is specifically contested and belongs to anyone who takes it as a site to form their own path' (quoted in Arnall et al., 2012: 296).

Initially it appears that all four films establish a comic distance between viewers and the action unfolding on screen. We do not empathise with Larry Abbott's (Gene Wilder's) fit of hysterics in *Haunted Honeymoon* but treat it as a comic reboot of that moment in *The Producers* when Max Bialystock (Zero Mostel) attempts to deprive Leo Bloom (Wilder) of his blue comfort-blanket. We are equally distanced from the fifty-nine-year-old Leslie Nielsen in the central role of *Dracula: Dead and Loving It*. With his white hair and statuesque manner, his very presence seems to emphasise the archaic nature of the material that seems ripe for parody by a performer popularly identified with *Airplane!* (Abrahams and Zucker, 1980) and *The Naked Gun* trilogy (1988–94). Director Brooks emphasises the narrative's artificiality through Jam Pascale's garishly coloured studio settings – all greens, blues and reds – and the inclusion of sequences that seem especially incongruous in a Gothic parody. At one point the camera looks from above at a group of courtly ladies and gentlemen performing the kind of highly patterned dance sequences reminiscent of a heritage film. Groups of young men and women stand at the side marking their dance cards. While the scene is visually attractive, it contributes towards a cinematic structure based on the Broadway musical that typically juxtaposes songs, dance and drama to disrupt empathy (Taylor, 2012: 6). Another example from *Young Frankenstein* can be found in the justifiably famous sequence where Frankenstein (Wilder) and the Creature dress in top hat and tails and perform a version of Irving Berlin's 'Puttin' on the Ritz'.[2] Such moments carry a positive charge by reminding us of film parody's potential to offer 'a short-lived break from the security of routine', offering in its place 'a new truth' about our adaptability (Hutcheon, 1986–7: 187). If the Creature can perform on stage despite his vocal handicap then we all can.

Another way of disrupting viewer empathy is through deliberately incongruous material – for example, making fun of Dracula's fear of the cross in *Love at First Bite* as Jeffrey (Richard Benjamin) thrusts a Star of David into Dracula's face. The vampire laughs contemptuously and replies in a faux-Jewish accent: 'I would say, leave Cindy alone and find yourself a nice Jewish girl, Doctor.' Jeffrey looks at the star and mutters: 'Ah, shit! It's the other one, isn't it?' Later on, Dracula invites Cindy

(Susan Saint James) to accompany him on 'an airline ticket to romantic places', consciously quoting a line from the 1930s ballad 'These Foolish Things'. In *Dracula: Dead and Loving It* Professor Van Helsing (Brooks) speaks with a strangulated German accent, giving him the chance to mispronounce the word 'what' as 'vat', much to his interlocutors' confusion. In another blackly comic sequence Van Helsing performs an autopsy, flanked by a group of six or seven trainee doctors; he opens the corpse and brings out the organs one by one with a series of loud plops as the blood spills onto the operating-room floor. All that we can see is the sight of the doctors fainting one by one, unable to stomach the scene unfolding in front of them. As they lie on the ground, Van Helsing wipes his hands and grins at the camera, suggesting that that this was precisely the reaction he expected. In *Haunted Honeymoon* (Wilder, 1986) the haunted house plot has been framed at the beginning and end by a parodic radio play performed in the style of mid-twentieth-century anthology series such as *Suspense!* (1942–62). Larry Abbott and his cast are seen crowding round the microphone with a live orchestra in the background, a sound-effects engineer and a Host (Bill Bailey) introducing the proceedings in suitably macabre tones. The drama they are performing happens to be called 'Haunted Honeymoon'; what follows in the film is a visualisation of the radio narrative. For nostalgia buffs, the prologue and epilogue offer an idealised representation of a time when all radio dramas were performed live and the creative personnel often had a difficult time stifling their laughter, especially when they fluffed their lines. Director Wilder draws our attention to radio's imaginative appeal as the leading female role of Aunt Kate is performed by a man (Dom DeLuise). Little attempt has been made to make him up; he resembles a drag artist in his long skirts and coiffed wig. Yet this is perfectly acceptable in terms of the film's basic premise of 'Haunted Honeymoon' being a radio play.

The appeal to the imagination is perceived as highly important as a way of escaping from urban and rural decay. *Love at First Bite*'s representation of urban New York is as unforgiving as Martin Scorsese's *Taxi Driver* (1976), with violent streets thronged by criminals, prostitutes and other low-life. Faced with five menacing-looking African Americans armed with knives, Dracula picks them off one by one, and looks despairingly around him at the large limousines and luridly lit sex-shops peopled with women wearing impossibly short skirts. No one has heard of the vampire (one person describes him as a 'black chicken'), not even Cindy, who takes him for an insurance salesperson on their first encounter. Racism and sexism flourish: one African American bitterly invokes the stereotype that all blacks are considered potential criminals, while Jeffrey refers to his fiancée Cindy as 'Little Miss Hot-pants' who can only advance her career by showing off her charms as frequently as possible. No one contemplates reform; they keep themselves to themselves, driving up and down the myriad freeways that desecrate the urban landscape. Although treated more light-heartedly, the haunted house in *Haunted Honeymoon* portrays an equally dystopic environment. The camera peers inside through the lead-lined windows to reveal shadowy figures opening and closing doors. Larry imagines himself being menaced by a werewolf (which turns out to be one of the bad guys in disguise), and not one of the other guests are safe from attack, either inside or outside the property. The thunder and lightning outside enhance the sense of menace.

The only way to escape from these environments is to establish safe spaces to explore sensitive issues in the hope of becoming 'a better person and try to create a better world' (Cherry, 1999: 157). In a climactic sequence on New Year's Eve, *Love at First Bite* offers Cindy the choice of staying in New York or becoming a vampire herself. In a hair-raising car chase through the city outskirts, Jeffrey pursues Dracula and Cindy with the firm intention of 'rescuing' her from living death. The action switches to Kennedy Airport with a TWA plane about to take off for Jamaica (one of the 'romantic places' Dracula envisages). Faced with the choice between returning to the fashion industry or becoming a vampire, Cindy opts for the latter. The plane takes off, leaving Jeffrey with nothing except Dracula's black cloak with a red lining. He runs his hand across the fabric and puts it on with an uncharacteristic feeling of pride. Compared to Jeffrey's New York, the prospect of eternal life foregrounding politeness, security and old-fashioned courtesy exerts an irresistible appeal for a young woman tired of showing herself off in front of predatory males. Jeffrey's obvious pleasure with the cape suggests that other mortals might be persuaded to follow a similar route to self-improvement. *Dracula: Dead and Loving It* offers a similarly optimistic ending as Dracula and Mina (Amy Yasbeck) transform themselves into bats and fly off into an orange-coloured sky signalling the onset of dawn. All that is left of Dracula's worldly presence is the empty coffin and a handful of dust, into which Renfield (Peter MacNicol) draws a childish image of two eyes and a big smile to remind him of his erstwhile master. Dracula might be gone for good, but he has found a suitable partner in the quest for a better life.

The final sequence of *Haunted Honeymoon* returns us to the radio studio as Aunt Kate mispronounces the word 'passed' as 'pissed' and vainly tries to suppress a fit of giggling. The Host intones the closing credits, the musical director strikes up the series' theme, and the entire cast embrace before shaking hands and preparing to leave. Another seven days will elapse before the next live broadcast. There is an obvious nostalgia for the 'Golden Age' of radio – for the unpredictability of live broadcasting: despite the perpetual threat of something going wrong, this form of art values spontaneity and good fellowship. We are left with the unmistakable belief that the past can be used to foreground the significance of community values to our lives. Nostalgia has the power to motivate by boosting optimism, increasing inspiration, and cultivating creativity (Sedikides et al., 2008: 306).

One of the major characteristics of parody is its reflexivity, directing critical attention upon itself by combining apparently disparate elements – some of which are germane to the plot, others functioning as stand-alone comic set-pieces. Parodies eschew issues of textual fidelity, concentrating attention on themselves as well as their source texts and suggesting their own potential as a model or target, a work to be rewritten, transformed or parodied even further (Hannoosh, 1989: 116). We reflect on what we see, not just in critical but personal terms, as we try to make sense of what takes place on screen. The endings offer positive representations of humanity trying to transform itself. Although Dracula is ordinarily identified as a representative of evil corrupting his victims, *Dracula: Dead and Loving It* and *Love at First Bite* represent the vampire in more positive terms. As Cindy and Mina fly off into the distance, they have no idea what to expect from the future, but at least they have followed their positive instincts rather than embracing the status quo. The cast of *Haunted Honeymoon* understand that, notwithstanding the demands placed on them by the radio scripts, they should perform as an ensemble. Such 'new truth[s]' are available to us if we are prepared to admit their existence. These late twentieth-century cultural products rehearse a truism famously expressed by Joseph Addison in *The Spectator* of 1 July 1712. The Gothic, whether in 'straight' or parodic form, appeals to an imagination 'naturally fruitful and superstitious', that 'makes new Worlds of its own' by creating fictions of humanity beyond nature (Addison, 1712/2017: 150).

Recently Arthur Asa Berger observed that irrespective of genre, 'parody is defined and discussed as an example of explicit intertextuality' (119–24). The films bristle with intertextual references: *Love at First Bite* contains an extended disco dance sequence based on *Saturday Night Fever* (Badham, 1977), as Dracula and Cindy form an irresistible partnership dominating the floor. All the fellow-dancers form a circle around them offering encouragement and congratulation in equal measures. We appreciate Dracula's attraction: with his black and red cape and immaculate moves, he possesses that ineffable quality of style that no one can emulate. It is hardly surprising that Cindy should opt for a future with him rather than Jeffrey. *Dracula: Dead and Loving It* references the Universal cycle of horror films, as in Dr Seward's (Harvey Korman's) pale make-up and vocal tics reminiscent of Nigel Bruce (Dr Watson to Basil Rathbone's Sherlock Holmes). *Haunted Honeymoon* casts a crabby housekeeper Rachael (Ann Way) in the mould of Judith Anderson's Mrs Danvers in Hitchcock's *Rebecca* (1940); in another sequence the sinister magician Montego (Jim Carter), and Susan (Jo Ross) embrace in a hall of mirrors creating a series of distorted images echoing Orson Welles and Rita Hayworth in *The Lady from Shanghai* (Welles, 1947). This is a disturbing sequence indicating how the magician exerts an unearthly power over his fellow-guests. Allusions crop up thick and fast: Aunt Kate stands dowager-like at the top of a winding staircase and proclaims – 'This house is cursed!' – in ringing tones recalling Bette Davis's Margo Channing in *All About Eve* (Mankiewicz, 1950). Kate calms down sufficiently to deliver the Danny Kaye standard 'Ballin' the Jack' with Vickie Pearle (Gilda Radner), with Charles (Jonathan Pryce) at the piano. Witnessing the performance with obvious disapproval is the butler Pfister (Bryan Pringle) – a tall, black-haired figure with a gaunt look and bushy eyebrows referencing Boris Karloff. *Young Frankenstein* contains an equally broad range of cinematic quotations: Frankenstein bids a lachrymose farewell to his fiancée (Madeleine Kahn) in a smoke-filled railway station based on *Brief Encounter* (Lean, 1945). The obsessive police chief Inspector Kemp (Kenneth Mars) pursues the Creature despite a prosthetic arm that inadvertently jerks upwards, reminiscent of Peter Sellers in *Dr. Strangelove* (Kubrick, 1964). Mars's faux-German accent has strong vocal links to the actor's characterisation of the crazed Nazi Fritz Liebkind, author of 'Springtime for Hitler' in *The Producers*. When the Creature performs 'Puttin' on the Ritz', the emcee (Norbert Schiller) introduces him with a phrase borrowed from *Cabaret* (Fosse, 1972) ('Meine Damen und Herren, Mesdames et Messieurs, Ladies and Gentlemen'). One of the most memorable moments of the film appears in an alternative rendering of the famous sequence in Whale's *Frankenstein* where the Creature (Karloff) encounters a little girl (Marilyn Harris) and inadvertently kills her. Brooks has the Creature and the girl (Ann Beesley) sitting on either end of a see-saw; as the Creature sits heavily on one end, the girl is projected into the air, then flies through her bedroom window before landing safely on her bed, much to her parents' (Michael Fox, Linda Kristen) relief. This sequence emphasises Brooks's fundamentally good-natured approach to the source text, concentrating on the survival of human life rather than the Creature's destruction.

The impact of intertextual references on the viewers' consciousness can be assessed through some of the comments posted on Brooks's fan-sites. On the Mel Brooks Fans page of the Magic Café one correspondent quotes an innuendo from *Dracula: Dead and Loving It* uttered by Van Helsing ('she will become one herself') – a line leaving us uncertain whether he is referring to a vampire or a lesbian. Another offers several extracts from the screenplay of *Young Frankenstein*, including the 'Chattanooga Choo Choo' pastiche, the punning exchange 'Werewolf?/ There wolf/Werewolf?/There wolf', and the alternative version of 'Puttin' on the Ritz' ('Dressed up like a trooper. OOPER DUPER!' ('Magic Café Forum: Mel Brooks Fans'). The 'Favorite Mel Brooks Quotes' fan-site repeats the werewolf/there wolf exchange, plus a visual reference to famous hunchbacks such as Shakespeare's *Richard III* or *The Hunchback of Notre Dame* (1939), when Van Helsing says to Igor: 'You know, I'm a rather brilliant surgeon. Perhaps I can help you with that hump'. Igor replies quite innocently 'What hump' – a line which evidently had the theatre audience at a 2007 screening roaring 'with thunderous laughter' with some people 'speak[ing] the lines with the actors' ('Favorite Mel Brooks Quotes'). Buzzfeed's guide to the 'Most Ingenious Moments from Mel Brooks Movies' includes the 'Puttin' on the Ritz' sequence (Naidus).

The fan-sites create transnational communities where users share memories while participating in discussions about the films and their impact on individual fans' past and future lives. Such options are available at most fan-sites: Robert G. Dryden's essay demonstrates how users derive 'pleasure, passion, and possessiveness' from their online involvement with Jane Austen (2013: 103–19). This facility might not always yield benefits: Andrew Hoskins argues that increased online involvement outsources memories away from the individual in favour of technology. Memories become a part of public cultures, to be used (or abused) at will by others. We no longer have control over our individual pasts, rendering our online communications insignificant (2016: 19, 31). This sense of loss is certainly not evident from the Brooks fan-sites, where the repeated citation of intertexts not only brings pleasure to users but indicates the possibility of reshaping the future. The ability to recognize intertexts and subsequently quote them at will is a good example of how new cinephilia vindicates the potential of Gothic past and present to offer new possibilities as well as increasing our self-confidence. Whatever form it might take – costume, music, painting, as well as films in parodic form (Eckart, 2005: 547–62) – the Gothic stimulates reflection, as we come to accept the artificiality of many of the conventions that permeated the classic horror cycles of the past. As we watch Dracula flying away into the distance with Cindy or Mina, or witness Frankenstein exchanging brains with the Creature (in *Young Frankenstein*), we understand how the respective directors aim to show how humour can encourage audiences to consider whether they could instigate similar escapes from the workaday world, whether physical or imaginative.

All four films are very much products of their time, when the disco craze was at its height and the screen careers of Brooks and Wilder – as actors and directors – were at their zenith. We cannot look at *Young Frankenstein* without taking the performers' work in *Blazing Saddles* (Brooks, 1974) into consideration. *Haunted Honeymoon* would seem very different if we had never encountered *The Producers*. Intertexts, both visual and verbal, informed the screenplays' respective structures. Although *Love at First Bite* was made by a different studio, the film has clear verbal and visual resemblances to *Young Frankenstein*. In terms of their approach to the Gothic genre, the films deal with issues raised in the contemporary television series *Penny Dreadful* (2014–16). Written by John Logan, the series draws on classic Gothic tropes and characters and invests them with a contemporary twist, while acknowledging the current popularity of neo-Victorianism in terms of style as well as script. The result is a series that reflects on the past through the present and vice versa. We are invited to consider where Gothic resides in this inter-textual work – in the bodies, the stories, the history, the cinematic style or all of them. That process of identification influences our response to the four parodies, wherein mock-Gothic elements underpin the style, the stories and the simultaneous histories represented onscreen. I use 'histories' rather than 'history' in the singular, as it is evident that films such as *Young Frankenstein* reference the early nineteenth-century world of the Shelley novel as well as the Classical Hollywood era. Likewise *Love at First Bite* and *Dracula: Dead and Loving It* encompass Bram Stoker's imaginative Transylvania of the late nineteenth century, as well as the Classical Hollywood and disco eras. History is perceived as fragmentary with past, present and future deliberately conflated, inviting audiences into active participation to ascertain their own perspectives on the material. Although *Penny Dreadful* offers a more contemporary (and gory) take on the Gothic with its speculations on female monstrosity and its relationship to the construction of gender, it retains its basic objective of using the genre to stimulate imaginative speculation on the human potential for good as well as evil. This dictum applies as much to the creative workers behind the series as the characters involved in the drama. It is this speculative capacity that renders *Young Frankenstein* (and the other three parodies) so watchable despite their age, as they prove beyond doubt the transhistorical popularity of the Gothic genre.

Notes

1. For further analysis of Graham-Dixon's three-part television series, see Laurence Raw, 2016. 'Mesearch and the Gothic Imagination', *Linguaculture*, 1, pp. 36–41. Print.
2. This device is familiar from Brooks's earlier films: 'Springtime for Hitler' in *The Producers*, or Madeleine Kahn's Lili von Shtupp taking off Marlene Dietrich in *Blazing Saddles*.

References

Addison, J. 1712. 'The Gothic', *The Spectator*, 1 July. *Mnstate.edu*, 2006. Web. 22 May 2017.

Arnall, G., Gandolfi, L. and Zaranella, E. 2012. 'Aesthetics and Politics: An Interview with Jacques Rancière', *Critical Inquiry*, 38: 2 (Winter), pp. 289–97.

Austen, J. *Northanger Abbey*. 1817. Introduced by Margaret Drabble. Afterword by Stephanie Laurens. New York: Penguin Random House, 2008. E-book.

Baumbach, N. 2012. 'All that Heaven Allows', *Film Comment*, 48: 2 (March–April), pp. 47–53.

Beer, J. and Horner, A. 2003. 'This Isn't Exactly a Ghost Story: Edith Wharton and Parodic Gothic', *Journal of American Studies*, 37: 2, pp. 269–85.

Berger, A. A. 2016. 'Intertextuality: Parody', *Applied Discourse Analysis: Popular Culture, Media and Everyday Life*. Basingstoke: Palgrave, pp. 119–24.

Cherry, B. 1999. 'The Female Horror Film Audience: Viewing Pleasures and Fan Practices.' Dissertation, University of Stirling.

Dryden, R. G. 2013. 'Inventing Jane: Pleasure, Passion and Possessiveness in the Jane Austen Community', Law, L. and Dryden, R. G. (eds), *Global Jane Austen: Pleasure, Passion and Possessiveness in the Jane Austen Community*. New York: Palgrave, pp. 103–19.

Eckart, G. 2005. 'The German Gothic Subculture', *German Studies Review*, 28: 3 (October), pp. 547–62.

'Favorite Mel Brooks Quotes', 1968. *DunEdinRanger*, 6 September 2008. Web. 31 May 2017.

Gallon, D. N. 1968. 'Comedy in *Northanger Abbey*', *Modern Language Review*, 63: 4 (October), pp. 802–9.

Goethe, J. W. von. *Faust*, 1829. Trans. Albert G. Latham. London: J. M. Dent, 1854. *Archive.org*. Web. 22 May 2017.

Hannoosh, M. 1989. 'The Reflexive Version of Parody', *Comparative Literature*, 41: 2 (Spring), pp. 113–27. Print.

Hoskins, A. 2016. 'Archive Me! Media, Memory, Uncertainty', in Hajeck, A., Lohmeier, C. and Pentzold, C. (eds), *Memory in a Mediated World: Remembrance and Reconstruction*. Basingstoke: Palgrave Macmillan, pp. 13–36.

Hutcheon, L. 1986–7. 'The Politics of Postmodernism: Parody and History', *Cultural Critique*, 5 (Winter), pp. 179–203.

'Magic Café Forum Index: Mel Brooks Fans'. 2017. *Magic Café*, 2011. Web, 31 May.

Naidus, A. '29 of the Most Ingenious Moments from Mel Brooks Movies', *Buzzfeed*, 30 August 2013. Web, 31 May 2017.

Raw, L. 2016. 'Mesearch and the Gothic Imagination', *Linguaculture*, 1, pp. 36–41.

Sedikides, C., Wildschut, T., Arndt, J. and Routledge, C. 2008. 'Nostalgia: Past, Present, and Future', *Current Directions in Psychological Science*, 17: 5 (October), pp. 304–7.

Shakespeare, W. 1592. *Richard III. The Complete Works of William Shakespeare. mit.edu.* 2001. Web, 31 May 2017.

Taylor, M. 2012. *Musical Theatre, Realism, and Entertainment.* Abingdon: Routledge.

Turner, M. R. 2003. 'Cowboys and Comedy: The Simultaneous Deconstruction and Reinforcement of Generic Constructions in the Western Parody', *Film and History*, 35: 2, pp. 48–54.

Chapter 9

The Gothic Sensorium:
Affect in Jan Švankmajer's Poe Films
Anna Powell

Jan Švankmajer's *The Fall of the House of Usher* (1980) and *The Pendulum, the Pit and Hope* (1983) encapsulate Gothic affect. They do this sensationally via images of terror and horror based on touch. Drawing on experiments with Tactilism (touch-based art) in sculpture and animation, these dissident films, made by Czech Surrealists under a repressive, Soviet-led regime, express what Gilles Deleuze calls 'a touching specific to the gaze' and present basic tropes of Gothic cinema in small form (1986: 12). Švankmajer's films adapt Edgar Allan Poe's tales for their uncanny *mise-en-scène*. *The Pendulum* evokes the tactile terrors of the Spanish Inquisition and *Usher* shifts sentience to the 'thing-world' as the animated Gothic House comes to life.

Švankmajer's adaptations use intensive compression of time and space analogous to Poe's prose poetry. The tales' perversely erotic plots and dream-like narratives understandably invite psychosexual reading. By linking Poe with Surrealism, Švankmajer's films might appear to be 'about' psychoanalysis. Yet, Gilles Deleuze's ideas about what a film *does* as an experiential event rather than what it means can open up a different kind of Gothic. He consistently refutes the symbolic 'archaeology' of psychoanalysis that digs out repressed familial desire. Art is, rather, the language of sensation, 'composed of percepts, affects, and blocs of sensation' (Deleuze and Guattari, 1994: 176). A schizoanalytic Deleuzian approach to horror film, viewing brain and viscera as a continuum, looks elsewhere than plot and theme. Its focus is the affective images of fear and terror as they impact upon screen/viewer. The Gothic cinema of sensation works via intense affects and shocks that break habitual response and re-imagine the generic formulae they revisit. As well as Deleuze's cinematic insights, I consider theoretical reflections on touch by Švankmajer and artist Eva Švankmajerova and contextualise them via broader studies of corporeal affect.

Švankmajer's films mix genres and stylistic techniques, including live-action footage, puppets, object animations and claymation. Much of his *oeuvre* has a Gothic inflection, seen most overtly in his literary adaptations, including the playful homage to Horace Walpole, *The Castle of Otranto* (1979). Švankmajer's Gothic-flavoured films include 1968's *The Flat* (entrapment and claustrophobia), 1970's *The Ossuary* (morbid religiosity), 1983's *Down to the Cellar* and 1988's *Alice* (the vulnerable child in a threatening environment), 1994's *Faust* (magic and the occult), 2000's *Little Otik* (the uncanny thing-world) and 2005's *Lunacy* (de Sade, madness, cruelty).

The Gothic theme of concealment dominates Švankmajer's films and is shaped by the political context of their making. The underground Prague Surrealist group used art to subvert the Stalinist regime in Czechoslovakia (1948–89), forcibly reinstated after the 'Prague Spring' of 1968 and the subsequent invasion of Czechoslovakia by the Soviet Union and Warsaw Pact Allies. After the suppression of Dubček's progressive Communism, attacks on *The Castle of Otranto* by the Krátký Film censor led Švankmajer to shift from film-making to tactile art. In 1980, when a relative 'thaw' enabled him to film only 'classic' literary adaptations, he chose Poe's 'psychological studies of pathological behaviour', where touch 'at times of psychic strain becomes hugely amplified' (Švankmajer, 2014: xxii). In these dark fantasy films, subversive ideological messages are barely hidden by masquerade, magic and puppetry. The suppression of a political critique with obvious contemporary targets ironically fuelled the subversive aesthetic of Gothic. Settings are subterranean and claustrophobic and thematic monstrosity comes cloaked in expedient disguise. Parallel to political concealment, and enhancing its force, is the seminal Surrealist agenda, shaped by Freudian psychoanalysis, to make art express unconscious desire. The Švankmajers' Gothic has a perversely erotic inflection, visible in Eva's set designs of *The Pendulum, the Pit and Hope*. Her painted scenery for the dungeons of the Spanish Inquisition features a sinister tactility that foreshadows physical torture.

Central to the films' affective impact is the use of suspense to induce terror. In Gothic, direct depiction is eschewed for elision, suggestion and part-objects rather than overt revelation. The literal 'undeath' of Gothic vampires and zombies also manifests in the uncanny 'life' of animated objects (Wells, 2002: 4). As Cathryn Vasseleu suggests, Švankmajer

> awakens the senses to animate objects. Film animation is just another alchemical aid to the performance of a magic ritual in which Švankmajer summons forth the immanent vitality that resides in inert material. (Vasseleu, 2008: 11)

Alongside this is the economical use of direct sensory horror which maximises visceral feelings via shock and disgust. Writing of cinematic affect, Antonin Artaud contends that 'no matter how deep we dig into the mind, we find at bottom of every emotion, even an intellectual one, an affective sensation of a nervous order' ([1927], in Sontag 1988: 150). Within the French theoretical context for Deleuze's work, others have foregrounded the experiential centrality of physical affect. Maurice Merleau-Ponty identifies 'the corporeality of all conscious experience' (Merleau-Ponty, 1998: 14) and Luce Irigaray positions touch as the 'the substratum of all the senses' with particular resonance for women (Irigaray, 1991: 108). Deleuze's affective model of art is developed further in the film-philosophy of the Cinema Books when he asserts the corporeal nature of cinematic thought:

> The body is no longer the obstacle that separates thought from itself, that which it has to overcome to reach thinking. It is [. . .] that which it plunges into or must plunge into, in order to reach the unthought, that is life. (Deleuze, 1989: 189)

Deleuze and Film Affect

Deleuze considers the non-material and virtual nature of moving images, yet these onscreen shots have physical affects, both corporeal and conceptual at same time. Cinematic images stimulate neuronal networks as biologically quantifiable events on internal and surface organs. As well as the actual physical impact of moving images and sounds, the cinematic sensorium includes a virtual 'sense' of physically absent sensations. By these multi-layered acts of incorporation, the simulation of other senses as well as sight and hearing produce affective thoughts. In the case of Švankmajer, touch is the most crucial of these 'absent' sensations.

In *Cinema 1: The Movement-Image*, Deleuze maps a general typology of images including affects, percepts and concepts. Affection-images (frequent in Gothic) prioritise affect over representational content. They are 'pure singular qualities or potentialities' (Deleuze, 1986: 102). Deleuze exemplifies them in the German Expressionist *Pandora's Box* (Georg Wilhelm Pabst, 1929) via the scene before Pandora (Louise Brooks) is murdered by Jack the Ripper. In a crucial affection-image, the gleam of the Ripper's knife is intensified by close-up and darkness. Deleuze explains that emotions (terror) and optical sensations (brightness) are virtual 'power-qualities' awaiting actualisation and mobilisation, in this case by the complex affect of compassion (1986: 102).

Gothic film often recycles plots as common 'cultural capital'. Yet, the mode's intensive images are far from being reducible to plot action or narrative themes. In our experience of moving images, formless space and restless motion exceed the eye's capacity and dismantle the purely optical. Deleuze's work on the 'tactile optical function' explores how art uses haptics to elide the visual and the tactile (Deleuze, 2003: 151). For Henri Bergson, seminal to Deleuze's thinking here, affect is a qualitative feeling, an 'intensive vibration' on a 'sensible nerve' (Bergson, 1991: 55–6) or, as Deleuze puts it, a 'motor effort on an immobilised receptive plate' (1986: 12). Cinematic images of touch are tactisigns, intensive sensations of touch made possible if 'the hand relinquishes its prehensile and motor functions to content itself with a pure touching' (Deleuze, 1989: 12). *In Cinema 2*, Deleuze offers a more developed typology of images via opsigns, sonsigns tactisigns. These categories are not rigid, but the film experience happens in the interstices between them. Within the sensory spectrum, touch and sight interconnect. Deleuze identifies three types of linkage between tactile and visual images: digital, manual and haptic. In the digital image, the hand is subordinated to the eye. The optical retains the manual sense of touch in virtual form via depth, contour and relief. The manual reverses the customary dominance of eye over hand to prioritise the tactile sense. Characters touch onscreen objects and close-ups have a tactile quality which foregrounds texture and relief. Because onscreen images are virtual in nature, we touch them not by an extensive act of the hand but by the intensive sensation of the tactile-optical function.

Tactilism, the aesthetic exploration of touch in which 'hands would become organs as knowing as brains, penetrating into the true essence of matter' (Classen, 2005: 332), was initially a Futurist project instituted by Filippo Marinetti. Despite their radical political divergence from Futurism, Tactilism was crucial to the Prague Surrealist group. Drawing on Merleau-Ponty's work with tactile memory, the experiments led by the Švankmajers used sensory encounter with objects as a stimulus to further artistic creation. As well as producing art works Jan Švankmajer and Eva Švankmajerova explored the affective phenomena of tactile imagination via group experiments with dreams, erotica and childhood memories (Vasseleu, 2008). Like Deleuze with tactisigns, Švankmajer asserted that the crucial tactile organs were not hands but 'the 'passive' parts of our bodies, and their connections to the entire surface, cavities, internal organs and mucous membranes, which act as a link to our most intensive sensory experience' (Vasseleu, 2008: 1). Švankmajer describes his own tactile obsession via a kind of 'becoming-hand', as Deleuze might say:

I am a hand [. . .] a tool for giving and receiving emotions. On the palm of my soul are engraved my life-lines [. . .] I am a victim of tactilism. I have too many erogenous zones for one body. I am a hand with six fingers with webs in between. Instead of fingernails, I have petite, sharp, sweet-toothed little tongues with which I lick the world. (Švankmajer, 2002)

Discussing his animation techniques, Švankmajer contends 'I don't actually animate objects, I coerce their inner life out of them' (Švankmajer, 1992). The Gothic figure of alchemist-magician controlling the thing-world points back to the Prague Golem (*The Golem*, Karl Boese and Paul Wegener, 1920) as well as the Faustus of German and Polish legend, who Švankmajer returns to in *Faust*. Contemporary political and psychic suffering is at once displaced and made more potent in the Gothic milieu of ruined castles and torture chambers. Švankmajer's adaptations of Poe's short fictions relocate them into a Surrealist milieu both mordant in its political critique and terrifying in its affective impact. Švankmajer was able to foreground the intimate connections of touch with vision and use both with sound to make the tactile experience even more visceral.

Švankmajer, Poe and Deleuze: Thinking Tactile Gothic

As well as the Surrealist penchant for the early Gothic visions of de Sade, Lautréamont and Baudelaire, Švankmajer relished Poe's sensuousness. The Švankmajers' study *The Tactile Imagination* (2014) valorises the

enormous role touch played in [Poe's] psychological studies of pathological behaviour [. . .] the sense of touch, which we are barely aware of in everyday life, at times of psychic strain becomes hugely amplified [which is] why his stories are teeming with descriptions of tactile sensations. (2014: xxi)

Švankmajer asserts the affective power of the cinematic above the literary medium, contending that:

for readers these sensations are second hand, not directly experienced with their own bodies, but the tactile imagination is capable of recreating them quite intensely. I worked quite deliberately on evoking these neglected or hidden tactile feelings and tried to enrich the emotional arsenal of filmic expression [after all] we have all been seeking the sense of tactile security since our birth . . . before we could see, smell, hear or taste. (Švankmajer, 2014: xxi)

Deleuze's ideas about the dissolution of the egoic self in the art encounter offers a useful way of thinking through the tactile Gothic of Švankmajer's films. Deleuze contends that 'the brain is the screen' (Deleuze, 2000), but this brain is already an embodied organ that thinks as well as feels. Both during and after the affective experience of Gothic film, our feelings of anxiety, nausea, dejection, arousal or fear work in a shifting assemblage with our thoughts. Švankmajer's Gothic films are affective events experienced by 'my' shifting singularity in assemblage with them. Here, the formal properties of cinematography and sound effects operate in the interval of feeling and thought and send out lines of flight between them, undermining their distinction as we think through style. So what kind of affective techniques are mobilised in *The Fall of the House of Usher*?

The Fall of the House of Usher (1980)

Poe's original tale (1850) presents an uncanny thing-world of non-human affects, ideal material for Švankmajer 'to let objects speak for themselves' (Hames, 1995: 66). His film is about 'a swamp in motion and the life of stones. And of course horror, unmotivated horror' (Hames, 1995: 66). The neurasthenic sensibility of Poe's Usher, who perceives the vegetable and mineral world as sentient, inspires Švankmajer 'to animate the inanimate, to bring to life that which is lifeless, in a world devoid of human beings . . . a world consisting of only nature and that which man has created' (White and Winn, 2006: 6).

The visual mastery of establishing shots is refused from the start. The film's world is spatially closed in and close up, to focus sensory attention on enlarged details and exaggerated textures, while black and white film stock reduces extensive colour stimulus. External locale is minimal, just a few brief location shots. The broader milieu for these vivid tactile events is obscure: a conical tower glimpsed in mist, a weed-choked tarn and bare-branched trees. The impressionistic background makes the interior thing-world more expressive. One result of spatial enclosure is to stretch the sense of time so that fifteen minutes running seems experientially longer. As Bergson suggests, time can be intensive not extensive, becoming Aeon (duration) not Chronos (clock-time) (Bergson, 1991). Sequences alternate animation and hand-held tracking shots. The camera moves through self-opening doors into dim passageways where shadows throw objects into relief and the gleam of reflective surfaces sharpens sensation. The fluid camera tracks deeper into the house, penetrating its texture by extreme close-up. The grain of wood, peeling paint and lichen-stained walls blur matter in a textural mix that leads us into the intensive impact of animation. Like the building, these shots are not 'for' humans but map a vivid sensation-scape of autonomous objects.

Voice-over extracts from Poe both complement and counterpoint visual images (word/image incongruity is a classic Surrealist device). The voice evokes a 'dull, dark, and soundless' day, yet we hear haunting violin notes (Poe, 2003: 245). The narrator's invisible approach is reduced to hoof prints in the muddy ground. Rather than depicting human characters, Švankmajer shows only traces of their movements, a rocking chair or a closing door. As Poe writes, characters are 'altered' indeed. Only Roderick's empty chair commands attention. Its gleaming wood and elaborate curves lend substance and vitality to inert things. Poe's evocative description of Roderick's face shifts here to Švankmajer's anthropomorphised chair. The film's human characters attain the condition of what Deleuze calls 'becoming imperceptible', the ultimate goal of a series of increasingly molecular becomings away from the rigid entity 'man' (Deleuze, 2007: 66). Poe's characters, Roderick, Madeleine and the unnamed narrator, remain imperceptible here. Their 'absent presence' works on us mainly by the traces of moving objects.

Textured cinematography and claymation destabilises divisions of inside and out, human and object. Usher's 'superstitious impressions' of the mansion's sentience are materialised by animated sequences of cracking plaster and writhing mud, which furls and unfurls. Fast-motion makes us feel the dampness of a dark stain seeping across plaster and the violent impact of rock-like balls defenestrating themselves. The gloomy grandeur of Poe's poem, 'The Haunted Palace', is deflated as Švankmajer's mud balls unroll gleefully to expose inner abjection. Poe's shadowy '[e]vil things in robes of sorrow' are grossly materialised by mud fingers prodding themselves erect and squirming like maggots (Poe, 2003: 258). Poe's 'discordant melody' becomes the barely audible chords of Usher's guitar (258). The 'hideous throng' that 'laugh but smile no more' is parodied by clay, fingered into labia that open and shut before melting into lumpy mush, our nausea increased by reverse footage (258). Švankmajer details his intense engagement when working the clay into a tactile analogue to Usher's psychological struggles, 'a kind of "tense interpretation" of the poem . . . applying a brake on the tension amplified these emotions, they became cumulative, even leading to cramping of the fingers [which] led to considerable mental exhaustion' (Švankmajer, 2014: 151). Švankmajer manifests Usher's belief in vegetable sentience via textural extreme close-ups of knobbly trees with whorls and knots. Usher's extension of feeling to the 'kingdom of inorganisation' is expressed in the shifting 'collocation of stones' in walls mirrored by the undulating swamp (Poe, 2003: 258). These phenomenal hallucinations recall Deleuze and Guattari's evocation of Carlos Castaneda's hallucinatory vision in which the world 'appears supple, with holes in fulness, nebulas in forms, and flutter in lines' as animation undermines the stability and form of things (1988: 227–8).

Marks left by Švankmajer's hands after palpating the clay leave clear indentations of fingers and palms. The effects, not the actions, are presented, so we feel more corporeally engaged than through character identification. The efforts of his bare hands as they strive with the clay is paralleled by the undead Madeleine, likewise scrabbling at her coffin lid. Madeleine's own 'presence' is limited to a roughly outlined skull on the wall, a literal reduction of the human face to Deleuze and Guattari's figure of 'white wall/black hole', used to dismantle signification and subjectivity (1988: 168). In *Cinema 1*, the face, defamiliarised by extreme close-up or by non-human objects being 'facialised', epitomises the 'unextended' affection-image with its intensive qualities of 'the pure affect, the pure expressed' (Deleuze, 1986: 103). Roderick's parallel defacialisation is evoked by a close-up brick wall, showing that the 'luminousness of his eye had utterly gone out' (Poe, 2003: 261). Švankmajer has literalised the 'stony rigidity' of Usher's body by a becoming-stone (268).

Madeleine remains imperceptible in her coffin which, impelled by unnatural *élan vital*, inters itself in the family vault with a scraping and banging of wood. This sound is amplified and transformed as a thunderstorm breaks out. Nails and a hammer on the lid are set in motion by the shaking of the coffin. An out-of-sequence shot of the coffin splintering prefigures its later disintegration. Outside the house, tree roots shoot out in random directions, materialising Deleuze and Guattari's hybrids of rhizome and arborescence (1988). These roots are match-cut with jagged lightning, the force of which brings inanimate objects to life. Twigs erect themselves from the undulating ground. A pair of dried roots like stags' locked horns engage in combat, churning up mud with violent energy. Cracks appear in the ground as the earth itself bursts open. Madeleine's name, briefly etched on the wall, suggests her simultaneous emergence from the tomb. Her subjectivity has been subsumed by the house and her resurrection inevitably brings it crashing down.

Tension mounts as Poe's spurious Gothic yarn 'The Mad Trist of Launcelot Canning' is side-lined by cracks in the ceiling as the house starts to split (Poe, 2003: 264). For Deleuze, the crack is a figure of delirium and subjective dissolution. In the early stages of drug or alcohol addiction, intoxicants produce a 'silent, imperceptible crack' as a 'unique surface Event', which is 'imperceptible, incorporeal, and ideational', at least in its early stages (Deleuze, 1990: 155). Yet the crack's location is neither internal nor external but 'at the frontier' between (155). Cracks on the virtual plane can produce actual change. These literal cracks in the House of Usher express psychic disintegration in disturbed characters. Their affects also work on the 'viewer' to split the carapace of ossified responses in a 'shattering and bursting' that lets new feeling and thought emerge (155). The coffin nails twist into maggot forms as the voice-over describes Canning's door cracking and ripping, yet Švankmajer undermines our expectation by withholding sound-effects at this point. Only later, when a gaping hole appears in the coffin, is the sound of wood tearing actually heard. Like water or autumn leaves, the mud swirls threateningly around Roderick's chair. The hammer splinters, then the coffin completely disintegrates to reveal only an empty space of grass, wood and shards. Inside and out change places as roots spread into the house and walls burst open. Madeleine's approach is heralded by a fast-track upstairs, but the open door reveals only emptiness in Roderick's waiting chair. The darkness beyond is intensified by a close-up blood stain seeping through muslin cerements. The last, invisible embrace of Roderick and Madeleine is concealed by disintegrating masonry as the house immolates itself in the tarn. The stone walls self-destruct and the furniture drags itself outside only to sink into the primal ooze. The raven of the opening sequence undergoes time-lapse death and decay in the final shot.

Usher's Gothic mode veers towards imaginative terror at the threat of the uncanny thing-world, although the gut-churning claymation images of mud are intensely visceral. Švankmajer's second Poe adaptation incorporates Villiers de l'Isle Adam's short story, 'A Torture by Hope' (1888) which focuses mainly on psychological torture. The Gothic mode of *The Pendulum, the Pit and Hope* combines the terror of entrapment and impending doom with the horror of torture and abjection. In keeping with de Sade's lionisation by Surrealism, and Švankmajer's own admiration of de Sade, this is a Sadean film structured by degrees of cruelty.

The Pendulum, the Pit and Hope

Poe's first-person tale of torture in the Dungeons of the Inquisition, 'The Pit and the Pendulum' (1843), is excruciatingly sensational as sound, motion and touch blank out thought. The protagonist recounts the 'odor of the sharp steel' as the pendulum's 'acrid breath' approaches (Poe, 2003: 282). The terror of not-seeing is strongly evoked while darkness removes vision and intensifies touch as his hand registers texture, temperature and volume. As the blade approaches, the hypersensitive narrator ponders 'upon the sound of the crescent as it should pass across the garment – upon the peculiar thrilling sensation which the friction of cloth produces on the nerves [until his] teeth were on edge' (283). His tactile revulsion and emotional distress at rats swarming over him is detailed:

> They writhed upon my throat; their cold lips sought my own; I was half stifled by their thronging pressure; disgust, for which the world has no name, swelled my bosom, and chilled, with a heavy clamminess, my heart. (286)

So, how does Švankmajer operate an analogous sensory encounter?

Only fourteen minutes long by clock time, the film's affective intensity and 'vertical' temporal movement makes it seem much longer. Minimal set changes and repetitive shot-content further impede linear progress, as do the sensuous distractions of high-contrast chiaroscuro and textural close-ups of flesh, stone and fur. It features more live-action and less animation than Švankmajer's other Gothic films. It is shot from the victim's – or more properly, from the camera's – point of view, enhancing affective directness by removing intermediate character identification. As with *Usher*, the protagonist is not facialised and only visible in parts. Voice-over quotations are confined to the prologue and epilogue and the lack of language intensifies sensory affect. Ambient sounds grate on the ears and set the teeth on edge. They include the metallic whirring of machines, the scream of a victim and the squeal of a rat. Pixilation is used sparingly, as the rats scuttle and machinery grinds to a halt. This subtly uncanny motion actually exacerbates the impact of live-action suffering as the protagonist struggles against environmental factors with a mysterious life of their own.

Švankmajer explains how he uses touch to produce terror:

> Tactilism was actually a kind of central character [by] using the point of view of the camera instead of the real hero, showing only the hands and bare feet that map out and 'touch' the limited space of the cell ... Various torture implements, above all the pendulum, evoke the feelings of 'coming' (nearing) pain. Torture as the extreme limit of tactilism. (Švankmajer, 2014: 170)

Amid ambient darkness and the blur of hooded monks, tactility is foregrounded from the start. The protagonist's hands are brightly lit at centre-frame as he is led along by his wrists. Medium close-up emphasises skin texture and bloody lesions. The skeleton mural incorporating the torture device emphasises pain by exposing the body's interior and its bony digits splay in painted agony. The large, curved blade of the pendulum protrudes from the mouth like a fiendish grin. The camera pans down from the ceiling to the victim's bound torso then returns to close-ups of jointed bones as the machine's workings are examined in obsessive detail.

The victim's hand meets a plate of food resembling excrement, and his palm opens in revulsion. By inadvertently touching a dangling sandbag, the machine starts up and the pendulum descends. The textural close-up of hessian ripped by a nail displaces an image of pierced flesh. The swinging blade, dominating the frame as it nears the victim's torso, is brightly lit to emphasise the steel's sharpness. In desperation, he daubs his bonds with food to tempt the rats. One rat, sliced open by the blade, is immediately devoured by his companions. The animals demonstrate (slightly pixilated) agility in dodging the blade. As they gnaw through the ropes, the mechanism grinds to a halt and the victim escapes.

In the next stage of the torture, the metal walls, covered with Eva's infernal paintings, slide inwards. The use of rapid-fire editing and zip pans as demons devour their human prey makes us back away. The demons' mouths and eyes gleam with the flicker of flames behind them. As the walls cave in, the victim backs nearer the central pit, his naked feet treading the stone floor which glistens as though with sweat. Close-ups of his hands and feet dominate the shots. He tries to push the walls back, but their force and heat repel him. In a shock close-up, his hand is penetrated by the brightly lit, retractable blade of a demon's tongue, its prominence recalling Deleuze's evocation of the Ripper's knife cited earlier. The mural springs into animated action as puppet-victims jig their limbs while dismembered by monsters. One naked woman is torn by the beak of an enormous bird. As the protagonist nears the pit, the victim jams the metal plate into the torture mechanism. The walls' frantic pace slackens in the unnatural slow-motion of pixilation and they recede.

The heretic emerges into a long, gloomy corridor, but his tentative steps heighten unease as does shaky hand-held camerawork. He is ignored by the hooded Dominicans passing by, but this deception is part of his psychological torture. His fingers feel their way along the walls to a studded wooden door that opens to reveal the injured feet of another victim bound on a torture bench. The protagonist's horror mounts and he flees along blurred walls to the end of the corridor, which he finds blocked by rubble. Tantalised by the gleam of daylight, he digs out the stones with his bare hands, only to emerge into the final horror of despair. A waiting Dominican moves towards the camera, arms and hands outstretched to embrace the unrepentant heretic before his delivery to an auto-da-fé.

I have used Deleuze's ideas to explore how Gothic film affects operate in assemblage with percepts and concepts. In considering the tactility of terror, I have reversed Švankmajer's own process in adapting Poe's tales, by turning cinematic affect back into words and concepts. The molecular flux of affective images acts to dismantle outworn structures of feeling and thought, as new formations emerge from their own premature burial. Švankmajer's tactile imagination works not just to visualise the sense of touch, but to bring out particular Gothic tropes and contradictions. Images of imprisonment and torture can, through the power of affect, work to mobilise anti-totalitarian desire.

References

Artaud, A. [1927] 1988. 'Cinema and Reality', in Susan Sontag, *Antonin Artaud, Selected Writings*. Berkeley and Los Angeles: University of California Press.

Bergson, H. 1991. *Matter and Memory*, trans. Paul, N. M. and Palmer, W. S. New York: Zone Books.

Classen, C. 2005. *The Book of Touch*. Oxford: Berg.

Deleuze, G. 1986. *Cinema 1: The Movement-Image*, trans. Tomlinson, H. and Habberjam, B. Minneapolis, MN: University of Minnesota Press.

Deleuze, G. 1989. *Cinema 2: The Time-Image*. London: Athlone.

Deleuze, G. 1990. 'Porcelain and Volcano', in *The Logic of Sense*, trans. Lester, M. and Stivale, C. New York: Columbia University Press.

Deleuze, G. 2000. 'The Brain Is the Screen', in Flaxman, G. (ed.), *The Brain Is the Screen: Deleuze and the Philosophy of Cinema*. Minneapolis, MN and London: University of Minnesota Press.

Deleuze, G. 2003. *Francis Bacon: The Logic of Sensation*. London and New York: Continuum.

Deleuze, G. 2007. 'On the Superiority of Anglo-American Literature', in Deleuze, G. and Parnet, C. (eds), *Dialogues II*. New York: Columbia University Press.

Deleuze, G. and Guattari, F. 1988. *A Thousand Plateaus: Capitalism and Schizophrenia*. London: Athlone.

Deleuze, G. and Guattari, F. 1994. *What Is Philosophy?* London and New York: Verso.

Hames, P. 1995. *Dark Alchemy: The Films of Jan Švankmajer*. Westport, CT: Greenwood Press.

Irigaray, L. 1991. 'The Limits of the Transference', in Whitford, M. (ed.), *The Irigaray Reader*. Oxford and Cambridge, MA: Basil Blackwell.

Merleau-Ponty, M. [1968] 1998. *The Visible and the Invisible*. London and New York: Routledge.

Poe, E. A. [1850] 2003. 'The Fall of the House of Usher', *Tales of Mystery and Imagination*. London: Collector's Library.

Poe, E. A. [1843] 2003. 'The Pit and the Pendulum', *Tales of Mystery and Imagination*. London: Collector's Library.

Švankmajer, J. 1992. 'The Magic Art of Jan Švankmajer', tx BBC2. 1992. Produced by Rose, C.

Švankmajer, J. 1995. 'Thinking Through Things: The Presence of Objects in the

Early Films of Jan Švankmajer', in Hames, P. *Dark Alchemy: The Films of Jan Švankmajer.* Westport, CT: Greenwood Press.

Švankmajer, J. 2002. 'An Alchemist's Nightmares: Extracts from Jan Švankmajer's Diary'. *Kinoeye*, 2 (1). http://www.kinoeye.org/index_02_ 01.php (accessed 20 October 2016).

Švankmajer, J. 2014. *Touching and Imagining: An Introduction to Tactile Art.* London and New York: I.B. Tauris.

Vasseleu, C. 2008. 'The Švankmajer Touch', *Animation Studies*, 3. http:// journal.animationstudies.org/cathryn-vasseleu-the-svankmajer-touch/ (accessed 21 October 2016).

Villiers de l'Isle-Adam, A. 1888. 'The Torture by Hope'. https://dmdujourword-press.com/2016/04/03/auguste-villiers-de-lisle-adam-the-torture-by-hope/ (accessed 4 May 2017).

Wells, P. 2002. *Animation: Genre and Authorship.* London: Wallflower Press.

White, T. and Winn, J. E. (2006), 'Jan Švankmajer's Adaptations of Edgar Allan Poe', *Kinema: A Journal for Film and Audiovisual Media.* http://www. kinema.uwaterloo.ca/article.php?id=400&feature#ViewNotes_22.

Chapter 10

Dracula in Asian Cinema: Transnational Appropriation of a Cultural Symbol

Andrew Hock Soon Ng

The focus of this essay is the vampire in Asian cinema. By vampire, I do not mean a monster native to Asia that academic and popular writings have come to associate with it, like the Filipino *aswang* or the host of blood-drinking Indian demons (such as the *vetala*, the *yakshi* and the *rakshasha*),[1] but Dracula himself – or rather a vampire based on Stoker's design. His representation, moreover, can be direct or indirect: obviously a replication of the Anglo-American prototype, or a hybridised configuration, like the Malaysian *pontianak* and the Chinese *jiangshi*, that nevertheless palpably manifest his characteristics (usually his fangs and blood-drinking). As we shall see, the latter strategy can sometimes transform the hybrid into an effective motif bearing allegorical implications, but at others potentially undermine the cultural meaningfulness of the film. Hence, the subject of my inquiry is Asian cinema's appropriation of Stoker's vampire as a Western icon itself. Admittedly the lack of films featuring Dracula or a Dracula-hybrid potentially signals the lack of the phenomenon's importance to the development of Asian horror. However, my concern here is not so much with *how often* Dracula appears in Asian films (although I will briefly address this point) but *why he appears at all*. By clarifying the symbolic role Dracula performs in Asian horror films, I hope to establish a possible reason why he is adopted as a motif other than the allegation that his appropriation is mainly for profit.

This chapter explains Dracula's apparent adaptability to Asian cinema. After briefly reviewing Dracula's claim as a pre-eminent symbol in Anglo-American popular culture, I demonstrate Dracula's inherent versatility and ambiguity as a symbol capable of accommodating multiple, constantly shifting and even contradictory meanings corresponding to the nation's evolving culture at different points in history. As I will argue, it is precisely these qualities that render his ideological loyalty uncertain on the one hand and enable his transcendence of national borders to become a transnational, multicultural symbol on another, and hence his attractiveness to Asian cinema. This chapter also considers a common, if deleterious, perception regarding twentieth-century Asian horror (with the exception of Japanese and Korean or J- and K-horror) that could also apply to Dracula's presence in its films. This perception, or more allegation, implies a propensity in Asian horror cinema to imitate or heavily rely on Hollywood (what is known as 'rip-off') because it either lacks creativity and technical innovations when it comes to the genre, or wants to capitalise on the latter's popularity by refashioning it for local productions to make a profit. One can see how this view would seem particularly pertinent to films featuring a foreign monster, whether he is represented overtly or (perhaps especially) subtly. This allegation has admittedly a ring of truth, but to construe it as the sole reason behind Asian horror's appropriation of Hollywood iconography would be myopic. Nevertheless, if a lack of scholarly and mainstream interest in twentieth-century non-East Asian horror films is any indication, it is likely this remains the prevalent view even today.

Thus the objective of the second and longest part of this essay is to establish an alternative motivation for Asian horror's appropriation of Dracula that focuses on his symbolic rather than use value. Reading exemplary films from South East Asia, India and Hong Kong against Michel de Certeau's concept of poaching, I want to argue that Dracula's appropriation by Asian cinema should be rethought as cultural innovation, not copyright violation, akin to fandom's appropriation of artefacts from popular media texts as a means for reworking the monster's significances to reflect fans' desires. I will show how Dracula has been cinematically adapted to different cultural situations in order to symbolically highlight the ideological tensions affecting them, often with a degree of ambiguity that obscures the position(s) he is reifying.[2] But while these productions are, I contend, collectively important as historical resource testifying to the vampire's multicultural symbolic use, their small number potentially also begs the question of his effectiveness in this manner. As a response, I will speculate on why Dracula's Asian screen presence, sporadic to begin with in the twentieth century, will become even less likely in the twenty-first.

Dracula as Multicultural Symbol

According to James Twitchell, the Victorians 'rarely, if ever wrote about vampires as vampires; instead the vampire was the means to achieve various ends' (Twitchell, 1982: 38). Twitchell's point suggests that

Stoker's Dracula was designed as a symbol from the outset, a function for which he will grow increasingly competent in twentieth-century Anglo-American culture. As Nina Auerbach observes in her influential study, *Our Vampires, Ourselves*:

> We all know Dracula, or think we do, but ... there are many Draculas – and still more vampires who refuse to be Dracula or to play him. An alien nocturnal species, sleeping in coffins, living in shadows, drinking our lives in secrecy, vampires are easy to stereotype, but it is their variety that makes them survivors. They may look marginal, feeding on human history from some limbo of their own, but for me, they have always been central: what vampires are in any given generation is a part of what I am and what my times have become. (1995: 1)

Auerbach's views are, of course, largely based on her reading of Anglo-American literature and film, but more importantly, as the passage above establishes, it is not any vampire but Dracula himself that is the focus of her investigation. Among the qualities she identifies, albeit indirectly, that make him a potent cultural symbol are his liminality (appearing marginal while occupying the centre), his versatility (reflecting stereotypes and hence bearing a 'variety' of meanings to different people), his adaptability to the rapidly evolving Anglo-American culture and, hence, his survivability. Interestingly, despite the singularity of his representation that is now recognised worldwide, there is multiplicity in the way he signifies symbolically; or to restate this in Auerbach's phrasing, '[t]here is no such creature as "The Vampire"; there are only vampires' (5). A final quality derivable from those mentioned above is Dracula's ambiguity. His capacity to reflect a range of symbolic meanings would necessarily implicate a preoccupation with contradictory ideological positions, thus rendering his loyalty uncertain as a result. For this reason, he can be simultaneously deployed to subtly attack, while appearing to reinforce, an ideology. What the vampire fundamentally signifies in the end is our sense of collective identity – 'who we are' – at any given period in history. As Auerbach attests, he 'matters because when properly understood, [he] make[s] us see that our lives are implicated in [his] and our times are inescapable' (9). That Dracula continues to fascinate and terrorise us in equal measure even today is arguably due less to his monstrous qualities or awesome screen presence, and more to his symbolic capacity to reflect cultural anxieties and, hence, embody our fears. As scholarship has often reminded us, he is the quintessential 'other' – whether sexually, racially, politically and so forth – against whom 'we' and our historical moments are defined. And if the recent popularity of the *Twilight Saga* (both the trilogy of novels by Stephenie

Meyer and its film adaptations) and the television series, *True Blood* (based on a series of books featuring recurring characters by Charlaine Harris), is any indication, it is obvious the vampire's profound service to culture remains unabated even today.

However, as this article aims to show, Dracula's cultural symbolism transcends his national borders and can therefore be appropriated for multicultural purposes. In the twentieth century, this seems to be the strategy undertaken by a number of Asian horror films, although intermittently and with varying degrees of effectiveness. That English language scholarship has hitherto shown limited interest in Dracula's appearance in Asian films can possibly be attributed to either unfamiliarity with, or dismissal of, them as nothing more than rip-offs capitalising on a Hollywood icon for profit, or to a lack of creativity and ideas. In fact, the latter view encompassed much of Asia's horror genre, with the exception of East Asian cinema, in the previous century and this has resulted in generally negligible critical attention directed at it.[3] The implication is that twentieth-century Asian horror's appropriation of Hollywood somehow deprives it of cultural value and historical import. Even the handful of critics who focus on pre-twenty-first century Asian horror appear to concede to this view; Stephen Gladwin, for instance, argues that some of Indonesian cinema's collaborations with (read deference to) Hollywood – he gives the example of *Bercinta dengan maut* (*Dangerous Seductress*, H. Tjut Djalil, 1983) – blatantly revealed a dilution of its core significance, 'namely the history and culture of one of the world's most diverse countries' (Gladwin, 2003: 229). In a somewhat similar vein is Mauro F. Tumbocon Jr's comparison of Filipino horror films to 'gothic melodramas' (Tumbocon Jr, 2003: 256) in relation to both theme ('love, perversion and lust' (256)) and setting (a large, dimly lit mansion), thereby implying their dependence on Hollywood tropes. Admittedly, the allegation that Asian horror is largely imitative is not unwarranted; there are numerous films evidently inspired by Hollywood to the point that ideas and even entire scenes from the latter are replicated with minimum attempt to disguise the fact. Examples include *The Exorcist* (William Friedkin, 1973) rip-offs; *Seytan* (Metin Erksan, 1974) from Turkey and *Bhoot* (Ram Gopal Varma, 2003) from India; and *Pembalasan Ratu Pantai Selatan* (*Lady Terminator*, J. Tjut Djalil, 1989), an Indonesian film whose English title clearly betrays its incorporation of ideas from James Cameron's renowned science fiction film, *The Terminator* (1984).[4] In the end, whether the phenomenon is the result of an absence of local talent or due to an impetus for profit does not matter since both views similarly reduce the cultural value of twentieth-century Asian horror cinema.

The allegation noted above seems particularly warrantable when it comes to films that feature a monster undoubtedly borrowed from Hollywood. The more direct examples represent a vampire who is unmistakably Dracula, not just in terms of his undead nature and blood-thirstiness, but also in form (including wardrobe), habit (sleeping in a coffin, nocturnal), power (hypnotism, shape-shifting) and weaknesses (fear of sunlight and holy objects), in varying combinations but usually all of the above. They include titles like *Kulay dugo ang gabi* (*The Blood Drinkers*, Gerardo de Leon, 1964) and *Ibulong mo sa hangin* (*Blood of the Vampire*, Gerardo de Leon, 1966) from the Philippines; *Bandh Darwaza* (*The Closed Doors*, Shyam and Tulsi Ramsay, 1990) and *Wohi Bhayaanak Raat* (*That Frightening Night*, Vinod Talwar, 1989) from India;[5] *Noroi no yakata* (*Lake of Dracula*, Michio Yamamoto, 1971) from Japan; and *Chom mekhin* (*Southern Cloud*, Chalermchatri Yukol, 1985) from Thailand, some of which clearly identify with, or strongly allude to, Stoker's prototype. Less direct are films that feature a Dracula who has been crossbred with a native monster, mainly by superimposing some of his more pronounced characteristics – especially his fangs and, by extension, his blood-drinking – onto the latter that, in turn, mutes its unique qualities. Examples include Malaysia's *Pontianak* (Roger Sutton, 1975) and the series of *jiangshi* (hopping corpse) films from Hong Kong collectively known as the *Mr. Vampire* saga (*Jiangshi xiān sheng*) (Ricky Lau, 1985–92), in which the creature indigenous to the respective regions (the *pontianak* or *jiangshi*) is cinematically endowed with attributes otherwise unfamiliar to it, apparently for greater terror-inducing effect. Despite the obviousness of their appropriation, to view the subgenre of Asian vampire films as nothing more than imitation (or imitative) for the sake of profit fundamentally prevents us from recognising the symbolic function the vampire may be performing, and by extension the allegorical potential of these films. As such, I want to proffer an alternative approach to understanding Asian horror's practice of appropriation that will, on the one hand, underscore the subgenre's cultural significance and, on the other, testify to Dracula's capacity as a multicultural symbol. By defining this practice more precisely as poaching, we can then see it is not so much disregard for media ownership but creative interpretation of Hollywood that is expressed by Asian cinema in order to indirectly comment on the ideological fault-lines underscoring respective cultures.

Cinematic Poaching: Rethinking the Hollywood Vampire in Asian Films

Michel de Certeau's notion of textual poaching (later refined by Henry Jenkins) is particularly useful as a conceptual framework for rethinking cinematic appropriation. Admittedly practices with dissimilar goals, they nevertheless share several interesting points of convergence. A concept linked initially to reading, poaching implies an act of 'inventiveness' (de Certeau, 1988: 172) that expands (i.e. through interpretative work) a text's meaning in multiple new directions (174), while always remaining deferential to its authoritative meaning. Jenkins, who in turn applies the concept to fan culture, argues that poaching encourages fans to ascribe meanings related to their desires onto favourite media texts, such as television programmes, that are otherwise disallowed by the texts' producers; in this regard, fans are then able to challenge or resist (although they could also conform to) what is purportedly a text's only correct, or official, meaning (Jenkins, 1992: 26). Poaching, as Jenkins sees it, is thus a tactical activity (45) involving thoughtful deliberation on what materials to poach and why. A favourite target for poaching are characters from television shows whose identities (usually sexual) become reconstituted to correspond with the alternative universes created by fans in their own creative work, such as fan-written fiction; these universes parallel, but are dissimilar to, the universe of the parent text. Fan fiction categorised by television shows is posted on websites created specifically to be shared with, and enjoyed by, other fans; in this way, a community devoted to a single media text, becomes engendered. From poaching, its members derive, as Jenkins asserts, 'not simply borrowed remnants snatched from mass culture, but their own culture built from the semiotic raw materials the media provides' (Jenkins, 1992: 49). In this regard, poaching is also an empowering act whereby fans gain a measure of control over a cultural product's significance that accords with their individual and collective visions without disrespecting the authority and ownership of the product's original creator(s).

Although poaching unquestionably implicates a degree of reliance on the parent text, reading Asian horror's appropriation of Hollywood iconography as poaching helps to shift the focus of the appropriation away from profiteering alone to what de Certeau calls 'inventiveness'. Of course, unlike textual poaching in fan culture, poaching as an Asian cinematic practice in the twentieth century was aimed at local financial returns, since most of the region's horror films before the era of transnationalism were primarily made for native audiences. Notwithstanding this fundamental disparity, it is undeniable there are several striking similarities between Jenkins's notion and poaching in Asian cinema. First, although media-producers themselves, film-makers of Asian horror are also consumers of Western popular culture who, like many fans, poach materials from their favourite Hollywood media texts for their own fan-produced work, which in this case happens to be motion pictures. Second, as fans often poach popular characters from media texts, who would be more appealing for appropriation by Asian horror film-makers than Dracula, whose versatility and adaptability as a symbol could be aligned with different cultural scenarios (or alternative universes) and made to accord with the respective desires of film-makers without compromising the vampire's significance within an Anglo-American context? That Dracula is rarely represented as 'Asianised' (or if hybridised, it will be his characteristics that are emphasised) even in films that attempt to align his origin with indigenous beliefs can be interpreted in a twofold way. On the one hand, it is to maintain the audience's familiarity with the Western monster without, on the other, compromising its authority as prototype at the same time. This leads to a third similarity: like a favourite character's significance for fans, Dracula is not simply a remnant 'snatched' by film-makers of Asian horror from Western mass culture but, to use Jenkins's terms, serves as 'semiotic raw material' provided by Hollywood that helps them, not so much to 'build' in this case, but to 'interrogate', symbolically speaking, their own cultures to expose ideological anxieties.

Precisely what symbolic work is Dracula made to perform in the horror films of South East Asia, Bollywood and Hong Kong?[6] Turning first to Malaysia's *Pontianak*, it is necessary to read the film against the country's cultural context in the 1970s to understand the symbolic meanings accommodated by its featured monstrous hybrid, a cross between the vampire and the *pontianak*, a creature – always female – indigenous to the South East Asian region. Simultaneously experiencing an aggressive form of Islamisation and undergoing modernisation (read Westernisation) during this period, Malaysia was invariably pulled in opposite directions by two equally powerful ideologies, resulting in a conspicuous assumption of duplicity in its relationship with culture, such as its horror cinema. While local productions of horror were gradually, albeit unofficially, banned throughout the 1970s (ceasing altogether by 1981, since horror represented what Islam denounced),[7] foreign imports, mainly from Hollywood, continued to enjoy considerable screen time in local cinemas across the country (possibly to avoid jeopardising trade relationship with the West).[8] Interpreted in the light of this historical moment, the vampire-hybrid in *Pontianak* could arguably symbolise the state's uncertainty in its negotiation with either its own culture and the West or both; is the vampire-hybrid a relic from the past that has no place in a progressive Islamic nation, or is it an incrimination against the state's hypocrisy regarding its own relationship with the West?

If the cultural anxiety symbolised by the vampire in *Pontianak* is politically motivated, in the English-language Filipino horror, *The Blood Drinkers*, it is informed by religion. Here, the monster, Marco, is not a Dracula-hybrid, but a Dracula incarnate as evident in his lineage, profile, wardrobe and supernatural prowess. Only in one respect is Marco distinct from Stoker's vampire: he is not completely evil; he kills not because he is a predator driven by hunger, but because he desperately wants to save his beloved Katrina from permanent death. This motivation is in fact impressed on the viewer from the outset of the narrative, thereby establishing Marco as what Margaret Carter terms a 'sympathetic vampire' (Carter, 2001: 16) long before the latter was popularised by Anne Rice's fiction. Because Katrina's fate can only be reversed with the heart and blood of her twin sister, Christine, Marco must seek her out and, in the process, destroy anyone standing in his way. The film's intriguing, if complex, narrative has much to offer by way of analysis, but two episodes will suffice for my purposes. The first occurs immediately after Christine implores a priest to pray for Katrina, whose undead nature she has since discovered; with a voice-over narrator commenting on the power of intercession following thereafter, the scene suddenly cuts to a surreal moment during which Marco and Katrina are shown experiencing an epiphany as they step into a beautiful garden in broad daylight, struggling to come to terms with the possibility that God has miraculously delivered them from their accursed existence. Their salvation, however, is short-lived: in professing to Katrina that 'no power in heaven or hell can make me stop loving you', Marco has unwittingly overturned their redemption as we see an injured Katrina reverting to her deteriorated condition while the background abruptly changes to a menacing forest at night. The voice-over narrator serves to clarify Marco's misstep in what he claims, the significance of which must be understood in the context of the island state's official religion, Catholicism:

> Dr. Marco had said that no power in heaven or in hell could kill his love for Katrina. The devil does not give up ever. There is no power in prayer without faith, and faith must be in our own selves. And so the devil again has his way.

Telling is the way blame is doubly shifted, first to the devil when it is God – conspicuously unmentioned as opposed to the two times the devil is named – who giveth and immediately taketh away. Second, the blame is aslo shifted to the lovers for their apparent lack of faith when the supplication to God that momentarily restored them was never theirs in the first place, but rather a priest's on Christine's request.

Consider also a moment near the end of the film where Marco, having lost Katrina and his followers to angry villagers, finds himself surrounded as they attempt to burn him alive. A similar scene will be repeated in *Blood of the Vampire*, another Filipino feature produced two years after *The Blood Drinkers*, where villagers led by a deacon trap the vampire and those he has infected within his mansion and proceed to burn it down. Unlike in the latter, however, in which the vampire is unquestionably destroyed (implied with an image of burning wood over a pile of ashes), the fate of the vampire in the former is more ambiguous. In disappearing before the crowd, Marco leaves the narrative inconclusive since it could mean either extirpation or escape. Along with the first episode's inconsistencies and Marco's representation as a sympathetic vampire, *The Blood Drinker*'s denouement arguably critiques Catholicism's value system even as the film apparently supports it. While reinforcing the link between the vampire and an abomination that must be extinguished, the film is also ambivalent in promoting Christianity's teaching concerning God's goodness and the religion's simplistic views about good and evil. Marco, as such, may be figuratively deployed to reify the state religion's authority on one level, but also to compromise it on another, thus demonstrating the vampire's versatility and ambiguity as a multicultural symbol once again.

Ideologically, through its village setting, *The Blood Drinker* is also allegorically concerned with class, with Marco symbolising the wealthy and the villagers the oppressed who would have been at the vampire's mercy if not for the intervention of some urban, middle-class visitors who arrive to comfort Christine after her parents are killed by Marco for protecting her. However, to explore the vampire's class symbolism, I turn instead to the film *Bandh Darwaza* (*The Closed Door*, Shyam Ramsay and Tulsi Ramsay, 1990),[9] a Bollywood production in which class ideology is palpably articulated. Like Marco, the vampire in *Bandh Darwaza*, Nevla ('mongoose', denoting villainy) is perceptibly another Asian incarnation of Dracula.[10] And as with the case of Dracula, whom Franco Moretti deems a consummate bourgeois, Nevla is also 'impelled towards . . . an expansion of his domain' by exploiting 'the labour-power from others' (Moretti, 1982: 73), mainly young women (thus overlaying a gender dimension to the issue of class) to achieve this aim. Importantly, Nevla's subjugation of women consistently reflects a twofold purpose premised on a capitalist logic: accumulation and monopoly. The former is evident in the way his victims are invariably transformed into workers who 'renounce all enjoyments of life' and serve him completely by seeking out others for his subjugation; hence the vampirism repeats until Nevla finally establishes a 'new order of beings'. Accordingly, Nevla's motivation is not to destroy humans, but to '*use*' (73, emphasis in the original) them as means to his ends. Tellingly, the women Nevla overpowers are often initially 'clients' who had *first* contacted him for personal favours (e.g. to bear a child, to cast a love spell on someone and so forth), and thereafter become contractually bound to his term – to submit to him as labour – in the process. In bargaining for, rather than forcefully taking, what he wants, the Bollywood Dracula undeniably reveals a capitalist propensity for accumulation.[11] His accretion, moreover, also reflects a monopolistic dimension that parallels Dracula's, at least according to Moretti, who contends that 'Dracula is a true monopolist: solitary and despotic, he will not brook competition . . . He no longer restricts himself to incorporating (in a literal sense) the physical and moral strength of his victims. He intends to make them his forever' (74). This view arguably applies to Nevla as well, whose choice of victims is clearly meant to ensure the working class, symbolically speaking, can never aspire to become his equal because its capacity to reproduce is slowly being nullified.

Bollywood horror has always been a low-budget affair and constitutes 'India's poverty row productions' (Tombs, 2003: 243), which, unlike higher-end productions, is primarily targeted at what Sara Dickey terms 'the urban poor', whose conscious and unconscious desires film-makers will attempt to satisfy to ensure healthy financial returns (Dickey, 1995: 135). As an escapist fantasy, Bollywood horror exhibits clear demarcations between good and evil, and its heroes invariably provide the points of view with which the audience sympathises, identifying the entity as 'one of us'. In this regard, just as Nevla represents the oppressive bourgeois capitalist, the protagonist Kumar reflects, to a point, the working-class hero.[12] While he may not be an underdog oppressed by a wealthy and corrupt landowner or political leader, his situation in confronting a 'hitherto-unassailable villain' clearly mirrors the underdog motif. In any case, as Vamsee Juluri has noted, despite his status, the working class hero

> hardly ever works in the film. He lives a life of a status above the reach of his peers. His solutions are ultimately about individual superman-like action and not about any kind of collective change. He kills the villain because his grouse is always with the bad individual, not so much with the system. (Juluri, 2013: 78)

From holding no demonstrable occupation and single-handedly fighting off a band of weapon-bearing henchmen, to irrevocably ending the reign of the monstrous capitalist, Kumar's character does not merely allude to, but patently resembles, the working-class hero based on Juluri's observation. Nevla, on the other hand, analogously embodies qualities despised by the urban poor, whose disenfranchisement in India's highly polarised society (as class is also linked to caste) involves various forms of exploitation by the rich. As a symbol of the *noblesse oblige*, Nevla is 'powerful' and clearly 'beyond the reach of law' (77). For this reason, his defeat can only be guaranteed by a man angry enough to bring about his comeuppance using means often equally impermissible by law: in *Bhand Dharwaza*, it is not until Kumar's best friend, Anand's, brutal slaying that the hero – by now armed with the knowledge of how Nevla can be eliminated – finally decides to end the vampire's existence permanently.

Asian cinema's poaching of Hollywood's Dracula for its own productions demonstrates a degree of inventiveness in his function as a transnational symbol. Nevertheless, that there is hitherto only a small number of such films may point to this horror subgenre's limited significance. This is possibly because Western-inflected vampires are usually culturally awkward, illustrating starkly the difficulty of deploying a Hollywood icon within an Asian setting in a cinematically convincing or meaningful way. It is often, moreover, the final confrontation between the hero and the vampire that most palpably reflects this discordancy; for example, in the *Bandh Darwaza*, there is a scene that cuts in quick succession from a crucifix to the Koran before finally settling on the *om* (or *aum*), arguably Hinduism's most potent symbol, as if implying a textual uncertainty regarding which religion's paraphernalia to use in battling Nevla. Alternatively, the Thai film, *Chom mekhin* (*Southern Cloud*, 1985), relinquishes religious iconography altogether and replaces it instead with an assortment of vampire-fighting items, including a jasmine flower and a virgin's blood, which must furthermore be wielded by a holy person – interestingly, a Buddhist nun in this case – for these paraphernalia to be effective. Coupled with the fact that the film's Dracula incarnate is given a backstory aligned with Thai mythology (i.e. the vampire is actually a spirit), the end result is a curious cinematic blend of East and West that is reductive to both cultures.

As a transnational symbol, Dracula would arguably function more effectively when his qualities are intermixed with those of an indigenous Asian being. This would not only result in the ensuing creature's embodiment of duality that negates cultural incompatibility, but also helps to tease out of the film's implied ideology or ideologies based on its intercultural monstrous referent. Such is certainly the case with the vampire-hybrid in *Pontianak* discussed earlier. Unfortunately, due to the film's poor production values, the symbolic quality of its monster would most likely be (dis)missed by viewers who would primarily perceive her as fulfilling a market function instead. The most recognisable vampire-hybrid of Asian cinema is arguably the *jiangshi* (or hopping corpse), which is featured in a series of Hong Kong films produced before the island's reclamation by China after more than one hundred and fifty years of British rule. The five films produced between 1985 and 1992 comprising the *Mr. Vampire* saga (*Jiangshi xiān sheng*) all feature culturally crossbred vampires that embody both Chinese and Western characteristics – the former suggested by attire reminiscent of a Chinese mandarin's and a method of transport associated with a Qing dynasty legend,[13] and the latter (excepting the first *Mr. Vampire* instalment) by their protruding fangs and bloodthirstiness.[14] Importantly, these vampiric figures were hugely popular both locally and across the Chinese diaspora in their time, garnering (particularly in the case of the original film) generous box office returns[15] and becoming enduring classics of Hong Kong cinema. I will not go into details concerning the *jiangshi*'s multicultural adaptability as a symbol in the *Mr. Vampire* saga since the subject has already been covered by several scholarly articles;[16] suffice it to say, however, that this series of films' acclaim is likely due in part to the monster's figurative role in reflecting, possibly unconsciously, the island's anxieties over its impending return to China and its relationship with imperialism in the final years before 'The Handover' in 1997. As a symbol, the vampire-hybrid was also ambiguous enough to confuse its allegiance since he could either suggest a nostalgia for a past rooted in tradition (and hence a repudiation of present foreign intrusion) or fear that the communist state will eventually – to extend the vampire's metaphor – suck the island's hitherto economic and social vibrancy dry despite China's promise to allow Hong Kong's capitalist system and way of life to remain unchanged for fifty years following 'The Handover'. In relation to the latter, the ascription of Anglo-American vampire's characteristics to the *jiangshi* could also then imply a desire for continuing British presence that cannot be otherwise articulated.

Conclusion: Dracula and Twenty-First-Century Asian Horror

It is difficult to see how Asian films featuring Dracula or a hybrid version of him, intermittent in the last century, can survive in the present one, since such a figure would be deemed culturally intrusive and unsuitable, and therefore unprofitable, from a perspective of transnational cinema.

Admittedly, it is still too early in the century to know for sure, but if the dissimilar degrees of success between two recent Dracula-hybrid films – Malaysia's *Pontianak Harum Sundal Malam* (*Pontianak of the Tuber Rose*, Shuhaimi Baba, 2010) and Hong Kong's *Jiang shi xin zhan shi on* (*New Age Vampire Warriors*, Dennis Law, 2010) – are any indication, it is likely this subgenre of Asian horror will eventually disappear altogether in the twenty-first century. In the former, which marked the return of local horror to Malaysian cinema, the monstrous feminine no longer bears characteristics borrowed from a foreign monster but is restored to her cultural distinctiveness reminiscent of the *pontianak* in film versions produced during the 1950s. *Pontianak Harum Sundal Malam* would go on to become not only the year's major box-office hit in the country, but an international success as well, winning in several categories at the Estepona Horror and Fantasy Film Festival (Spain) and the best actress award at the Asia Pacific Film Festival. By contrast, *New Age Vampire Warriors*, which retains a Dracula/*jiangshi* crossbreed as the titular monster, grossed earnings, both locally and internationally, below those of its predecessors,[17] possibly indicating the monster's symbolic and market devaluation and the fact that the efficacy of the Dracula-hybrid in the earlier *jiangshi* films was clearly propelled by their historical moment, beyond which it can no longer signify meaningfully.

Dracula's periodic appearance in Asian horror films since the 1960s demonstrates the continent's attempts to poach a world-famous Hollywood icon for its cinema, thereby stretching the vampire's versatility as a cultural symbol beyond his national borders. The effectiveness of this strategy has been, at best, uneven. However, while the vampire, as argued, is certainly able to reflect the ideological tensions affecting different nation states, his distinctiveness as 'other' often makes him awkwardly suited to the task as well. And because horror films in Asia were, up until recently, usually also 'B-movie' type affairs, whatever symbolic value he expressed was likely subsumed by his use value from most viewers' perspective. This circumstance has been, to an extent, reversed by the rise of J- and K-horror and the global interest in world cinema in the twenty-first century. Coupled with better film-making technology and a greater respect for the genre (largely because of its marketability), contemporary horror films, especially from South East Asia and Bollywood, have clearly undergone a revival. They are no longer low-budget affairs featuring mainly unknown, amateur actors in a predictable plot, but expensive and intelligent cinematic works of quality. More importantly, unlike in the previous century where horror films were largely aimed at native consumption, in the present era, horror is produced with a transnational market in mind *but always with a focus on the local* to ensure a degree of cultural specificity so as to attract international audiences who also want a cultural experience alongside being vicariously terrorised. Pieter Aquilia (2006), for example, argues that the Singaporean horror film, *The Maid* (Kelvin Tong, 2005) exemplifies Olivia Khoo's observation of how the island-state's contemporary 'film-makers actively work to produce a vision or version of the local that is also able to engage the international audiences the country is so keen to capture' (Khoo 2006: 82). Similarly, Mae Ingawanij notes how the Thai horror, *Nang Nak* (Nonzee Nimibutr, 1999),[18] transforms the indigenous into pleasurable aesthetics for an audience predisposed to Hollywood by self-exoticising, projecting 'for the enticement of the "native" gaze a "native" object of desire as if it were foreign' (Ingawanij, 2007: 185). The examples of *The Maid*, *Nang Nak* and many others clearly demonstrate that Asian horror (and Asian cinema in general) can no longer remain culturally insular if it wishes to be relevant and compete in an international market that is looking for something different from Hollywood,[19] including the latter's monsters.

Notes

1. For examples in scholarship, see Ramos (1969) and Thundy (1999) respectively.
2. There are very few criticisms that consider specifically Asian vampire films, but a good spread of essays on the subgenre can be found in the edited volume by Browning and Picart (2009).
3. Of particular interest is the growing number of studies on South East Asian horror cinema that rarely discuss pre-twenty-first century productions. A case in point is the special issue of *Horror Studies* (5: 2) edited by Katarzyna Ancuta and Mary Ainsley on Thai cinema published in 2014, in which only one of its seven essays is specifically concerned with films produced in the previous century.
4. The genres (and premises) of the American and Indonesian films are, however, rather dissimilar in that the former is science fiction while the latter is mythic horror – a point obviously underscored by a literal translation of the Indonesian feature's title, i.e. *Revenge of the Queen of the Southern Seas*.
5. As the title indirectly indicates, the film is inspired by Tom Holland's *Fright Night* (1985).
6. Unless there are designated English titles, I will use the original titles when discussing the various Asian films throughout this article.
7. This ban would remain for nearly two decades until it was finally lifted in 2004.
8. Or alternatively, a strategy to subtly convey the idea of Western decadence as part of the government's 'Look East' policy (which was adopted in 1981 and continued until the then-Prime Minister, Mahathir Mohamad, stepped

down in 2001), the goal of wich was to gradually reduce relations with the West while forging stronger partnerships with neighbouring and other developed Asian countries, i.e. Japan.

9. The title alludes to one of the film's musical numbers, which are a staple in Indian cinema regardless of genre.

10. In fact, Pete Tombs asserts that *Bandh Darwaza* 'was . . . the Dracula story' (Tombs, 2003: 247) according to the Ramsay brothers who have directed many of Bollywood's horror films to date.

11. This echoes Moretti's point that, despite his courtly title, Dracula is essentially bourgeois, not an aristocrat (Moretti, 1982: 72).

12. This figure, in Vamsee Juluri's assessment, was made prominent by the famed actor, Amitabh Bachchan (Juluri, 2013: 76), due to his role as the angry young man in a series of films produced especially during the 1970s and 1980s.

13. This image of a hopping dead person is related to the legend of the corpse drivers, who used esoteric magic to reanimate those who died far away from their ancestral villages in order to transport them back home for burial. As Pamela Kyle Crossley notes, 'corpse drivers would be engaged to come in the night, bind up the corpse and join it with a herd of other corpses to be driven to their home villages. Then, using a long stick, the drivers knew how to prod the corpses so that they would hop forward' (Crossley, 2010: 44).

14. The *jiangshi* in the original *Mr. Vampire* (1985) adheres to the monster according to legend in that it kills its victims by stealing their breath.

15. For details, see individual film entries at www.hkmdb.com (accessed 5 January 2017).

16. For example, see especially essays by Ng Ho (1989) and Dale Hudson (2009) respectively.

17. According to Boxofficemojo, in total *New Age Vampire Warriors* earned about HK$14 million locally, less than the final instalment of the *Mr. Vampire* saga, and which, after currency adjustment, amounts to around HK$24.9 million (or HK$17 million in 1992)

18. Although released in 1999, *Nang Nak*'s international success would only be apparent in the following years to come.

19. It is Hollywood that now turns to Asian horror for ideas, as evinced by its remakes of several successful films such as Japan's *Ringu* (1998, dir. Hideo Nakata, remade as *The Ring* in 2002, dir. Gore Verbinski) and *Ju-On* (2002, remade two years later as *The Grudge*, both by Takashi Shimizu), Thailand's *Shutter* (2004, directed by Banjong Pisanthanakun and Parkpoom Wongpoom and remade using the same designated English title in 2008, directed by Masayuki Ochiai) and South Korea's *The Tale of Two Sisters* (2002, directed by Kim Jee-woon, remade as *The Uninvited* but with substantial modification in 2009, by Charles and Thomas Guard).

References

Ancuta, K. and Ainsley, M. (eds) 2014. *Horror Studies*, 5: 2: Special issue on Thai Horror.

Aquilia, P. 2006. 'Westernizing Southeast Asian Cinema: Co-productions for "Transnational" Markets', *Continuum: Journal of Media and Cultural Studies*, 20: 4, pp. 433–45.

Auerbach, N. 1995. *Our Vampires, Ourselves*. Chicago: Chicago University Press.

Boxofficemojo. www.boxofficemojo.com/movies/intl/?page=&country=HK&id=_fNEWAGEVAMPIREWAR01 (accessed 7 January 2017).

Browning, J. E. and Caroline J. P. (eds) 2009. *Draculas, Vampires, and Other Undead Forms: Essays on Gender, Race, and Culture*. Lanham, MD: Scarecrow Press.

Carter, M. 2001. 'Revamping of Dracula in Contemporary Fiction', *Journal of Dracula Studies*, 3, pp. 15–19.

Crossley, P. K. 2010. *The Wobbling Pivot: China since 1800*. Malden: Wiley-Blackwell.

De Certeau, M. 1988. *The Practice of Everyday Life*, trans. Randal, S. Berkeley, CA: University of California Press.

Dickey, S. 1995. 'Consuming Utopia: Film Watching in Tamil Nadu', in Breckenridge, C. A. (ed.), *Consuming Modernity: Public Culture in a South Asian World*. Minneapolis, MN: Minnesota University Press, pp. 131–56.

Gladwin, S. 2003. 'Witches, Spells and Politics: The Horror Films of Indonesia', in Schneider, S. J. (ed.), *Fear without Frontiers: Horror Cinema across the Globe*. Godalming: FAB Press, pp. 219–30.

Ho, N. 1989. 'Abracadaver: Cross-Cultural Influences in Hong Kong Vampire Movies', in Li Cheuk-to (ed.), *The 13ᵗʰ Hong Kong Film Festival: Phantom of the Hong Kong Cinema*. Hong Kong: HKIFF/Urban Council.

Hong Kong Movie Database. www.hkmdb.com (accessed 5 January 2017).

Hudson, D. 2009. 'Modernity in Crisis: *Goeng Si* and Vampires in Hong Kong Cinema'. in Browning, J. E. and Picart C. J. (eds), *Draculas, Vampires, and Other Undead Forms: Essays on Gender, Race, and Culture*. Lanham, MD: Scarecrow Press, pp. 203–34.

Ingawanij, M. A. 2007. '*Nang Nak*: Thai Bourgeois Heritage Cinema', *Inter-Asia Cultural Studies*, 8: 2, pp. 180–93.

Jenkins, H. 1992. *Textual Poachers: Television Fans and Participatory Culture*. London: Routledge.

Juluri, V. 2013. *Bollywood Nation: India through Its Cinema*. New Delhi: Penguin.

Khoo, O. 2006. 'Slang Images: On the Foreignness of Contemporary Singaporean films', *Inter-Asia Cultural Studies*, 7: 1, pp. 81–98.

Moretti, F. 1982. 'The Dialectic of Fear', *New Left Review*, 1: 136, pp. 67–85.

Ramos, Maximos (1969), 'The Aswang Syncrasy in Philippine Folklore', *Western Folklore*, 28: 4, pp. 238–48.

Thundy, Zacharias (1999), 'Indian Vampire: Nomen et Numen', in *The Blood Is the Life: Vampires in Literature*, eds Heldreth, L. G. and Parr M. Bowling Green, KY: Bowling Green State University Popular Press.

Tombs, P. 2003. 'The Beast from Bollywood: A History of the Indian Horror Film', in Schneider, S. J. (ed.) *Fear without Frontiers: Horror Cinema across the Globe*. Godalming: FAB Press, pp. 243–55.

Tumbocon Jr, M. F. 2003. 'In a Climate of Terror: The Filipino Monster Movie', in Schneider, S. J. (ed.), *Fear without Frontiers: Horror Cinema across the Globe*. Godalming: FAB Press, pp. 255–65.

Twitchell, J. B. 1982. *The Living Dead: A Study of the Vampire in Romantic Literature*. Durham, NC: Duke University Press.

Part III

Gothic Film Traditions

Chapter 11

The Italian Gothic Film
Mikel J. Koven

To try and synthesise all the explicit and implicit definitions of what constitutes 'the Gothic' would make one as insane as Ambrosio in Lewis's *The Monk* (1796) or one of Poe's narrator/protagonists. Gothic at once refers to a very definite set of creative choices and expectations, while it also can, seemingly, refer to anything with a graveyard or a cobweb in it. Baldick and Mighall (2012) noted how the term has become so overextended as to render it almost completely meaningless: so that anything vaguely scary or sensational is labelled as Gothic (280). Botting (2008: 12) noted, citing Levy, such a proliferation [of different kinds of Gothic] ... threatens to gothicise the entirety of human experience. The word becomes meaningless if it can refer to anything. I have no doubt that many of the articles published in this volume proffer better definitions than I could hope to articulate, so I defer to them. In lieu of a proper definition of the Gothic, I will fall in with Gilda Williams (2014: 412) who simply identifies the Gothic as anything which depicts a lurid interest in the macabre: 'works typically featuring skulls, gore and other "spooky" iconography'. Later on, Williams (417) focuses her definition slightly, seeing the Gothic 'as a synonym for the aesthetic of the dark, the grotesque, the macabre and the supernatural'.

Work on Gothic *film* tends to suffer from a similar epistemological malady which attempts to keep the definition open until it becomes almost synonymous with the entire horror genre itself. Consulting Halberstam (1995), Hervey (2007), Hopkins (2005), Kay (2012), Morgan (2002), Aldana Reyes (2014) and Spooner (2006), few could give a concrete definition of what Gothic *film* actually was. Many of the scholars just noted contain their research by looking only at specific film adaptations of a priori Gothic literary texts, suggesting that Gothic film is an adaptation of a particular Gothic novel. Worland (2014) provides a useful overview and contextualisation distinguishing between Universal Pictures' cycles of Gothic horror in the 1930s and 1940s, the

British Hammer Gothic movies from the 1950s through the 1970s, the Roger Corman-directed Edgar Allan Poe adaptations of the early 1960s and, albeit only slightly, the Italian Gothic films I will be discussing here. I am drawing much of my understanding of Gothic film, and particularly the Italian Gothic horror film, from two recent volumes: Roberto Curti's *Italian Gothic Horror Films: 1957–1969* (2015) and Jonathan Rigby's *Euro Gothic: Classics of Continental Horror Cinema* (2017).

What follows is a discussion of the Italian Gothic horror movies produced in the early 1960s but put into the context of the larger debates about the Gothic, sometimes outside of film studies. Space and time only permit me to explore a few films, and so my selection is meant to be representative, not definitive. Therefore I shall be discussing *Black Sunday/La maschera del demonio* (Mario Bava, 1960), *The Horrible Dr. Hichcock/L'Orribile segreto del Dr. Hichcock* (Robert Hampton [Riccardo Freda], 1962), *The Whip and the Body/La frusta e il corpo* (John M. Old [Mario Bava], 1963) and *Castle of Blood/Danza macabra* (Gordon Wilson Jr [Sergio Corbucci] and Anthony Dawson [Antonio Margheriti], 1964), and examining these films within the discourse of the Gothic.

There are some minor discrepancies in fully identifying the beginnings of the Italian Gothic film: while Hughes (2011: 77) gives the years 1960–5, for example, Curti (2015) casts his net wider, discussing a range of films produced between 1957 and 1969. Danny Shipka (2011) identifies key continuities between the films produced in the 1960s and film production through the 1970s, and Rigby (2017) discusses the European Gothic film (including those made in Italy) from the very beginnings of cinema history to the present day. Trying to nail down, definitively, any period of film production is notoriously difficult; however – and typical of the scholarship on Italian genre cinema – a more useful approach is to see the Gothic in terms of *filone*, an Italian word literally referring to a seam of precious metal or a tributary of a river in its larger context. Rather than seeing the Italian Gothic film as a distinctive period in Italian horror film-making, it is, perhaps, advantageous to refer to a Gothic *tradition* within the genre. Such an approach recognises a period in vogue (in the early 1960s), while also recognising that, like Dracula himself, the Gothic never truly dies.

Before looking at an overview of the Italian Gothic horror films produced in the early 1960s, further context is needed. As the domestic box-office underperformance of *Black Sunday* suggested, Italian audiences had little interest in Italian horror films. *Black Sunday* gained its audience largely through American International Pictures (AIP) buying the rights and putting the film out on the grindhouse and drive-in circuits in the US (Rigby, 2017: 123): so, given the apparent lack of domestic interest, most of these films were produced for international *export*. The international casts many of these films (featuring American, British, German, Spanish as well as Italian actors) not only reflect this international distribution, but also the international co-production of many, often being Italian-Spanish or Italian-German co-productions. As Francesco Di Chiara noted, 'this formula allowed companies located in different countries to pool resources and production experience in order to make bigger, more competitive films, which were able to attract a European audience typically keen on consuming American films' (2016: 34). Furthermore, because of European (Italian, in particular) audiences' desire to watch American films, many of the Italian film-makers (and writers and actors) worked under English-sounding pseudonyms. So, for example, Mario Bava (after the financial failure of *Black Sunday* under his own name) directed *The Whip and the Body* (1963) as John M. Old. Other relevant pseudonyms (for this chapter) include directors Robert Hampton (Riccardo Freda), Anthony Dawson (Antonio Margheriti) and screenwriter Julian Berry (or Julyan Perry).[1]

Rigby (2017) saw Italian Gothic horror films as having, at least in the historical context I am working here, two distinct waves of production: one following on the heels of the Hammer horror films beginning with *The Curse of Frankenstein* (Terence Fisher, 1957) and *Dracula* (Terence Fisher, 1958) (see Di Chiara, 2016: 35), and the second in response to the AIP adaptations of Edgar Allan Poe stories directed by Roger Corman, starting with *House of Usher* (1960). As Rigby noted:

> For, just as the first wave had been set in motion by Hammer Films, the second took its cue from Roger Corman's sequence of Poe adaptations for AIP, specifically his 1961 smash *Pit and the Pendulum*, which made as big an impact on Italian audiences as Fisher's *Dracula* had a few years earlier. Henceforth no Italian Gothic seemed complete without a diseased family at its centre, garnished if possible by torture devices in the basement and prolonged, candlelit corridor-wanderings for the beleaguered heroine. (2017: 125)

This patterning reflects the initial wave of Gothic production in 1960, including Bava's *Black Sunday*, and then another apparent wave around 1962–3, including Freda's *Dr Hichcock*. The following analysis is intended simply as a representative sampling of this period of Italian genre cinema.

While critics like Curti and Rigby trace the Italian Gothic films back to, at least, 1957 and *I Vampiri* (Riccardo Freda [and Mario Bava], 1957),[2] most histories put the start of this *filone* with Mario Bava's 'official' directorial debut, *Black Sunday*. Bava's film opens with an Inquisition-like auto-de-fé condemning Satanists Asa Vajda (Barbara Steele) and her lover Javutich (Arturo Dominici) to be burned at the stake after the 'Mask of Satan' (the title of the film in Italian, *La maschera del demonio*) has been nailed to their faces. A sudden rainstorm puts out the fires and Javutich is buried in unconsecrated ground, while Asa is taken to the Vajda family crypt. Jumping ahead two hundred years, Dr Kruvajan (Andrea Checchi) and his young assistant, Dr Gorobec (John Richardson), are on their way to a conference when their carriage breaks down near Castle Vajda. The two doctors explore a nearby crypt and discover Asa's tomb. Dr Kruvajan removes the 'mask', and accidentally cutting his hand on the broken glass of the coffin, drips a tiny amount of blood on the corpse. This is enough to begin Asa's resurrection. The two doctors decide to stay at a nearby inn for the night, but as they are leaving the crypt, they encounter Asa's descendent, Katia Vajda (also played by Steele), who mentions that she lives at Castle Vajda with her father, Prince Vajda (Ivo Garrani), and her brother, Constantine (Enrico Olivieri). Later that night, Prince Vajda is taken seriously ill and Dr Kruvajan is sent for. The partially resurrected Asa calls forth Javutich, who emerges from his unconsecrated grave to do her bidding. Javutich is sent to intercept Kruvajan and bring him to the vampire-witch. Asa seduces and kills Kruvajan, turning him into a vampire like herself. Kruvajan, in turn, kills Prince Vajda. All of this is part of Asa's grand plot to destroy the Vadja family who condemned her to die two hundred years earlier, as well as her desire to possess the body of Katia so she can be fully alive.

Unlike other horror films produced in Italy around this time, like *I vampiri* (Freda and Bava, 1957), all of which took place in the present, Bava's film takes place in a nineteenth-century past; this is a significant Gothic setting, especially given the publication history of Gothic novels, at least in English. Bava's *mise-en-scène* is filled with the images one stereotypically associates with the Gothic. Howard Hughes noted: 'The ruined chapel has crumbling arches, cobwebs, tombs and a crypt, and the castle interior, with its great hall dominated by an ornate fireplace and portraits of Asa and Javutich, conceals a network of secret passages and trapdoors' (2011: 79). But we can identify other elements of the literary Gothic throughout the film too: despite the film's setting in Moldovia, and the designation of the Church as Eastern Orthodox rather than Roman Catholic, the film's opening with hooded monks torturing and then burning alive the two Satanic witches echoes the (British) Gothic's anti-papal litany of Roman Catholic excesses in previous centuries. If the British Gothic was anti-papal, as suggested by Botting (1996: 3), then Bava, coming from a Catholic country himself, displaces these abuses of the past to an alternative European Other, namely the Eastern European, with its echoes of Dracula's Transylvania.

The key Gothic theme of a long hidden past erupting into an unstable present, regardless of whether that 'present' is the mid-twentieth century or within the story-world itself, is explored by Bava in Asa's persistent disruption of the Vajda family's existence. The events of *Black Sunday* coalesce around the anniversary of Asa's and Javutich's executions. As Curti commented, 'the present is continually menaced by a past that hangs and waits, ready to take back what belongs to it' (2015: 45). As Botting elsewhere has noted:

> The projection of the present onto a Gothic past occurred, however, as part of the wider processes of political, economic, and social upheaval: emerging at a time in bourgeois and industrial revolution, a time of Enlightenment philosophy and increasingly secular views, the eighteenth-century Gothic fascination with a past of chivalry, violence, magical beings, and malevolent aristocrats is bound up with the shifts from feudal to commercial practices in which notions of property, government, and society were undergoing massive transformations. (2012: 13–14)

Kruvajan and Gorobec embody a contemporary bourgeoisie: while the Vajda's aristocratic family persists, they fulfil no apparent purpose than to suggest the tenacity of the aristocracy itself. The two doctors, however, are men with trades, men who work for their living, even if such educational privilege was open only to the lucky few who had the economic resources to take advantage of it. Asa and Javutich, as Botting's 'malevolent aristocrats', return from the dead to feed off the living. As vampires, they literally live on the blood of the living; as vampires, they are, what Punter (1996: 183) identified as, 'barbaric' – symbols of the chaos of the past attempting to disrupt the equilibrium of the present, much like the barbaric hordes did to Rome. As Curti noted in detail:

> *Black Sunday* evokes a fear of past times which is typical of Gothic literature, by reworking the awe of the aristocracy which was the basis of the legends on vampires. Through Asa, Bava synthesizes one of the Gothic's fundamental themes: the fear of a 'return to the past.' Time becomes an obsessive presence, and produces a sense of vertigo and inevitability: just as the barriers between life and death become blurred, the same happens between the past and the present. The returning past takes the form of a curse launched centuries earlier, whose oppressive legacy has an impact on the present. (2015: 45)

Italian Gothic horror cinema is filled with idle aristocracy juxtaposed to 'contemporary' men of education and employment. The Gothic, itself, can be seen as an anxiety regarding the epochal shift between these two organising principles from aristocracy to bourgeoisie.

In many respects, aristocracy and bourgeoisie can be seen as each other's double, reflecting the opposition between the two. This doubling is also a standard motif within Gothic literature, which Bava could not be unaware of. In casting Barbara Steele as both Asa and Katia, *Black Sunday* visually connects the two. Like Stevenson's Dr Jekyll and Mr Hyde, the *sine qua non* of doppelgänger motifs in Gothic literature, Asa is the wicked witch to Katia's 'virginal heroine' (Curti, 2015: 45). Across the corpus of Italian Gothic horror cinema, this doubling becomes a standard feature in many films, as noted below.

Italian horror cinema screenwriter Ernesto Gastaldi, who would go on to write some of the seminal Gothic and *giallo*[3] scripts of the 1960s and 1970s, noted in the Forward to Curti's book that as beginning screenwriters, they were 'called on to make up stories set in gloomy crumbling castles, isolated villas, dark crypts and foggy cemeteries packed full with crooked crosses, in the shade of cypress tress just like in an [Italian Gothic nineteenth-century poet] Ugo Foscolo poem – even better if those cypresses were shaken by a howling wind that recalled the echo of wolf packs or the gnashing teeth of damned souls' (in Curti, 2015: 1). While Gastaldi does not use the word 'Gothic' to describe these films – in fact, the vernacular term used at first by (at least) the screenwriters themselves was 'cinema di paura' (cinema of fear, or 'scary cinema') (Curti, 2015: 1) – he does evoke the Gothic poet Foscolo as an allusion for these films. Gastaldi continued, noting that he first encountered these films referenced as 'Gothic' by director Riccardo Freda, who described his *The Horrible Dr Hichcock* (written by Gastaldi) as 'a Gothic film, due to its mixture of romance and horror' (Curti, 2015: 2).

Having learned from *Black Sunday* the coldness Italian movie-goers had towards Italian horror films, *The Horrible Dr Hichcock*, a film which Danny Shipka noted 'stands out as one of the seminal Italian Gothics' (2011: 56), hid its Italianate elements behind a facade of English-sounding pseudonyms. I've already mentioned that Riccardo Freda is credited as 'Robert Hampton' and Gastaldi as 'Julyan Perry'; I will note in square parentheses a listed actor's real name when relevant. The Italian title of *Dr Hichcock* alludes to a 'horrible secret' (a 'L'orribile segreto') of the titular character, Dr Bernard Hichcock (Robert Flemyng): necrophilia. All credit to a film made in 1962 which not only references necrophilia, but opens with a newly interred coffin dug up, opened and the body of a young (dead) woman fondled. Dr Hichcock has a regular ritual with his wife, Margaretha (Teresa Fitzgerald [Maria Teresa Vianello]): he injects her with an anaesthetic he has developed, thereby rendering her body absolutely prone, in order to satisfy his urges. However, by administering too large a dose, he accidentally kills her. He leaves his stately home and university hospital position to get over his widowhood, but returns twelve years later with a new wife, Cynthia (Barbara Steele). Upon his return he also re-employs his housekeeper, Martha (Harriet White), whose mentally ill sister she is responsible for. Margaretha seems to haunt the Hichcock household; her portraits remain in what appears to be every room, always watching Cynthia. The new bride is even convinced she has seen the first Mrs Hichcock's ghost walking in the garden. A recovering mental patient herself, Cynthia's hold on her sanity becomes increasingly more difficult.

There are two key literary texts that Gastaldi (and Freda) appear to allude to in *Dr Hichcock*: Daphne du Maurier's *Rebecca* (1938) is evoked in the roles of the three central characters. Hichcock fills Maxim's position within the narrative, Martha is the film's Mrs Danvers and Cynthia is clearly 'the second Mrs' Hichcock. The second allusion is to Charlotte Brontë's *Jane Eyre* (1847), specifically Martha's mentally ill sister, who, like Brontë's Bertha, is another Gothic 'mad woman in the attic'. In a move evocative of Brontë's Bertha, it is revealed that Martha's 'sister' is in fact Margaretha, and that Cynthia is to be sacrificed so her blood will rejuvenate Hichcock's first wife. But these Gothic novels (from different periods of Gothic literature) are not the only allusions: clearly the titular doctor is a reference to film-maker Alfred Hitchcock and his films are referenced. The plot recalls his film adaptation of du Maurier's *Rebecca* (film, 1940), and the spiked milk drink that Hichcock brings to Cynthia is reminiscent of *Suspicion* (1941). There may even be an echo of the story of the Hungarian Countess Elizabeth Báthory (1560–1615), who murdered hundreds of women in whose blood she bathed to keep herself young, by way of the film's allusion to *I vampiri*, one of director Freda's first films, which featured a vampiric version of Báthory.

While David Punter (1996: 183–4) recognised 'taboo' as one of the 'aspects of the terrifying to which Gothic constantly, and hauntedly, returns' – and necrophilia is, in most polite circles, a taboo subject – it is rare to find the practice quite so explicitly depicted in *Dr. Hichcock*. Punter identified these key literary Gothic sensibilities as 'constantly approach[ing] areas of social-psychological life which offend, which are suppressed, which are generally swept under the carpet in the interests of social and psychological equilibrium' (184). Taboo in the Gothic tradition, then, manifests itself as the return of the repressed. The pleasures inherent in breaking these taboos within the safe and contained contexts of a novel or a film feeds what Botting identifies as our 'fascination with transgression and the anxiety over cultural limits and boundaries, [and which] continue to produce ambivalent emotions and meanings in their tales of darkness, desire and power' (1996: 1). Despite this fascination, a lurid interest in the macabre is, as Botting noted, 'less an unrestricted celebration of unsanctioned excesses and more an examination of the limits produced [in these texts] . . . to distinguish good from evil, reason from passion, virtue from vice and self from other' (1996: 5). The theme of necrophilia in *Dr Hichcock* is disarmed by an almost ludic self-reflexivity (cf. Hurley, 2007: 142–3) and a sense of the comic (cf. Horner and Zlosnik, 2012): as Rigby (2017: 110) noted, Hichcock's perversions require the epitome of the docile sexual object – taking 'lie back and think of England' to its furthest conclusion. The 'Englishness' of the Gothic novel is also played with in these films by frequently having Britain as a setting; *Dr. Hichcock*, for example, takes place in 'London, 1885', as we are told at the beginning of the film.[4] However, as these films were produced mainly for export, what we see is less a presentation of Britain than a depiction of how Italy *sees* Britain; it is a distorted Britain, filled with sexual repression and Gothic angst. English women are cold to the point of being cadaverous and the men are so sexually repressed they look like they're going to explode in a miasma of jism and blood. Necrophilia then, from an Italian perspective, is the quintessential *perversione inglese*.

To be sure, the necrophilia in *Dr Hichcock* produces a visceral reaction to this day; the physicality of Asa's seduction of Kruvajan suggests necrophilia, but Dr Hichcock's perversion is not only onscreen; Margarethe is aware of and complicit in his necrophiliac indulgences. Such explicitness further suggests a Gothic in the Lewisonian tradition, as, in the words of Andrew Smith, an 'explicit physicality of horror' (2007: 147). This physicality, what Jack Morgan (2002: 7) called the 'bio-psychological', is a key device in the Gothic, and with a loosening up on censorious limits of what could be shown in a film (Curti, 2015: 15; also Shipka, 2011: 39), these Gothic film-makers were able to exploit the limits of Gothic cinema, specifically with regard to the perverse play with sex and death. Although discussing *Black Sunday*, Peter Bondanella noted how Barbara Steele embodied this sex/death connection: 'Steele's high cheekbones suggest that there is a skull barely concealed under her beautiful face . . . combining the suggestion of death behind the face of a woman embodying the traits of both virgin and temptress – and thus associating the themes of sex and death – certainly serves the many related themes found in the horror film quite well' (2009: 313). In *Dr Hichcock*, Steele still embodies those qualities Bondanella saw in *Black Sunday*, and, while not stated directly, certainly suggests how Cynthia functions as a sex-death fetish for Hichcock. But it is not simply connecting sex and death that these Italian film-makers achieve so well, but that, as Judith Halberstam (1995) noted with regard to the Gothic, these abstractions were viscerally felt by the audience. As Roberto Curti pointed out, 'Excess, in these films, meant not only a more direct approach to horror but also the presence of a strong emotional element which was a direct result of the Italian tradition of melodrama' (2015: 15). The excess and perversion in the Italian Gothic horror film plays upon the physical, visceral reaction to the horror, while also leading viewers to connect emotionally with it: a bio-psychological experience.

Mario Bava's *The Whip and the Body* may very well be the most beautifully filmed Italian Gothic horror film. Instead of necrophilia, this time screenwriter Gastaldi explicitly uses the Gothic as a means to explore sadomasochism.[5] Prodigal son, Kurt Menliff (Christopher Lee), returns to his costal castle after leaving in disgrace many years before. His departure had something to do with his seduction of housekeeper Giorgia's (Harriet White) daughter, Tanya, and Tanya's suicide. Giorgia blames Kurt explicitly for her daughter's death, and she keeps the still bloody dagger Tanya used as a memento, under glass. Kurt is into the sadomasochistic scene rather heavily, wherein he enjoys savagely whipping his lovers into ecstasy. He finds a more than willing partner in his brother Christian's (Tony Kendall [Luciano Stella]) wife, Nevenka (Daliah Lavi), and they begin an affair. Kurt is mysteriously killed one night with the bloody dagger, although the murderer is unseen. Thereafter Nevenka claims to see Kurt through her window or his muddy footprints in the crypt. Kurt appears to Nevenka sufficiently to continue their sadomasochistic affair. At first, only Nevenka can detect Kurt's ghost (assuming Kurt is really dead), but soon after, Christian also claims to hear his brother's laughter in the echoing halls.

Castle Menliff is filled with secret passages down to the crypt, and a wind storm ravages the coastline; this setting is right out of a classic Gothic novel, a point also noted by Rigby (2017: 131) and Punter and Byron (2004: 259). Curti noted how this setting all too frequently reflects the emotional state of the characters, most notably Nevenka's 'tormented soul and psyche' (2015: 105). If *Dr Hichcock* was Lewisonian in its physicality, *The Whip and the Body* (while also quite physical in its own right), is more Radcliffian in how 'an overwrought (and therefore Gothic) imagination can become overly stimulated by fantastical ideas' (Smith, 2007: 147). There are questions throughout the film about the extent to which this haunting is entirely in Nevenka's head, a key theme and preoccupation in the Gothic (Curti, 2015: 5). Scott Brewster, discussing the theme of madness in the Gothic, noted:

> We compulsively interpret random signs, haunted by the possibility that we may be deluded, that we have not seen enough or have seen too much. To pursue delusion leads nowhere but, as these Gothic texts have suggested, we cannot help but undertake this pursuit. The madness we find resides in us: madness in the Gothic lies in the reading. (2012: 493)

The Gothic text is, as these critics have suggested, a hysterical text; we are sutured into a narrative told by a madman (or woman). The world, as we see it, is told from their subjective experience. At least, these narratives challenge our assumed omniscient perspective, either as a reader or a film viewer. Perhaps, most particularly, the Gothic film challenges this assumption of omniscience as we are too quick to assume what we *see* is some form of objective (narrative) reality. In this way, Bava's breathtakingly beautiful cinematography shapes the subjectivity of the film experience. Without going so far as to say *all* films that present their narrative from such a distorted subjective perspective are, *ipso facto*, Gothic, the films discussed frequently play with that visualised subjectivity. This perspective is what Punter called, in his three key aspects of the Gothic, 'paranoiac fiction': 'fiction in which the "implicated" reader is placed in a situation of ambiguity with regards to fears within the text, and in which the attribution of persecution remains uncertain and the reader is invited to share in the doubts and uncertainties which pervade the apparent story' (1996: 183). Until the film's conclusion, Kurt's haunting of Nevenka remains ambiguous; it is the final revelation that not only was she responsible for Kurt's murder, but that the entire 'haunting' has been in her mind, which confirms that we've experienced the film text as free indirect discourse, a subjective position presented to us as objective.

The elite French film journal, *Cahiers du Cinéma*, referred to Antonio Margheriti's *Castle of Blood* as a '*poème nécrophilique*' (cited in Rigby, 2017: 129), which is a lovely way of framing a film which is so typical of the Italian Gothic cinema that its charms can be overlooked. The film begins with a bizarre wager: Lord Thomas Blackwood (Raul H. Newman [Umberto Raho]) wagers £10[6] to journalist Alan Foster (Georges Rivière) that he cannot spend one night (that night) in the Blackwood stately home. As witness to this bet is the American writer Edgar Allan Poe (Montgomery Glenn [Silvano Tranquilli]) who Foster is supposed to interview. Not long after arriving at the Blackwood estate, Foster meets Elisabeth Blackwood (Barbara Steele), Blackwood's sister, and the two fall madly in love with each other almost instantly. However, Foster finds himself in a complex melodrama of adulteries, passions and murders: while Elisabeth (seems to) love Foster, she is married to William (Ben Steffen [Benito Stefanelli]) and is having an affair with the gardener, a shirtless hunk of a man (Johnny Walters [Giovanni Cianfriglia]) and the object of desire for Julia (Margaret Robsham [Margrete Robsahm]). Not long after Foster and Elisabeth consummate their mutual passion for each other, she admits to being dead (necrophilia again), and Foster then witnesses the other ghostly residents in the house reliving their deaths. Also present in the house is Dr Carmus (Henry Kruger [Arturo Dominici]), a scientist studying the supernatural, who also repeatedly experiences his own murder. These ghostly inhabitants of the Blackwood estate feed on the blood of the living, which gives them this one day of life every year. It was Blackwood's plan to find someone each year to stay in the house overnight to feed these hungry ghosts.

Castle of Blood is a veritable checklist of Gothic motifs: old mansion filled with dusty furniture and cobwebs, ghosts, crypts, adultery, passion, murder, necrophilia ... one could go on. While the film is easily dismissed as simply ticking off the motifs as it goes through the motions, Gothic scholars, like Catherine Spooner, saw these similarly transparent Gothic mechanisms as part of the genre's self-reflexivity. In other words, the 'checklist-like' litany of motifs in the film is a Gothic device itself, letting the reader/viewer in on the joke from the very beginning. Spooner likewise noted how the Gothic

> is also ... profoundly concerned with its own past, self-referentially dependent on traces of other stories, familiar images and narrative structures, intertextual allusions. If this could be said to be true of a great many kinds of literature or film, then Gothic has a greater degree of self-consciousness about its nature, cannibalistically consuming the dead body of its own tradition. (2006: 10)

Consider the function of Edgar Allan Poe in the film. *Castle of Blood*'s Poe is simply a referent to the Gothic; Poe is a writer so associated with the nineteenth-century macabre that the simple evocation of his name is sufficient to make the connection. Certainly, Poe's inclusion in the film is a further reference to the Roger Corman-directed adaptations which were popular at the time. The film-makers even claim that their movie is based on a short story by Poe (it's not). As Curti (2015: 110) noted, Poe's inclusion was 'mostly as a commercial gimmick and sometimes just as a vague reference'. Be that as it may, while in the coach on route to the Blackwood estate, Foster is able to interview Poe who comes along for the ride although he's not spending the night. During this interview, or as much of it as we see, Poe relates the famous dictum from his essay 'The Philosophy of Composition' (1846), namely that 'the death of a beautiful woman is the most poetical topic in the world', a statement that clearly foreshadows Foster's encounter with the striking Elisabeth. But in this self-reflexive sense, the aggregate of Gothic horror motifs, or the film's apparent clichés, are part and parcel of the Gothic itself.

Furthermore, *Castle of Blood* plays less with the horror motifs than with the erotic. While the passion Foster and Elisabeth have for each other is clearly physical and fully unrepressed, it is still necrophiliac – while Elisabeth may be ghost, she is still dead. But, Elisabeth is not decomposing like Asa or in a drugged catatonia like Margaretha Hichcock; she is the beautiful, and physical, body of Barbara Steele. But we can add to the film's list of erotic excesses, like Julia's explicit desire for Elisabeth. While the word 'lesbian' is never used, the relationship between the two women was clearly sexual, at least at one time, although Julia is rejected for Foster and the heteronormative. Elisabeth is constructed as the bisexual subject of the film; in addition to the strong suggestion of a previous sexual relationship with Julia and her current focus on Foster, we see Elisabeth having a quick fumble with the shirtless gardener and, from the construction of the shots in this sequence, particularly its focus on the ecstasy on Elisabeth's face, it is strongly suggested that he has gone down on her. As the bisexual subject, Elisabeth can be read within the context of queer theory, namely in how her character can be seen as a 'radical deconstruction of sexual rhetoric as a form of resistance to sexual normalization' (Hanson, 2007: 175). Elisabeth rejects the traditional role of heteronormative sexuality of an aristocratic married woman through her bisexuality, adultery and her continued sexuality after her death.

The ghosts in *Castle of Blood* are different from many of the spectres that haunt supernatural fiction and film: in order for their single night of physical revels, they need the blood of the living to sustain them. Dr Carmus was one such victim, who, having succumbed to the Blackwood ghosts, is cursed to forever join them. The same fate awaited the Perkinses, a newlywed couple who were the previous year's victims, although we are 'treated' to the surprising (for 1964) image of Elsie Perkins (Sylvia Sorent [Sylvia Sorrente]) topless as she undresses before the fireplace – an image which evokes the physical eroticism Margheriti is trying to covey. In this regard, the Blackwood ghosts are, in Kelly Hurley's phrase, 'abhuman': according to Punter and Byron, 'a body that retains traces of human identity but has become, or is in the process of becoming, something quite different' (2004: 41). The traces of their former lives are indelibly trapped in the estate, but their physicality, their bodies, are at once physical and ephemeral; they can interact with the material world around them, but only for the one night. As Foster, ignoring Elisabeth's pleading that she cannot go with him, drags her from the house at the film's denouement, she dissolves into dust before his (and our) eyes.

By no means has this current chapter exhausted either the aspects of the Gothic that could be discussed in reference to these films, or the number of Italian Gothic horror films which could be discussed. The topic is much larger than a single chapter could hope to cover. The Gothic never dies, and despite these films falling out of favour in the mid-1960s, there were frequent attempts to, if not resurrect the *filone* in its entirety, then to draw from it, cross-pollinating other *filone*. Mario Bava returned to the Gothic with *Kill, Baby . . . Kill/Operazione paura* (1966), *Baron Blood/Gli orrori del castello di Norimberga* (1972) and *Lisa and the Devil/Lisa e il diavolo* (1972) while Antonio Margheriti remade his own *Castle of Blood* in colour as *Web of the Spider/Nella stretta morsa del ragno* (1971). We can see evidence of the Gothic in *gialli* like *All the Colors of the Dark/Tutti I colori del buio* (Sergio Martino, 1972) and in director Dario Argento's 'Three Mothers Trilogy' – *Suspiria* (1977), *Inferno* (1980) and *The Mother of Tears/La Terza madre* (2007). As a literary genre, the Gothic has been going for more than 250 years; I would anticipate we have not seen the end of the Italian Gothic horror movie either.

Notes

1. While the Anglicisation of the Italian names was to disguise the films' national identity, I could extend this argument to say that such duplicity is further part of the Gothic traditions. Citing Jerrold Hogle, Botting notes that with regard to *The Castle of Otranto* specifically, is 'a fake translation by a fake translator of a fake medieval story by a fake author, the novel turns on a false nobleman unlawfully inheriting both title and property through a false will and attempting to secure a false lineage through nefarious schemes' (2012: 14). While I am not suggesting that such was intentional for these film-makers, it does, however, suggest a nice parallel. That being said, despite such a lack of intention, Mario Bava's son, film-maker Lamberto Bava, has occasioned to use a pseudonym as well, and when he does, he goes by John M. Old, *Jr*, effectively creating a 'false lineage' started by his father, 'John M. Old'.
2. Bava was cinematographer on *I Vampiri* and completed the film when Freda walked off set.
3. *Giallo* (*gialli*, pl.) as a film genre refers to Italian murder mystery-horror movies popular in the 1970s. These movies are frequently gory, sexy and the best of them are deeply sleazy too.
4. The most ludicrous setting of any of the Italian Gothic horror films is in *The Hyena of London* (*La jena di Londra*, Gino Mangini, 1964), in which we are told the film takes place in Bradford, which apparently (according to the title card) is a 'village' just outside of London.
5. Rigby noted: 'As Gastaldi admitted 30-odd years later, "The producers . . .

showed me an Italian print of *Pit and the Pendulum* before I started writing it. "Give us something like this" they said . . .' (2017: 130).

6. The wager was originally for £100. However, Foster says he cannot afford that, so the wager was reduced to £10. This is only worth mentioning as some critics confuse the original wager with the accepted bet.

References

Aldana Reyes, X. 2014. 'Gothic Horror Films, 1960–present', in Byron, G. and Townshend, D. (eds), *The Gothic World*. London: Routledge, pp. 388–411.

Baldick, C. and Mighall, R. 2012. 'Gothic Criticism', in Punter, D. (ed.), *A New Companion to the Gothic*. Oxford: Wiley-Blackwell, pp. 267–87.

Bondanella, P. 2009. *A History of Italian Cinema*. London: Continuum.

Botting, F. 1996. *The Gothic*. London: Routledge.

Botting, F. 2008. *Limits of Horror: Technologies, Bodies, Gothic*. Manchester: Manchester University Press.

Botting, F. 2012. 'Gothic Darkly: Heterotopia, History, Culture', in Punter, D. (ed.), *A New Companion to the Gothic*. Oxford: Wiley-Blackwell, pp. 12–24.

Brewster, S. 2012. 'Seeing Things: Gothic and the Madness of Interpretation', in Punter, D. (ed.), *A New Companion to the Gothic*. Oxford: Wiley-Blackwell, pp. 481–95.

Curti, R. 2015. *Italian Gothic Horror Films, 1957–1969*. Jefferson, NC: McFarland.

Di Chiara, F. 2016. 'Domestic Films Made for Export: Modes of Production of the 1960s Italian Horror Film', in Baschiera, S. and Hunters, R. (eds), *Italian Horror Cinema*. Edinburgh: Edinburgh University Press, pp. 30–44.

Halberstam, J. 1995. *Skin Shows: Gothic Horror and the Technology of Monsters*. Durham, NC: Duke University Press.

Hansen, E. 2007. 'Queer Gothic', in Spooner C. and McEvoy, E. (eds), *The Routledge Companion to the Gothic*. London: Routledge, pp. 174–82.

Hervey, B. 2007. 'Contemporary Horror Cinema', in Spooner, C. and McEvoy, E. (eds), *The Routledge Companion to the Gothic*. London: Routledge, pp. 233–41.

Hopkins, L. 2005. *Screening the Gothic*. Austin, TX: University of Texas Press.

Horner, A. and Zlosnik, S. 2012. 'Comic Gothic', in Punter, D. (ed.) *A New Companion to the Gothic*. Oxford: Wiley-Blackwell, pp. 321–34.

Hughes, H. 2011. *Cinema Italiano*. London: I.B. Tauris.

Hurley, K. 2007. 'Abject and Grotesque', in Spooner, C. and McEvoy, E. (eds), *The Routledge Companion to the Gothic*. London: Routledge, pp. 137–46.

Kay, H. 2012. 'Gothic Film', in Punter, D. (ed.), *A New Companion to the Gothic*. Oxford: Wiley-Blackwell, pp. 239–51.

Morgan, J. 2002. *The Biology of Horror: Gothic Literature and Film*. Carbondale & Edwardsville, IL: Southern Illinois University Press.

Punter, D. 1996. *The Literature of Terror: A History of the Gothic Fictions from 1765 to the Present Day*, Vol. 2: *The Modern Gothic*. London: Routledge, pp. 183–4.

Punter, D. and Byron, G. 2004. *The Gothic*. Oxford: Blackwell.

Rigby, J. 2017. *Euro Gothic: Classics of Continental Horror Cinema.* Cambridge: Signum Books.

Shipka, D. 2011. *Perverse Titillation: The Exploitation Cinema of Italy, Spain and France, 1960–1980.* Jefferson, NC: McFarland.

Smith, A. 2007. 'Hauntings', in Spooner, C. and McEvoy, E. (eds), *The Routledge Companion to the Gothic.* London: Routledge, pp. 147–56.

Spooner, C. 2006. *Contemporary Gothic.* London: Reaktion Books.

Williams, G. 2014. 'Defining a Gothic Aesthetic in Modern and Contemporary Visual Art', in Byron, G. and Townshend, D. (eds), *The Gothic World.* London: Routledge, pp. 412–25.

Worland, R. 2014. 'The Gothic Revival (1957–1974)', in Benshoff, H. M. (ed.), *A Companion to the Horror Film.* Oxford: Blackwell-Wiley, pp. 273–91.

Chapter 12

Gothic Science Fiction

Geraint D'Arcy

In the late 1950s Richard Hodgens lamented that Science Fiction (SF)[1] films had come close to 'ruining the reputation of the category of [literary] fiction from which they have malignantly sprouted' (1959: 30), citing films like *Destination Moon* (Irving Pichel, 1950) or *The Thing from Another World* (Howard Hawks and Christian Nyby, 1951) as 'strange throwback(s) of taste to something moldier and more "Gothic" than the Gothic Novel' (30). Hodgens's increasingly savage attack on Science Fiction film finds him dissatisfied with cinematic versions of a genre that he considers 'the only kind of writing today that offers much surprise' (31). Hodgens is frustrated in particular with the horror elements of what he appears to categorise as some kind of arch-Gothic (no pun) present in the Gothic tradition, but not in the literary Gothic. Ostensibly Hodgens's issue was with the apparent 'cheapness' of Science Fiction cinema at that time where not only did the 'special effects . . . not deceive a myopic child in the back of the theatre' (38), but where the producers were deliberately hybridising the worst parts of each genre to make money: making horror films with a Science Fiction skin. Hodgens ends his criticism on a positive but defeatist note though, stating that 'an audience for good Science Fiction probably exists, but it is unlikely that producers will take that chance now' (38).

Present a text and say 'that is a Gothic Science Fiction film' or 'a Science Fiction Gothic film' and watch the academy roll its eyes. It should be nigh on impossible to take a 'highly unstable genre' with many different 'scattered ingredients' (Hogle, 2010: 1) and marry it to another genre, where attempts to define it are anything but conclusive (Evnine 2015: 1), in order to simply respond to 'the nagging conviction . . .' that one '. . . ought to define (a genre) before describing it' (Sobchack, 1998: 17). The Gothic is hard enough to cleanly identify as a mode, let alone a genre and Science Fiction is equally awkward academically. So, to bring two 'contested concepts' (Evnine, 2015: 16) together for the academic purpose of furthering the discussion of both fields seems like a futile task. Equally, any work trying to coin a new genre from the pieces of two separate ones would have to defend itself pretty fiercely against fields which have over a long period of time been defensive and territorial themselves.

Despite Hodgen's objections to it, the blending of the Gothic with Science Fiction is quite well recognised in literary SF, the most famous early example being the prevalence of 'imaginative' fiction at the forefront of Romanticism (Roberts, 2006: 42–50; Bratlinger, 1980), a trend coinciding with the publication of Mary Shelley's 1818 novel *Frankenstein; or, The Modern Prometheus* (Aldiss, 1973: 18). Despite there being earlier examples of work that could be considered SF, the most significant of which is Margret Cavendish's *The Blazing World* (1666), the idea that SF developed from the Gothic, or from *Frankenstein*, can be historically contested. In formalist terms (Botting, 2005: 111–26) the 'issue is not so much whether SF grows out of the Gothic . . . but rather how responsive SF texts would be to an interpretation informed by Gothic practices' (Seed, 2005: 3). In a book about Gothic film, this would seem to be a very good place to start when constructing a definition of SF film. Eventually, of course, 'the conjunction of two hybrid genres composed from diverse literary and mythical precursors breeds monstrosities' (Botting, 2005: 111), especially as the task of identifying either is itself monstrous. The definition this chapter posits is itself contestable, but it offers a language derived from Darko Suvin and Vivian Sobchack that can be used to examine the Gothic elements of Science Fiction films which, when they manifest, appear often as one of two aspects: either visually in the production design, or thematically within the dramatic narrative. To explore how the Gothic elements of 'transcendental . . . religion and magic' (Sobchack 1998: 63) work in Science Fiction, this chapter will first examine and define the presence of visual Gothic conceits in Ridley Scott's *Alien* (1979) and then look at how Gothic themes appear in the visuals and dramatic narratives of Duncan Jones's *Moon* (2009) and Alex Garland's *Ex Machina* (2015).

Defining Science Fiction in Film

Eventually any popular form can be studied academically, but forms like the Gothic or Science Fiction are ever popular and ever changing, and over time fluctuate between reputability and disreputability (Hoppenstand, 2005: 603; Roberts, 2006: 12). For SF, the debate is essentially about 'taxonomies' (Roberts, 2006: 21), the academy's agreement on what makes up an SF text and where the boundaries lie between it and similarly non-realist genres such as Fantasy. For some the difference is moot and it can instead be labelled 'speculative fiction', a genre familiar to any 'authentic card-carrying science fiction and fantasy nerd' (Hoppenstand, 2005: 603). Some see this definition as anathema to the historical traditions of a genre (Clayton, 1987: 204–5), or as Simon Evnine claims: 'the victory of entropy in the literary field', which sees the 'loss of generic distinction' as an inevitable part of experimentation in a form (2015: 26). In Evnine's example, the writers of the SF New Wave in the 1960s and 1970s (Michael Moorcock, J. G. Ballard, Pamela Zoline et al.) were experimenting and trying to become more 'literary', consequently increasing the academic respectability of the genre through its integration with other genres. That Science Fiction has its 'high art' and its 'low art' in the topography of its literature is a consequence of those debates, and SF in literature now seems secure within this landscape. Film studies are considerably less secure, and it is here where the anxiety of definition is perhaps more keenly felt in a form based on an industry which is driven by popular commercial demand to 'remake' its texts for newer audiences, updating, refreshing or rebooting films on a regular basis either as sequels, prequels or remakes. The briefest survey of the *Star Wars* (1976–), *Star Trek* (1966–) and *Alien* (1979–) franchises are enough to see that after the 'original' proved popular enough to warrant further investment, the generic components of each franchise have widened radically while still essentially remaining 'Science Fiction'. Each franchise has become almost an individual genre with visual and thematic indicators transferring between its texts transmedially; defining such transfers, however, exceeds this chapter's scope. At any rate, the audience that Hodgens wished but did not dare hope for in 1959 was certainly located by the producers.

Vivian Sobchack's book *Screening Space* (1998) deals with the anxiety that film studies has about defining Science Fiction by pinning down the genre using the definitions provided by literary studies, before ultimately lamenting that critics have only ever made the most 'specious connections' (20) between film and literary definitions of the genre. In her attempts to define film SF, Sobchack re-stages many of the literary debates – the perpetual association of film Science Fiction with horror and monsters (Sobchack, 1998: 26–38), the question of its status as work of 'substance' (24) or its lack of profundity compared with literary versions (25) – before finally admitting that literary definitions are inadequate (63) and that any definition of film horror must 'gladly' recognise 'these hybrid forms as part of a spectrum which moves – on a sliding scale – from the sacred to the profane' (63). The definition of

SF she eventually posits is one which 'emphasizes actual, extrapolative, or speculative science and the empirical method, interacting in a social context with the lesser emphasized, but still present, transcendentalism of magic and religion, in an attempt to reconcile man with the unknown' (63). For film, this definition works well enough, although it could probably look to the literary world one last time for simplification from one of the key academics of Science Fiction studies, Darko Suvin. Suvin's formalist work provides a sometimes dismissed (Clayton, 1987) but always useful set of terms centred upon an idea of novum or 'an exclusive interest in a strange newness' (Suvin, 1976: 58–9) which covers Sobchack's 'actual, extrapolative, or speculative science and empirical method' (1998: 63) quite neatly. Suvin also posits two aspects which combine to articulate the attitudes of Science Fiction quite handily: the first is *cognitive estrangement*, which can be here defined against Sobchack 'interacting in a social context . . . in an attempt to reconcile man with the unknown' (63). Cognitive estrangement is the sense that what is 'known' (scientifically or socially) or 'normal', and therefore cognitive (related to the 'normal' of any given age including its own), is made 'strange' or 'new' to an audience and is consequently estranged (1976: 60–1). We could take Suvin's definition of 'SF as the *literature of cognitive estrangement*' (1976: 58) and apply it to film instead of Sobchack's rather more cumbersome definition but for the one part of Suvin's definition that does not cover what Sobchack offers: there is one subclause in Sobchack's definition which makes allowance for films which are consistent in their action but ever changing in their form. The clause allows for the hybridisation with other genres and styles: 'the lesser emphasized, but still present, transcendentalism of magic and religion' (1998: 63). Hybridisation in the literary form of SF is something that Suvin does not make allowance for and inevitably leads writers such as those referred to by Evnine to experimentation and to the generic entropy he describes. In literary terms, Suvin is quite clear: 'less congenial to SF is the fantasy (ghost, horror, Gothic, weird) tale, a genre committed to the interposition of anti-cognitive laws into the empirical environment' (1976: 62). For Suvin, the Gothic tale, even just a few 'scattered ingredients' (Hogle, 2010: 1) is enough to render in literary terms the text 'not SF', but for Sobchack this is that 'specious connection' (1998: 20) that differentiates between literary and film SF: literature can afford to argue for a pure Science Fiction form, but film Science Fiction as a genre is always a hybrid, 'part of a spectrum which moves . . . from the sacred to the profane' (63).

Suvin's definition is of course not perfect – if it were there would simply be no debate. What overlaying Sobchack's view onto Suvin's definition reveals here is that in film there is an expected extra element which will be present: the 'transcendentalism of magic and religion' (Sobchack, 1998: 63). That element could either be taken as emerging from the human protagonist, or in the concretising of an abstraction through a visual design decision. The human protagonist as the embodiment of such a concept would react emotionally and instinctually to a situation rather than empirically; in film, the protagonist is often dominant in a hierarchy of visual signification. In the efforts to create a SF film world visually, some aspects of SF, which would be abstract in the literary form and left to the reader's imagination (24–5), must, in film, be realised and therefore concretised through design choices.

If the design choice in an SF text concerned an anti-cognitive element, such as parts of an imaginary or fantastical world that is not empirically explained within the film's diegesis, it would become an element that 'escapes out of its horizons and into a closed collateral world indifferent towards cognitive possibilities' (Suvin, 1976: 62). Such an element in SF cinema is the production design, which is often mistaken for simple artifice or set dressing rather than an obvious source of signification within the film's diegesis. Charles and Mirella Affron regard the set designs of SF film as artifice, 'predominantly descriptive' and 'intent on defamiliarization', which enhances the estranging SF elements by appearing 'patently unreal' (Affron and Affron, 1995: 39). Should this hold true, and there is little to contradict Affron and Affron's work on set theory, set design in SF film is always anti-cognitive because it 'does not use imagination as a means to understand the tendencies in reality, but as an end sufficient unto itself and cut off from the real contingencies' (Suvin, 1976: 62). Set design, considered as artifice in Science Fiction film is already stretching the literary definition of SF, which depends upon imagination to envisage its worlds. The SF film realises this vision for us and offers no explanation for how it works so the viewer can assume that science or magic is what makes it work because '[d]ecors appropriate to these worlds are palpably invented realities' (Affron and Affron, 1995: 115) and not part of our own 'real' world.

Equally frustrating to Suvin's definition is the presence of the pro-filmic character acting as a protagonist. Suvin's definition depends upon its literary naturalism: a character struggles against other characters where the character's destiny exists only in other humans; the circumstances surrounding the central figures are passive or neutral and only change because of the novum they encounter. In film, however, the circumstance of the dramatic narrative is often positively or negatively focused on the protagonist. In an SF film, a person 'is capable of affecting [their] environment and [their] own destiny' (Sobchack, 1998: 61).

This is a difference that is a distinctly 'non-naturalistic, metaphysical' (Suvin, 1976: 65) variation that Suvin cannot account for, but for which Sobchack must.

It would seem that in the tenuous gap between literature and film, Science Fiction cinema has picked up an extra complexity peculiar to film: there is a perceptual visual element in film which literature can only evoke in the imagination. This causes a shift in the narrative focus from an internal personal (cognitive) viewpoint, to a sometimes-exterior protagonist-centred narrative. These complexities allow for the hybridisation of SF with other styles and genres, and where historically it has been the cause of critics to 'purify the genre of its horrific elements' (Sobchack, 1998: 63). To this end, the combination of Gothic and SF can be explored on 'a sliding scale – from the sacred to the profane' (Sobchack, 1998: 63), with the pleasures of their distinct elements celebrated in their union, and through their production of an exponentially larger combination of symbols. In the exploration of the SF films to follow, these unions will be examined, first, through a focus upon the visual Gothic within SF film production design, and then through a consideration of different constructions of the Female and Male Gothic in SF narratives.

Alien (Ridley Scott, 1979) and the Visual Gothic

A sense of the Gothic within Science Fiction cinema is most visibly and outwardly delivered through the film's production design: the visual signifiers and familiar architectures of the Gothic are deployed to evoke a sense of unease, decay or villainy. This much is evident in many Science Fiction films, such as the *Alien* franchise and the films influenced by its design, such as *Galaxy of Terror* (Bruce D. Clark, 1981), *Event Horizon* (Paul W. S. Anderson, 1997) and *The Chronicles of Riddick* (David Twohy, 2004). Even examples from the more culturally central Science Fiction franchises draw upon the Gothic in their iconic set designs such as *Star Trek: First Contact* (Jonathan Frakes, 1996) and the recent *Star Wars: The Force Awakens* (J. J. Abrahms, 2015).

Alien (1979) is rarely dealt with as a stand-alone text separate from its franchise or the worlds and sequels associated with the first film, and then only rarely by those interested in making connections between Science Fiction and Gothic elements in film. Most critical discussions instead favour the increasingly Gothic themes that can be found in later films and applied retrospectively to the beginning of the series (Roberts, 2006: 80–1; Botting, 2002: 289–90). In particular, these analyses draw connections between the concept of the alien or artificial reproduction and the figure of Ripley as an increasingly post-human mother/alien 'as sites of abjection, places where numerous cultural fears are thrown and dissolve together' (289). Such discussions usually begin with the series' later films, from James Cameron's action thriller, *Aliens* (1986), through David Fincher's *Alien 3* (1992) and Jean-Pierre Jeunet's *Alien Resurrection* (1997). These studies map how cultural fears are born, raised, killed and born again multiple times. Extensive discussion of Ridley Scott's recent and proposed additions to the franchise he began have yet to emerge at the time of this writing, though there is no doubt that as 'prequels', *Prometheus* (2012) and its successors will one day face academic scrutiny. The 1979 film, however, does not articulate these fears so explicitly, and studies which look at the original film regard it either as a Science Fiction text (Luckhurst, 2014; Matheson, 1992) or as a horror film (Creed, 1986), foreshadowing later expansions of similar discussions in the sequels. The central figure of the *Alien* franchise eventually becomes Lieutenant Ellen Ripley (Sigourney Weaver), but in the first film she is merely one of the crowd of victims in a film which Vivian Sobchack dismisses as one of a 'few contemporary echoes of the earlier period in which space was inscribed as deep, and invasion still possible' (Sobchack, 1998: 228), as well as an example of a throwback to the 'bug-eyed monster' (43, 228, 293) movies of the 1950s – the same movies which Richard Hodgens calls a 'strange throwback of taste to something moldier and more "Gothic" than the Gothic Novel' (1959: 30).

In the production design of *Alien*, it is clear from the very first shot of a human-made spaceship that the film is going to be a Gothic text. The establishing shot presents the film's first SF novum and simultaneously sets the style of the film: as the pseudo-journalistic caption informs the audience, the structure is the mining tug *Nostromo* towing an ore refinery through deep space. This object looks very distinctly like a massive space cathedral. Science fiction production design frequently presents the unreal or not yet possible considered sets which are 'artificial' but 'mediate the narrative relationships between the material and the emotional; they objectify a nexus between exterior and interior, between the physical and the psychological universe' (Affron and Affron, 1995: 115). If what is presented at the beginning of a narrative evokes a sense of the sublime (here the individual lost in the glorious and terrifying void of space) while also being indexically similar in appearance to medieval architecture (structures that signify the insignificance of the human against the glory of a creator), and as similar approaches have been used throughout the first seventy years of cinematic horror to evoke a sense of terror and the supernatural, then it may be fair to assume upon first viewing that *Alien* is going to be a Gothic horror narrative set in space.

Vast spaces of dark architectural grandeur, tangled mossy woodlands, ruined spaceships or long, high corridors with misty, cathedral-like lighting are not merely chosen by *Alien*'s production designers as suitable spaces for Science Fiction action, but as environments that draw upon other aspects and other examples of the visual Gothic to create an understandable and immediately 'readable' Gothic aesthetic that recalls the stormy backdrops for many different versions of Frankenstein's monster, the battlements across which versions of Dracula have raced and the staircases up which damsels in gossamer dresses have fled (Affron and Affron, 1995: 118–23; Sobchack, 1998: 30–5). We know what these things look like in literature, because they have at their core a real-world style familiar from the crumbling architectures of medieval European ruins which were once constructed in the architectural Gothic style. In visual terms, understanding this style is key to understanding how the visual Gothic pervades all those other texts and, consequently, *Alien* too.

Approaching a satisfying definition of what comprises the visual Gothic can be drawn from what is arguably the most extant visual Gothic form: architecture. This is not an attempt to historically attach the visual Gothic with the architectural form which evolved from the Romanesque in the twelfth and thirteenth centuries, although any sense of a visual Gothic may evoke the pointed arch, flying buttress and ribbed enclave; those architectural forms were responses to the functionality of the previous form of architecture. They may be recognised as Gothic forms historically but identifying the impetus behind the design and creation of those forms is more helpful to this discussion.

In medieval architecture, the Romanesque – the movement from which the Gothic grew – demanded 'to be seen frontally' (Crossley, 2000: 10) from views arranged perpendicularly to each other. Durham Cathedral (1093) is a clear and spectacular example of this style: looming squarely over the English city, all four elevations are equally impressive. In contrast to the Romanesque, Gothic architecture was designed around diagonal axes so that all superficial details could be seen from multiple angles and 'from a variety of points' (Crossley, 2000: 10). The effect was one that required viewers to regard structures separately from the demands of the mechanical architectural form (the layout, the utility, the structure); the architecture's decorative aspect 'touches upon the observer's perception of the building and deals with the mental images which the purely optical qualities of the architecture imprint on the memory' (9). The architectural Gothic developed from pre-existing structural forms, present in Romanesque architecture, which forced through its 'spatial division, the smooth flow of forces, and a predominance of diagonal views' (Frankl, 2000: 49) an impression of depth and an effect of 'growth as in plants' (49).

Examples of actual Gothic architecture (Frankl, 2000: 112–15) can be seen in the Cathedrals of Bourges (1193), Rouen (1200) or Reims (1210), but these architectural Gothic qualities are also evident in *Alien*'s set design. The refinery is a confusing labyrinth of dark, towering, interconnected spaces which starkly contrast with the endless, cramped, low corridors of the *Nostromo*, the space-tug in which the crew are quartered (Benson-Allcott, 2015: 271). When the monstrous alien escapes into the ducts of the *Nostromo* and the refinery, the crew are faced with the impossible task of trying to find it and survive. The audience is taken with them into the depths of an environment of uncanny 'post-human futurity' (271) full of multiple, interconnected spaces that have filled the 'spectator with horror well before the crew awakes or the alien starts wreaking havoc' (270). Such spaces provoke a sense of liminality through its 'spatial division', its 'smoothness of flow' and its sense of depth created by its 'predominance of diagonal views' (Crossley, 2000: 50) that encourage spectators to feel like every space flows into, or is connected with, another space beyond the one observed. This spatial arrangement gives rise to the liminal sense of contiguousness; each space is neither the 'inside' or 'outside' of the other, but rather a constantly moving state of 'between'. The liminality and verticality of actual Gothic architectures do not have to be physically present for the Gothic to be visually evoked, only alterations in the decorative qualities of the visual are enough to evince the Gothic, 'the memory of those impressions compressed into a single, synthetic mental "image"' (Crossley, 2000: 10).

The visual Gothic is concerned with the 'superficial qualities of architecture – light, colour, and surface effects' (Crossley, 2000: 10), and in *Alien*'s set design, Ridley Scott evokes these Gothic designs. One aspect of this is evidenced through the way in Scott lights the majority of the film's spaces: 'Light pours across the screen in a kind of phosphorescent mist; heavy back light and the use of incense smoke as a filter create a nostalgic-romantic ambience' (Andrews and Kennedy, 1979: 18). This lighting is used in conjunction with the labyrinthine spaces and muted colour pallet to enhance the sense of the Gothic. Scott, interviewed in 1979, admits: 'I prefer smoke, because a gauze or a filter has a tendency to flatten. Incense increases the depth and adds a three dimensional quality' (18) that enhances the sense that these spaces are not just divided, but rather flow into each other in the gloom producing zones of intensity which lure the spectator's gaze into 'spaces they cannot master, spaces that elude their powers of perception and reveal their limited agency' (Benson-Allcott, 2015: 272). If, as Fred Botting suggests, 'Gothic representations are a product of cultural anxieties about the nature of human identity' (2002: 280), then the Gothic spaces of *Alien* present environments filled with isolated terror, and in which there is nowhere to go but 'deeper in' (Benson-Allcott, 2015: 272). In *Alien*, it is enough that some of the visual and spatial qualities are present to evoke the impression of Gothic, and any visual element which does so also evokes all the other Gothic images the spectator is familiar with. These images are not just those associated with medieval church architecture, but the crumbling reimaginings of the half century of cinema since F. W. Murnau's *Nosferatu* (1922) and other early horror films. Evoking Gothic visuals is sufficient to call to mind all others experienced, and because of the predominance of its association with horror, it is the visual association that fills 'the spectator with horror' (Benson-Allcott, 2015: 270).

When the decorative aspect of the Gothic is considered as a visual component, it is not necessarily fixed to the architectural features of familiar medieval churches such as the pointed arch; it is merely the reason for the point in the Romanesque arch. The arch, of course, has an architectural function; the Gothic architectural approach applies a smoothness along a vertical access so that the arch looks like it is 'a vertically rising stream of force, an organism growing like a plant' (Frankl, 2000: 10). The arch's function has not changed, but the optical impression should add a decorative aspect to what is already there. Visually, then, the Gothic can be understood as an application of decoration to an architectural feature that provides it with a vertical quality that evokes a sense of organic growth. In *Alien* this is taken to the extreme. Scott employed the Swiss surrealist H. R. Giger, whose specialty was a 'machine-age eroticism' (Andrews and Kennedy, 1979: 19), to oversee the design and construction of the alien monster, the mysterious alien spacecraft, its (dead) attendant and the alien planet surface (Andrews and Kennedy, 1979; Scott, 1996: 18). Ron Cobb was the designer responsible for the Earth-based Gothic of the *Nostromo* and its refinery; Giger was responsible for the organic alien landscape reminiscent of 'strewn bones' and the alien spacecraft interior, which looked like a 'gigantic windpipe' (Scott, 1996: 18). If the *Nostromo* is spatially Gothic, flowing through liminal 'zones of horror' (Benson-Allcott, 2015), then the alien world created by Giger is certainly the organic Gothic, its decoration of the alien architecture achieving the flow of a 'vertically rising stream of force, an organism growing' (Crossley, 2000: 10) on an alien world that echoes Giger's famous 'anthropomorphic shapes' and 'machine parts' that 'writhe together in a futuristic bacchanalia' (Andrews and Kennedy, 1979: 19). This bio-mechanical design, based directly on Giger's H. P. Lovecraft-inspired *Necronomicon* paintings, extends to the depiction of the alien itself.

The imposition of the alien, the prime novum of the film, into the protagonists' space ship is perhaps the final visual Gothic element that should be addressed here. At the insistence of Dan O'Bannon, the film's screenwriter, the crew of the *Nostromo* are not the polished and fresh-faced astronauts familiar to Science Fiction cinema of this time, nor are they the youthful adventurers of the then recent *Star Wars* (1976), or the paramilitary pioneers of the *Star Trek* TV series (1966–9). The crew of the *Nostromo* have a 'weathered, lived in look' and reside in 'cluttered domesticity' (Andrews and Kennedy, 1979: 20). They are essentially blue-collar oil riggers. Such a shift in the class structures that a late twentieth century SF film like *Alien* depicts is reminiscent of a similar shift found in the literary Victorian Gothic (Warwick, 2007: 30–1), which saw a shift in the location and class of its protagonists from aristocratic castles to middle- and educated working-class domestic spaces. This shift appealed to the empathies of the Victorian Gothic's key audience, and it also resited the space of the Gothic and, consequently, the ambivalence and anxieties associated with the Gothic, from the castle to the household. In shifting the look of the *Nostromo* from the antiseptic 'realist' look of the vessels in *2001: A Space Odyssey* (Kubrick, 1968), the bridge of the *Enterprise* or the magical, well-lit space-tech of *Star Wars*, towards the grungy, cramped quarters of a blue-collar space ship, O'Bannon and Scott shift the social focus so that *Alien* achieves what Darko Suvin defines as a movement towards the known: what is socially normal and therefore 'subject to a *cognitive* glance' (Suvin, 1976: 61). Ironically, considering the Affrons' insistence that SF film set designs are 'patently unreal' (Affron and Affron, 1995: 39), the Gothic visual element here works towards the efficacy of *Alien*'s SF credentials despite objectifying the 'nexus between . . . the physical and the psychological universe' (1995: 115), and against the text's anti-cognitive elements (Suvin, 1976: 62–3).

Alien is perhaps the Ur example of a Gothic space horror. Thematically, however, it eschews many of the Gothic narrative elements we are familiar with in other Gothic texts: the damsels are not damsels, the super-males are not so super, the alien is not a supernatural beast, just a scientifically incomprehensible one; there is no romantic sub-plot and no painful memory of a lost love (Russ, 1973: 666–8). Apart from being in danger of evoking Hodgen's maligned 'moldier . . . "Gothic"' (1959: 30), the horror conventions resemble the conventions of the Male

Gothic narrative (Williams, 1995: 102–4). Anne Williams's formula for this collection of Gothic themes 'simply posits the supernatural as a "reality"' (102) and 'has a tragic plot' (102) where the survivors 'emerge from the concluding apocalyptic orgy of violence … permanently marked by what they have suffered' (103). In *Alien*, any semblance of a Female Gothic is side-lined or lost. The Female Gothic allows room for the themes of terror and not horror, and *Alien* downplays the terror created by moments of uncanniness and aspects of the sublime which are restricted to the spatial design of the text. With the arguable exception of the haywire robot, *Alien* is a Male Gothic Horror enhanced by all the elements of Williams's formula but explained away through the nova of the xenomorphic monster the crew find on a planet, or the malfunctioning of a robot on a clandestine mission, or the ruthlessness of a faceless corporation. Through these explanations, *Alien* does not feel overtly like a Gothic text beyond the 'look' of it. Many of the aspects of the horror can be explained as SF nova, but it is worth noting that the design leads us immediately to the discomfiture evoked by a visual Gothic, and those same nova can also be read as Male Gothic horror elements enhanced by a deliberately Gothic 'look'. That said, despite *Alien*'s apparent credentials as an Ur-Gothic SF horror text, not every hybridising of Gothic with SF will be horrific.

Moon (2009) and the Female Gothic

The Lunar Industries mining base in Duncan Jones's *Moon* (2009) looks like the *Nostromo*. This is deliberately done, as is the inclusion of a large leather armchair which looks anachronistically out of place in the otherwise high-gloss and white-base interior: a reference to the waiting room at the finale of *2001: A Space Odyssey* (1968) (Jones, D. et al., 2009). Although done with the intention of referencing its SF forebears, the design schema of white corridors with padded panels, inlaid and bas-relief hexagonal-motifs, and a system of symbolic graphic fonts placed against bulkheads and pressure doors do more than simply reference the functionality of Ron Cobb's interior designs from Scott's *Alien*. In echoing the visuals of the *Nostromo*, the production design also, unintentionally perhaps, references the Gothic elements in the *Nostromo* and the alien threat from that earlier SF text. In establishing the base as similar to the interiors found in *Alien*, Jones begins the story of Sam Bell in a suitably Gothic manner; he establishes a familiar Gothic visual as the backdrop to his Gothic tale. Sam Bell believes he is the sole custodian, save for an AI companion called GERTY, of a Lunar Industries automated mining base on the Moon that suffers from a spatial and temporal isolation from Earth. There seems to be a communications malfunction, which later turns out to be a deliberate blackout, so Sam can only send and receive recorded messages to Earth. Sam has two weeks remaining of his three-year contract and will soon be returning to his estranged wife and their daughter. Unfortunately, while attempting to fix one of the automated mining machines out on the lunar surface, he gets into an accident of which, when he wakes, he has no memory. His AI companion takes care of him through his recovery, and eventually Sam wants to resume work against GERTY and the Lunar Industries Executive Board's advice. By Tricking GERTY into letting him out of the base and onto the lunar surface, Sam Bell discovers a wrecked lunar rover inside of which is another Sam Bell – the original Sam Bell from the start of the film. The original Sam is rescued by his unwitting clone, and the two, with GERTY's help, uncover the conspiracy of the Sam Bells who have gone before them and the others who will come after them.

The theme of cloning, and the ontological and philosophical discussions (Sundvall, 2015; Wight, 2017) that are supplemental to this resurgently popular SF novum, has dominated contemporary musings on the social implications of a Science Fiction turned reality since 1997 and the successful cloning of Dolly the Sheep. Other recent explorations can be found in *Never Let Me Go* (Romanek, 2010), *The Island* (Bay, 2005), *Oblivion* (Kosinski, 2013), TV's *Orphan Black* (Fawcett et al., 2013–16) and Warner Brothers' DC Comics-inspired animation *Young Justice* (2010–present) and its associated DC comic series (Kane et al., 2011). Literary SF has long pondered the implications of scientifically enabled reproduction, with Mary Shelley's 1818 *Frankenstein; or, The Modern Prometheus* being the main example, and there are several literary Gothic texts exploring the idea of the double or doppelgänger (e.g. Edgar Allan Poe's 'William Wilson' (1839), Alexandre Dumas's *The Corsican Brothers* (1852), Charles Dickens's *The Haunted Man and the Ghost's Bargain* (1848)). Sigmund Freud rests part of his 1919 psychoanalytical essay on aesthetics, 'The Uncanny', upon an example drawn from the work of his colleague Otto Rank on H. H. Ewer's 1913 motion picture, *The Student of Prague* (Freud, 2003: 142), one of the earliest films to use a double exposure technique to have the same actor play two characters on screen at once. As with the set design, these references are evoked regardless of their intention, and *Moon* is an uncanny text as much as it is a Science Fiction text. The novum of cloning is simultaneously an SF conceit and a central Gothic tenet. What makes *Moon* 'more' Gothic, however, is not just the visual allusion to a previous Gothic SF work depicting cloning, but the frame into which the novum is worked. The audience is offered a mystery tale; the original Sam Bell that we meet is a haunted person: he has visions of a mysterious young woman, who first appears in his armchair and then, later, standing on the lunar surface, an action that causes his accidental collision with the automated mining vehicle. This young woman, clothed in a yellow floral summer dress with loose dark hair, is a vision of his grown daughter, but Sam Bell believes his daughter is only three years old down on Earth. Thus the vision of the strange young woman haunts him. As Sam struggles to bear separation from his infant daughter, he is also haunted by vivid intimate memories of his courtship of her mother, and as he nears the end of his 'contract' with Lunar Industries, his desperation to return home becomes manifest in his actions: he is tired and irritable with GERTY, frustrated with his employers and impatient with his surroundings. When the new Sam is vivified after the original Sam's accident, we see what a fresh-faced and eager Sam resembles, and the contrast between the original Sam and the new Sam becomes more pronounced as it becomes increasingly clear that the older clone's viability is declining. Sam's 'contract' is a lifespan of servitude, like that of the Robots in Karel Capek's *Rossum's Universal Robots* (1920) or the replicants in *Blade Runner* (Scott, 1982). Here again the duality of the central novum as both SF device and Gothic device becomes clear: the artificial body is artificially finite as a method of control; eventually Sam Bell would want to return to earth, presumably as the true Sam Bell once did. His clones are given artificial memory implants to keep them motivated to work and complete their mission. As his body decays, however, those memories become too present, haunting his conscious mind and opening his unconscious mind in ways that are not fully explained by the novum's scientific aspects. A clone vivified with pre-set knowledge could, or rather should, have no access to information that it does not awake with, and yet the dying Sam Bell is somehow able to see visions of his grown daughter. This is a transcendental Gothic indulgence otherwise restricted by the metaphysical verisimilitude of SF.

Perhaps then it is worth revisiting *Moon*'s visual design. If, outwardly, the novum of the text might seem to be SF that functions as Gothic, then the outwardly visual SF might also function as a Gothic visual. *Moon* copies some aspects of the *Nostromo*'s interior very closely, from the concealed lighting at the peripheries of the corridors to the way the airlock doors function partly internally, partly externally. The resemblance is deliberate, but only the *Nostromo* is referenced; the other parts of the *Alien*'s principle sets are absent, and the exterior model shots of the lunar base imply that the interior of the base is not a synecdoche for larger industrial Gothic spaces which might be contiguous with Sam Bell's living quarters. The base is sprawling and squat; the refinery that the *Nostromo* tows is towering and cathedral-like. The lunar base is deliberately not Gothic in its appearance apart for the superficial interior decoration appearing like the *Nostromo*. However, this is itself an indication of the Gothic: the visual Gothic takes the pre-existing architectural form and draws attention to the detail and the decoration. If these decorations are flying buttresses and grotesques, that is one thing, but *Moon*'s design deliberately evokes the *Nostromo*'s cramped domestic social spaces. Like the class-shift in *Alien* from the presentable bourgeois imaginings of the future to the blue-collar, we are reminded once again what a blue-collar future may look like in *Moon*, a film released a few months after the very flashy, expensive and neat-looking *Star Trek* (2009) reboot from J. J. Abrams. The lunar base is grimy and lived-in, but it is also curiously open: each section of the base that we see is contiguous with the next, one end of the base can be seen easily from the other with no obstructions save those for the the bulkheads which divide it. Sam has to negotiate these trip-hazards if he is to travel any-where in the base, passing through the slightly more passable 'openings' which all lay to one side of a wider and narrower letter-box opening in each bulkhead. These openings resemble keyholes laid upon their sides and serve two functions: they make the space antagonistic to comfort-able domestic existence, and they provide divisions in a single space so that each 'room' appears individual, but also contiguous and liminal, neither one thing nor another. In short, they re-establish the Gothic sense of a divided space that flows spatially but not mechanically. It may lack an organic sense of verticality and the textures or lighting of the more visibly Gothic *Alien*, but spatially it is achieving a similar effect: it makes the lunar base antagonistic, liminal and draws our attention to the surface details, such as the visual references to another text – *Alien* – where almost everyone dies. The base is not tall, but still appears 'vaulted', and it is not until a 'secret room' is discovered that the set's Gothic becomes clear: the secret room found directly below Sam Bell's living quarters is the clone storage area. It is not an apse or basilica, but a tomb. Architecturally, it is the same as above, vaulted and liminal. But unlike the base above, it seems to stretch on forever, it is coloured granite-grey and it is dimly lit. Lining the walls are access chambers with sleeping clones ready to be awakened into duty. The chamber is a reverse mausoleum, full of potential Sam Bells. The space Sam discovers is quintessentially what Diana Wallace describes in her exploration of the Female Gothic as a 'womb and tomb' (Wallace, 2013: 26), a birthing space positioned beneath a haunted site of domestic decay. The duality of these spaces, one clearly visually more Gothic than the other, is the difference in realised form between the Male and the Female Gothic:

> [T]he Female Gothic Centralises the female point of view, and generates suspense through its limitation, the Male Gothic uses multiple points of view to generate dramatic irony ... [T]he Female Gothic explains the ghosts, the male formula accepts the supernatural as part of the 'reality' of its world. (17)

The lunar base in which the clones live as motherless constructs of science is the primary Male Gothic space of the narrative. It is here where we are introduced to the first of the SF nova: a lunar mining operation. As the narrative progresses and Sam becomes increasingly haunted by the past and by visions of a young woman, we assume – as Sam does – that this is part of the narrative of the SF world we are watching, accepting it as part of the quotidian existence of a solitary space lighthouse keeper in the Male Gothic 'tradition'. When the newer Sam discovers the older one, we uncover the ironic aspects of the dramatic plot through the revelation of the SF novum of cloning. In accepting, as they do, the complexities of their situation as part of their 'ontological stasis' (Sundvall, 2015: 28), as well as the spatial controls of their desires imposed by the communication restrictions on the base as part of the dramatic narrative, we could dismiss the Male Gothic elements of this text as texture that contributes to the SF discussion of the socio-political implications of the cloning novum. The discovery of the secret room, however, inverts this and forces us to consider this as an overtly Gothic text: in the womb-tomb, we are provided with an explanation for where the Sam Bells come from and the reason for their existence, a limitation, albeit an apparently vast one (the mausoleum stretches into the darkness), is provided. Until this point, the narrative of Sam Bell and his clone could still be accepted as SF. Peculiarly, though, this explanation is grounded in a sense by the vast quantity of 'back-up' Sam Bell clones, the narrative's explanation of how this is achieved and how the mining operation is maintained. This explanatory twist shifts *Moon* from an SF centred upon an acceptance of Gothic indicators towards a more Female Gothic narrative in which suspense is generated by 'limitations imposed by the chosen point' rather than the film's initial 'setup' and the eventual 'dramatic irony' accepted by both clones (Williams, 1995: 105). After the discovery of the womb-tomb, the situation is no longer accepted but explained and endured and eventually railed against. We are afforded an explanation for the older Sam's decay and for the haunting hallucinations, though not necessarily for the content of the hallucinations. There is still one transcendental problem that is unexplained by the Female

Gothic or literary SF definitions: how does Sam know what his daughter looks like before he sees her on the video call he finally manages to make to his 'home'?

In a final Female Gothic act, the newer Sam Bell climbs aboard a coffin-like (womb-like) transporter and is fired back to Earth just as a crew, who have been dispatched on an armed 'rescue' mission, land at the base and discover the dead original Sam Bell in his crashed rover. The shift in Gothic tone from Male Gothic to Female Gothic also shifts the film's SF dramatic narrative significantly from one of simmering horror, which may have ended up with the grisly deaths of one or both the clones at the hands of each other or their rescuers, to one of terror and suffering but eventual escape, with a seemingly happy ending (Wallace and Smith, 2009: 17; Williams, 1995: 103).

It would seem at this point that the position of Gothic as a hybrid genre or supplementary style can affect an SF narrative considerably. *Moon* is an example of SF hybridising with Gothic elements to create a narrative that is immediately recognisable as SF but is extensively affected by the shift between Male Gothic and Female Gothic narrative modes. The next section looks at Alex Garland's *Ex Machina* (2015) and asks: can the same be said for a Gothic text hybridising with SF conventions?

Ex Machina (2015) Female/Male Gothic SF

Ex Machina (2015) is very clearly a retelling of the Bluebeard tale combined with SF conventions that evoke, in narrative terms, a remodelled and updated Frankenstein in the figure of Nathan Bateman, who creates a female Artificial Intelligence. Essentially, though, *Ex Machina* is a film that, as Katie Jones argues, uses 'SF conventions' and alternate versions of the Bluebeard mythos (Jones, K., 2016: 15) to examine gender politics. Jones's use of this type of Gothic can broadly be identified with a Female Gothic framework. It involves the incarceration and eventual emancipation of a woman. In older versions of the Bluebeard tale, the young bride is given keys to every room and told to wander about her new husband's castle, but she is warned not to enter the one room that the smallest key fits. Given the opportunity, the bride transgresses her husband's wishes and enters the room in which her husband keeps the tortured bodies of his previous disobedient wives (Jones, K., 2016: 4). In terms of the Female Gothic, the Bluebeard narrative fits quite well; the emphasis is on terror, with all elements rationalised and explained, while the narrative is focused upon the female protagonist and her efforts towards self-emancipation (Williams, 1995: 102–4). The Female Gothic is not necessarily feminist, especially in the case of *Ex Machina*, as it is 'unsuited for transgressing the margins that constrict and confine a potentially limitless space for new ways of being, becoming and desiring as a woman' (Jones, K., 2016: 21). Although this may be the case where *Ex Machina* as a Female Gothic is concerned, Jones's dissatisfaction with the gender politics in this retelling of the Bluebeard myth may be because the 'major peaks' of the Female Gothic are usually 'connected with the waves of feminism' historically (Wallace and Smith, 2009: 19). As Jones points out, though: 'Ultimately the portrayal of passive femininity, repeated scenes of female nudity and the exploitation cinema aesthetics of *Ex Machina* merely duplicate and consolidate the cinematic tropes of fetishized/abject femininities' (Jones, K., 2016: 21). *Ex Machina*, despite resembling a Bluebeardian Gothic apropos of the Female Gothic, fails to be feminist in its application of SF nova.

Ex Machina's Female Gothic foundations present a plot about the emancipation of a woman from the physical and psychological abuse of her male imprisoner and creator, Nathan Bateman, a computer-age prodigy. Caleb, a computer programmer at Nathan's tech-giant corporation, 'BlueBook', is chosen by Nathan to assess the viability of an Artificial Intelligence. Created by a process of data-mining and a range of unspecified technologies, the Strong AI has been housed in the fragmented and uncanny body of Ava, a female android. Nathan keeps Ava in a subterranean glass and concrete apartment filled with security cameras, a modernised version of a glass cage for Nathan's monstrous prisoner (Gilbert and Gubar, 2000: 89). Caleb and Ava's discussions are scrutinised by the overly athletic, aggressively masculine, fully-bearded and often semi-naked Nathan. The Bluebeardian elements are so spelled out by Alex Garland, the film's director, that it becomes 'difficult to get past the hour mark without figuring out what is going to happen next' (Wright, 2015: 12). Caleb is positioned as Nathan's 'new bride' and offered the keys to the castle. In a knowing meta-textual twist common to contemporary re-imaginings of the Bluebeard story, he is told which areas he does not have access to (Mulvey-Roberts, 2009: 98–114).

In this sense, Caleb is positioned as the 'new bride', but only partially, until he is introduced to the other half: the gynoid Ava, who is already imprisoned and fulfils the more expected iteration of the 'new bride' role than Caleb does alone. The conflation of these two characters into a single Bluebeardian role is the first of several elements that make the reworking of this story problematic in terms of gender. As Ava asserts her humanity, Caleb questions his own; as Caleb's relationship with Ava becomes deeper, he increasingly empathises with her predicament and is repositioned as her rescuer. Furthermore, Nathan's relationship with Caleb, which began as mentorship, becomes more pressed and antagonistic as Nathan pushes to groom Caleb toward joining him in his Bluebeardian project, and as Caleb steadily becomes a Bluebeard figure himself (Jones, K., 2016: 12–15, 21).

Ex Machina is set in an immanent and recognisable future – a tech-modern, Frank Lloyd-Wright style country retreat-cum-lab. This modern concrete mansion is minimally decorated with high-design furniture and eclectic works of fine art. To contemporise the isolated castle motif further, the house is geographically secluded within an extensive and untouched wilderness of deliberately sublime natural beauty: glaciers are reachable upon foot and cascading waterfalls, pine jungles and unscalable mountains form the backdrop of Nathan and Caleb's constitutional rambles in the environs around the house.

Despite the often neat contemporising of the visual Gothic tropes of the mansion and the sublime environs, it is the SF conventions that make this text ultimately, as Katie Jones argues, a 'failure' (2016: 1) in feminist terms. It is unable to reconcile the aims of the Female Gothic (emancipation and resistance) cleanly because they are intermingled with too many layers of objectification and disembodiment of the central 'female' figure. Ava's body is constructed of a transparent material that displaces like flesh but shatters like glass, allowing views both through and into her body. Ava is not merely housed in a glass cage, but her body is also glass and fully transparent; only her hands, feet and face are flesh. Only the areas around her breasts and pelvic region, which are opaque and grey, are the exception. Ava is feminine but imprisoned within her own 'alien and loathsome body' (Gilbert and Gubar, 2000: 89). This disembodiment of her female form makes her ostensibly naked: this is an aspect of the character made more evident in various dressing and undressing scenes. In the first of these, demure clothes hide her transparency from Caleb but only serve to make her look more vulnerable and in need of saving. Later, in a scene that follows the murder of Nathan at the hands of his creations, Eva strips a deactivated predecessor of her synthetic flesh. Placing the 'skin' over her transparent frame Eva 'dresses' to appear as a fully nude (i.e. covered in human flesh and hair) young human woman under the ever-watchful gaze of Caleb, her would-be rescuer. When Ava escapes, clothed in a white dress, she walks past Gustav Klimt's portrait of Margaret Stonborough Wittgenstein (1905), overemphasising the 'male visions of femininity and the exchange of women through patriarchal institutions' (Jones, K., 2016: 19), and deserts Caleb in a glass prison of his own. In her escape, Ava becomes an objectified female body watched by her would-be rescuer and reflected by mirrors that hide Nathan's failures. '[S]he remains', in Jones's assertion, 'entombed by the patriarchal symbolic as she embodies the fetishized feminine subject' (Jones, K., 2016: 19), but the two new layers of clothing, one of flesh and one of patriarchal institution, cannot disguise to the audience that beneath the appearance of a 'nude, young, white woman' (Jones, K., 2016: 19) is a monstrous glass non-human female killer.

The gendering, sexualising, and scopohilic framing of this 'gynoid' (Jones, K., 2016: 1) renders 'her' eventual escape into a sublime, isolating landscape of mountains and forests a pyrrhic feminist victory. The compounding factor in this is Eva's betrayal of her Gothic counterpart, Caleb. After fooling him with his own trust and objectification of her multi-layered body, she leaves him to die in a glass prison of his very own. Eva becomes the site of technologised fears imposed upon her by her Frankenstein creator, a SF theme explored by many SF texts contemporary to *Ex Machina*, including *Humans* (Jonathan Brackley and Sam Vincent, 2015–18), and the very similar 2013 film by Caradog Williams *The Machine*.

Nathan creates Eva from scratch using unexplained scientific means, and we are even introduced to his laboratory and prototypes as he explains how his AI novum was created. When Caleb discovers the record of Nathan's horrifying previous attempts, the text shifts noticeably towards the horror associated with the Male Gothic. It is this SF imposition upon a Female Gothic text that stultifies and reframes it as a male horror: the Frankenstein conventions make *Ex Machina* another tale 'of the male overreacher' (Wallace and Smith, 2009: 2) plagued by his abject creation: a monstrous female 'other' who kills him and escapes into the world.

Conclusion

In *Ex Machina* we have a reverse example from *Moon* of the hybridisation of the styles and themes of Gothic and SF: if *Moon* is an SF with constructive and oscillating Gothic elements which drive the narrative, then *Ex Machina* is a Gothic psycho-drama with an interfering SF novum which produces a text that ultimately consolidates the objectification of women 'even though it may critique it' (Jones, K., 2016: 21).

It is interesting that in the case of *Alien* the Gothic elements are fixed in the visuals of the film. The thematic Gothic in *Alien* can be treated as a Male Gothic, but it can also be read as part of the SF constructions of the text. In *Ex Machina*, the SF conventions added to a Female Gothic text renders those themes problematic at best, forcing the narrative to present itself as a much more Male Gothic than it would otherwise be. In the shift between the Male and Female Gothic in *Moon* we are allowed a more thoughtful exploration of the SF nova than would otherwise have happened if the film had pursued the Male Gothic elements set up in the first act of the film.

Despite it being 'less congenial to SF' (Suvin, 1976: 62), the application of a Gothic element to SF adds to the 'transcendentalism of magic and religion' (Sobchack, 1998: 63) that functions in SF film, whether that element is a Female Gothic terror, a Male Gothic Horror or a visual Gothic which draws from the texts of both. If *Moon* handled its narratives with only Male Gothic aspects, we might be expected to accept it is 'pure' SF despite its exploration of the 'uncanny' double. *Moon*, however, seems to oscillate between the Male and the Female Gothic; outwardly it is an SF with few visually Gothic elements, but those that are there can be read retrospectively after the narrative shifts from a Male-centred Gothic to a Female Gothic. If any Gothic elements exist in the *Alien* narrative, they are most certainly Male ones 'specialising in horror' (Williams, 1995: 102): the alien is accepted as what it is while the multiple characters interact and antagonise each other until they meet their grisly ends. Outwardly it is a space horror with visually Gothic elements that draw upon intertextual sources, namely our memories and ideas about what Gothic looks like. This process is an unending one and is perhaps the most enduring aspect of the visual Gothic in SF, as can be seen by the many films influenced by the design of *Alien*, *Moon* included.

One of the interesting things forwarded in the introduction of this chapter was the hope from David Seed that the 'issue is not so much whether SF grows out of the Gothic . . . but rather how responsive SF texts would be to an interpretation informed by Gothic practices' (Seed 2005: 3). As a final point, and as testament to how enduring the intertextual influence of the visual Gothic is, we can consider the recent TV series *Orphan Black* (2013–17). In the fourth season of the show (aired 2016), one of the clone sisters, Rachel, is imprisoned in an intertextually familiar, tech-modern country retreat-cum-lab. This tech-modern concrete mansion is minimally decorated with high-design furniture and eclectic works of fine art. To contemporise the isolated castle motif further, the house is geographically isolated within an extensive and untouched wilderness of deliberately sublime natural beauty. It is also subterranean and bears a striking resemblance to the set of *Ex Machina*. If the visual Gothic is the addition of decoration to existing forms, add this 'mad scientist's lab' to the list of visually Gothic locations.

Note

1. 'SF' is the appropriate abbreviation used by current scholarship (cf. Roberts, 2006) and will be used interchangeably with Science Fiction throughout this chapter.

References

Affron, C. and Affron, M. J. 1995. *Sets in Motion: Art Direction and Film Narrative*. New Brunswick, NJ: Rutgers University Press.

Aldiss, B. 1973. *Billion Year Spree: The History of Science Fiction*. London: Weidenfield & Nicholson.

Andrews, N. and Kennedy, H. 1979. 'Space Gothic', *American Film*, 5, pp. 17–22.

Benson-Allcott, C. 2015. 'Dreadful Architecture: Zones of Horror in *Alien* and Lee Bontecou's Wall Sculptures', *Journal of Visual Culture*, 14: 3, 267–78. Web. Accessible: https://doi.org/10.1177/1470412915607926 (accessed 4 January 2017).

Bratlinger, P. 1980. 'The Gothic Origins of Science Fiction', *NOVEL: A Forum on Fiction*, 14: 1, pp. 30–43.

Botting, F. 2002. 'After Gothic: Consumption, Machines, and Black Holes', in Hogle, J. E. (ed.), *The Cambridge Companion to Gothic Fiction*. Cambridge: Cambridge University Press, pp. 277–300.

Botting, F. 2005. 'Monsters of the Imagination: Gothic, Science, Fiction', in Seed, D. (ed.), *A Companion to Science Fiction*. Oxford: Wiley-Blackwell, pp. 111–26.

Clayton, D. 1987. 'Science Fiction: Going Round in Generic Circles', in Slusser, G. E. and Rabkin, S. (eds), *Intersections: Fantasy and Science Fiction*. Riverside, IL: Southern Illinois University, pp. 201–4

Creed, B. 1986. Horror and the Monstrous-Feminine: An Imaginary Abjection', *Screen*, 27: 1, pp. 44–70.

Crossley, P. 2000. 'Introduction by Paul Crossley', in P. Frankl, *Gothic Architecture* [1962]. Revised edn by Paul Crossley. New Haven, CT: Yale University Press.

Dickens, C. 2016. *The Haunted Man and the Ghost's Bargain* [1848] [(Web). Accessible https://archive.org/stream/hauntedmanthegho00dickuoft#page/n11/mode/2up (4 January 2017).

Dumas, A. 2007. *The Corsican Brothers* [1844], trans. Brown, A. London: Hesperus Press.

Evnine, S. J. 2015. '"But Is It Science Fiction?": Science Fiction and a Theory of Genre', *Midwest Studies in Philosophy*, 39: 1, pp 1–28.

Frankl, P. 2000. *Gothic Architecture* [1962]. Revised edn by Paul Crossley. New Haven, CT: Yale University Press.

Freud. S. 2003. *The Uncanny* [1919], trans. David McLintock. London: Penguin.

Gilbert, S. M. and Gubar, S. 2000. *The Madwoman in the Attic: The Woman*

Writer and the Nineteenth Century Literary Imagination, 2nd edn. New Haven, CT and London: Yale University Press.

Hodgens, R. 1959. 'A Brief Tragical History of the Science Fiction Film', *Film Quarterly*, 13: 2, pp. 30–9.

Hogle, J. E. (ed.). 2010. *The Cambridge Companion to Gothic Fiction*, 8th edn. Cambridge: Cambridge University Press.

Hoppenstand, G. 2005. 'Editorial: Series(ous) SF Concerns', *Journal of Popular Culture*, 38: 4, pp. 603–4.

Jones, D., Shaw, G., Rothery, G. and Noble, T. 2009. *Moon DVD Commentary* [DVD]. Sony Pictures.

Jones, K. 2016. 'Bluebeardian Futures in Alex Garland's *Ex Machina*', *Gender Forum*, 28 (Web). Accessible: http://www.genderforum.org/issues/gender-and-captivity/bluebeardean-futures-in-alex-garlands-ex-machina-2015/ (29 December 2016).

Karel, C. 2016. *Rossum's Universal Robots* [1920] (Web). Accessible: https://ebooks.adelaide.edu.au/c/capek/karel/rur/ (4 January 2017).

Luckhurst, R. 2014. *Alien*. London: Palgrave Macmillan.

Matheson, T. J. 1992. 'Triumphant Technology and Minimal Man: *The Technological Society*, Science Fiction Films, and Ridley Scott's *Alien*', *Extrapolation*, 33: 3, pp. 215–29.

Mulvey-Roberts, M. 2009. 'From Bluebeard's Bloody Chamber to Demonic Stigmatic', in Wallace, D. and Smith, A. (eds), *The Female Gothic: New Directions*. New York: Palgrave Macmillan, pp. 98–114.

Poe, E. A. 1993. *The Complete Short Stories*. New York: Alfred K. Knopf.

Roberts, A. 2006. *Science Fiction*, 2nd edn. Abingdon: Routledge.

Russ, J. 1973. 'Somebody's Trying to Kill Me and I Think It's My Husband: The Modern Gothic', *Journal of Popular Culture*, 6: 4. pp. 666–91.

Scott, R. 1996. 'Alien', in Barany, L., Movie, G. T. and Cowan, J. R. (eds), *HR Giger's Film Design*. London: Titan Books.

Seed, D. 2005. 'Introduction: Approaching Science Fiction', in Seed, D. (ed.), *A Companion to Science Fiction*. Oxford: Wiley-Blackwell, pp. 1–8.

Shelley, M. 1992. *Frankenstein: Or, the Modern Prometheus*. London: Wordsworth Classics.

Sobchack, V. C. 1998. *Screening Space: The American Science Fiction Film*, 2nd edn. New Brunswick, NJ: Rutgers University Press.

Sundvall, S. 2015. 'Clonetrolling the Future: Body, Space and Ontology in Duncan Jones' Moon and Mark Romanek's Never Let Me Go', *Politics of Place* 2 [pdf]. Accessible: http://blogs.exeter.ac.uk/politicsofplace/files/2012/02/POP_Issue02_Sundvall.pdf (28 December 2016).

Suvin, D. 1976. 'On the Poetics of the Science Fiction Genre', in Rose, M. (ed.), *Science Fiction: A Collection of Critical* Essays. Englewood Cliffs, NJ: Prentice-Hall, pp. 57–71.

Wallace, D. 2013. *Female Gothic Histories: History, Gender and the Gothic*. Cardiff: University of Wales Press.

Wallace, D. and Smith A. 2009. *The Female Gothic: New Directions*. New York: Palgrave Macmillan.

Warwick, A. 2007. 'Victorian Gothic', in Spooner, C. and McEvoy, E. (eds), *The Routledge Companion to Gothic*. London: Routledge.

Wight, J. 2017. 'Reclaiming Virtue and Post Humanity in Moon', in Boone,

M. J. and Neece, K. C. (eds), *Science Fiction and the Abolition of Man: Finding C. S. Lewis in Sci-Fi Film and Television*. Eugene, OR: Wipf & Stock.

Williams, A. 1995. *Art of Darkness: A Poetics of Gothic*. Chicago: University of Chicago Press.

Wright, T. 2015. 'The Body Virtual', *The Lancet*, 385, p. 12.

Chapter 13

American Gothic Westerns: Tales of Racial Slavery and Genocide

Josef Benson

Nick Groom traces the roots of the Gothic tradition to barbarian tribes that emerged outside of Greco-Roman civilisation and eventually conquered the Roman Empire, ushering in the Middle Ages and marking a break between the classical and medieval periods in European history. Tribes such as the Visigoths and Ostrogoths sacked the Roman Empire, converted to Christianity and consequently linked with death, spirituality and a dark cultural aesthetic based on decay and rebirth. Where the European Gothic frequently symbolises an ancient past of barbarity and otherness that affected everything from architecture to politics, the American Gothic tradition reflects America's fairly recent but no less volatile and gory origins. Groom argues that the American Gothic draws on its historical legacy of racial slavery and the genocide of indigenous peoples, in addition to Europe's Gothic associations of violence, death and spirituality (2012).

The American Western genre is particularly well suited for American Gothic narratives since the genre itself emanated from both racial slavery and the genocide of indigenous peoples. This correlation is reflected in its common tropes of aestheticised violence and dehumanisation. While a classic American Western like *The Wild Bunch* (Sam Peckinpah, 1969) elevates violence to an aesthetic, functioning as imagistic residue of America's violent origins, a film such as *Django* (Sergio Corbucci, 1966) and later Westerns such as *Django Unchained* (Quentin Tarantino, 2012), *High Plains Drifter* (Clint Eastwood, 1973), *Dead Man* (Jim Jarmusch, 1995) and *Priest* (Scott Stewart, 2011) incorporate these elements ironically as rhetorical guerrilla warfare that harasses and parodies the genre itself.

The powerful associations of violence and death in relation to the European Gothic stems from barbarian tribes who conquered the Roman Empire and from the subsequent emergence of an architectural style that defined a sharp break with the classical period. As Groom notes, '[t]he spiritual meaning of architectural Gothic . . . ultimately led to a style associated with the darker side . . . a whole cultural landscape of death in the Mediaeval period' (22). Gothic architecture, characterised by ornate pillars, vaulting and pointed arches, literally pointed to God, and the more a structure reached towards the heavens the closer it was to God. As a demarcation point from classical antiquity, Gothic architecture also became a defining aspect of the Middle Ages in which, according to Groom, '[d]eath was omnipresent. This was not simply a fact of living with the terrifying mortality rates of the Black Death, which killed up to 60 per cent of the European population between 1348 and 1350 . . . [There] was also a culture of death that was centered on churches . . . [and] theological emphasis on Christ's suffering . . . The emphasis on mortality eventually developed into a cult of the macabre, reveling in the plight of the body' (22–3).

The American Gothic tradition inherited the European Gothic's associations of violence and spirituality that eventually burgeoned into macabre and fantastic images of ghosts, vampires and all manner of goblins and wraiths. These sensibilities variably combined with the added texture of America's unique and insidious spiritual vision of manifest destiny and frontier masculinity responsible for the victimisation of Africans and Native Americans. The American character of glorified violence informs Groom's contention that, '[d]omination and enslavement, torture and murder, rape and sexual violence . . . form the themes of American Gothic writing and later horror movies' (114) and that 'slavery, racial discrimination, and dehumanization are encoded in the . . . American Gothic' (121).

As the American Gothic points to the dehumanisation concomitant with the American colonisation of the New World, nowhere is this better illustrated than in the American Western. As Richard Slotnik notes, '[t]he myth of the Frontier is our oldest and most characteristic myth . . . According to this myth . . . the conquest of the wilderness and the subjugation . . . of the Native Americans who originally inhabited it have been the means to our achievement of a national identity' (9). The myth of the frontier pulls double duty in justifying not only westward expansion but also the primary dehumanising means by which the colonies developed into a powerful country. As Slotnik further points out, '[v]iolence is central to both the historical development of the Frontier and its mythic representation. The Anglo-American colonies grew by displacing Amerindian societies and enslaving Africans to advance the fortunes of White colonists. As a result, the "savage war" became a characteristic episode of each phase of westward expansion' (11). Violence, consequently, became the defining and necessary characteristic of the development of America as a global power. What distinguishes American violence is its mythic significance and symbolic power as the driving force toward progress and civilisation (13).

The archetypal American outlaw gunslinger's penchant for killing reflects America's belief that only through violence primarily directed at African slaves and Native Americans did America grow into a great nation. Mary Lea Bandy finds, '[t]he leading protagonist of the Western is pretty sure to be a man, but not a kindly, upright sort of guy ... He is likely to be a "good bad man"' (Bandy and Stoer, 2012: 2). Consequently, and perhaps absurdly, the symbol of the gun has developed into a marker of life and freedom instead of death and enslavement. Bandy further holds that '(e)ssential to the figure of the westerner is his weapon. Whether he carries a six-shooter or a rifle, Colt or Winchester, every man of the West has mastered the use of a gun ... Killing and avoiding being killed are ... his principal activities' (3).

The gunslinger protagonist and social bandit outlaw of the American Western has its roots in American slavery, emancipation and its aftermath. As Slotnik relates:

> The myths of social banditry are symbolic dramatizations of ... social conflicts ... In the South, this kind of conflict [arose] from the northern-imposed 'Reconstruction' of the former Confederacy: a complex of racial, political, and economic conflicts between freed slaves, poor Whites, former masters, and new plantation owners ... This latter type of conflict produced the James Gang. (1992: 129)

The James Gang provided America with its most famous outlaw, Jesse James, a southerner whose exploits were, at least initially, enacted in relation to the American government forcing southerners to adhere to the new laws of emancipation. The James Gang's post-war attempts to carry on the 'Lost Cause' of slavery developed into national stories carried by daily papers often depicting '[t]he anti-slavery forces, whose cruelties [drove] Jesse to rebellion and outlawry ... as "white trash", jealous of the Jameses' refinement' (136). The James Gang's transition from robbing banks to robbing trains in 1873–4 catapulted them to national stardom and muted their southern origins (137). Sealing this false narrative was 'Frank Triplett's *Life, Times and Treacherous Death of Jesse James*, which appeared just after Jesse's assassination in 1882 [and] was the foundation of the outlaw's literary mythology' (136). The association of banditry with train robbery became the central trope in cinema's very first Western, *The Great Train Robbery*: 'Edwin S. Porter's *The Great Train Robbery*, produced for the Edison Company in 1903, has long figured in the folklore of American mass culture as the progenitor of narrative cinema: "the first story film," the first to use a close-up, "the first Western"' (231). Jesse James symbolises not only the first famous American outlaw, an outlaw whose outlawry centred on his refusal to accept the freedom of black slaves, but he is also the inspiration for the first protagonist of an American Western.

All Westerns are to some degree violent and stem from American slavery, employing the civiliser/savage binary, but some Westerns elevate that violence to an aesthetic and employ these tropes ironically. Coupling elements of American Gothicity vis-à-vis American Western films with Linda Hutcheon's 'concept of irony as "counterdiscourse" . . . a "mode of combat" . . . "a *negative* passion, to displace and annihilate a dominant depiction of the world"' (1994: 30) wreaks havoc on a genre driven by white hypermasculine patriarchy. The Gothic mode has the potential to function as a counter-discourse that highlights the sexism, racism and homophobia endemic to a genre rooted in white supremacy and imperialism. Hutcheon asserts, 'irony has been seen as "serious play", as both a rhetorical strategy and a political method . . . that deconstructs and decenters patriarchal discourses. Operating almost as a form of guerrilla warfare, irony is said to work to change how people [engage in the process of] interpret[ation]' (32). Irony works as an interpretive mode, not a writerly mode. It makes no difference whether these films intended to be ironic or to undermine the genre. As Hutcheon argues, 'the final responsibility for deciding whether irony actually happens . . . (and what the ironic meaning is) rests, in the end, solely with the interpreter' (45). Some of these films hijack, appropriate and defamiliarise the genre by populating it with familiar characters – the stranger in town, the gunslinger and the avenger – whose hypermasculinity often manifests in rape, homosexuality, cannibalism and racialised sport-killing, all elements mostly hidden in more standard genre fare. As Hutcheon notes:

> The concept of irony as 'counter-discourse' . . . has been a mainstay of oppositional theories that take on such hierarchies – be they based on race, ethnicity, class, gender, sexuality . . . In this view, irony's intimacy with the dominant discourses that it contests . . . is its strength, for it allows ironic discourse both to buy time (to be permitted and even listened to, even if not understood) and also to 'relativize the [dominant's] authority and stability . . . in part by appropriating its power'. (1994: 30)

The risk is that the irony can be missed, in which case the film merely operates like a standard problematic Western. Hutcheon admits, 'all ironies, in fact, are probably unstable ironies' (1994: 195).

Sam Peckinpah's classic Western *The Wild Bunch* continually ranks near the top of the list of most violent films ever produced. Peckinpah elevated the Western trope of violence to new aesthetic heights. As Slotkin notes:

> Peckinpah ... [made] deliberate and sensational use of new special-effects technology to render as literally as possible the effects of bullets on human bodies ... giving the most violent scenes a balletic quality ... The 'exaggerated' display of bloodshed is in fact a truer representation of the real effects of violence. (1992: 593)

Peckinpah's attention to detail in relation to approximating the actual effects of bullets tearing through human flesh not only enhances the verisimilitude of the dramatic action but also humanises the action, making it difficult for audiences to gloss over the implication of mortal pain. The effect, while not necessarily macabre, anticipates what we might call a more mainstream use of the Euro-American Gothic style by accentuating the violence in the first place. Peckinpah's attempts at realism included the mutilation of women's bodies by violence in addition to eschewing archetypal Western heroes. As Slotkin notes:

> Since Peckinpah does not offer, within the film, an explicit denunciation of this kind of violence, the possibility is left open that the makers of this film will not scruple to show us forbidden actions and ideas, and that the heroes we will be asked to identify with may actually be monsters. (1992: 597)

Sergio Corbucci's 1966 film *Django* represents another motion picture that is both famous and controversial for its depiction of violence. While Corbucci's use of violence is not as realistic as Peckinpah's, images and symbols of violence and death exist as the focus of the film from the start. The opening sequence depicts Django, a former Union soldier, toting a coffin that he drags behind him in the mud. This scene, along with the opening credits that appear as though written in blood, situate the film as ironically Gothic in the Hutcheon sense of irony as a self-conscious counter-discourse. Furthermore, the heavy symbolism of a man dragging around what appears to be his own coffin, accompanied by 'bloody' credits and the Rocky Roberts theme song, is only made stranger and more overtly Gothic when Django happens upon a beautiful woman getting whipped and crucified. When one of the men refers to Django as a 'yankee' and says, '[w]e don't take much to folks who fought for the North. Get the idea?' we are firmly ensconced in the Euro-American Gothic style of violence, death, spirituality and dehumanisation.

The obvious correlation between Major Jackson's group of rebels and the KKK further demonstrates the American Gothic's penchant for echoing racial slavery. Maria, the mixed-raced woman at the centre of the film, says of Major Jackson, 'I think he hates anyone who isn't pale skinned and southern.' Jackson's extreme racism is underscored when he and his rebel gang are shown sport killing Mexicans by letting them see how far they can run before shooting them. While this scene does very little to advance the plot, it employs violence as a means of highlighting America's history of racial dehumanisation.

Django's violence and Gothic symbolism demonstrate the Western's most pernicious elements. This is not a love story. This is not a story about the Western landscape. This film does not romanticise the development of the frontier or seek to justify the violence used for Western expansion to fulfil the manifest destiny of US power stretching from coast to coast. Rather, *Django* exposes these elements and forces viewers to witness race-based atrocities. The film's use of violence is ironic and meant not only as a critique of racial violence but also as a critique of the Western genre.

Corbucci additionally appropriates European Gothic spiritual symbols, such as the coffin and (burning) crosses. The owner of the brothel where Maria works says of Major Jackson's rebels, who wear red hoods evocative of the KKK: 'Have you seen those strange hoods they wear? It's a religion with them. They're crazy.' Likening Major Jackson's extreme racism and refusal to accept emancipation to religion exemplifies the fusion of the European and the American Gothic, wedding both European spirituality with US slavery. Jackson says at one point, 'I got my own private war going on. I reckon maybe that's a war you haven't heard about.' Jackson's personal war reflects the lost cause of white supremacy, and his position as a rebel or bandit outlaw is reminiscent of the most famous bandit or outlaw of all time, Jesse James, the gunslinger, or cowboy, from which the future of Westerns derived.

Nearly a half century later, Quentin Tarantino released the film *Django Unchained* (2012), an American Western that operates as a parody of the Western genre and a pastiche of Corbucci's film. Tarantino's deployment of an American Gothic modality centres on slavery and classic Gothic symbols, such as the human skull. Tarantino channels Corbucci by co-opting the title as well as the lead character's name, Django, and employing the same theme song and sanguine opening credits. Ratcheting up the ironic use of violence by totally abandoning realism in favour of horror-style depictions of blood spatter, Tarantino, like Peckinpah, highlights the damage that bullets wreak on the human body. Unlike Peckinpah, however, Tarantino's effects are not geared toward realism. Bodies explode like water balloons in *Django Unchained*, drawing attention to the film as artifice and entertainment instead of historical fact. As G. R. Carpio argues, 'Django . . . [blows] bodies apart as he shoots, using dead white men as his shield . . . [making] blood spurt to high heavens in a violence that is so extreme it is hyperbolic' (2013: 112). Tarantino's hyperbolic special effects, especially his depiction of blood spatter, elevates the symbols of violence, firmly ensconcing *Django Unchained* within the American Gothic cinematic tradition. Perhaps the most explicitly Gothic scene in the film is when the plantation owner, Candie, saws the back of a skull belonging to a former family slave in order to advance a phrenological argument rooted in biological racism. Candie contends, and attempts to demonstrate, that black skulls are different from white skulls in that they have three dimples, signifying submissiveness and therefore justifying African enslavement.

In the film, blood frequently spatters against white backdrops like cotton or a white horse, signifying the brutalisation of black bodies against white backgrounds. Tarantino reserves the worst images of violence for black bodies that are alive. In one scene, dogs tear apart a black slave when he refuses to fight. In another, men whip Django's wife, Broomhilda, and she is later shown suffering in a hotbox as punishment for attempted escape. In yet another scene, black men are shown fighting to the death in the parlour of a plantation as white men who have made bets on the outcome urge them on.

Clint Eastwood's *High Plains Drifter* (1973) likewise weds the European and American Gothic traditions. The film employs aspects of the European Gothic in its use of ghosts, devils and coffins and the American Gothic in its focus on whipping and lynching as culturally specific forms of violence associated with American slavery and Native American genocide. While the film does not explicitly address the dehumanisation of African Americans or Native Americans, the constant flashbacks to the whipping of Marshall Duncan recall that history.

Similar to both *Django* films, the opening scenes of *High Plains Drifter* evoke the Gothic in the use of an eerie score and the ghostly emergence of the unnamed stranger. The film's primary critique of the genre centres on the anti-heroic nature of its protagonist. Clint Eastwood's character rides into town and within minutes kills three men and violently rapes a woman. One can argue that the stranger not only avenges the killing of the former marshal, for which the whole town is guilty, but also the Western genre itself by punishing its primary players.

When the unnamed stranger gallops into town out of the heat-waved horizon amidst a backdrop of mountains and to a chorus of eerily musical locusts, he rides past a prominent cemetery where the marshal is buried in an unmarked grave. Once in town, he takes note of a man making, or transporting, several coffins. These images and symbols of death are very much in line with the American Gothic tradition and symbolise America's history of human subjugation. The stranger is immediately startled by the sound of a bullwhip, foreshadowing what viewers soon realise to be the cause of the marshal's death as well as a primary signifier of America's history of slavery.

Alongside additional Gothic visual references, such as dwarfism,[1] the stranger is referred to as a 'devil' multiple times and seems to overtly turn the town of Lago into a living hell. As one of Lago's denizens remarks upon the stranger's arrival: 'Couldn't be worse if the devil himself had ridden right into Lago.' When the townspeople ask the stranger to protect them from their former protectors who took over the town and were subsequently jailed, they say to the stranger: 'What if we offered you anything you want?' To this, the stranger answers, 'Anything?' What the stranger means to take is their souls. Just before the marshal is whipped to death, he says to the townspeople who look on: 'Damn you to hell.'

The stranger orders the townspeople to paint the town red in anticipation of the former outlaws returning to seek revenge. One man says of this order, 'When we get done this place is gonna look like hell.' Later, when the preacher says that surely the stranger does not mean to damn the church, too, the stranger says, 'I mean especially the church.' The stranger then paints the word 'Hell' under the sign for Lago. Later in the film, one of the corrupt mining executives has a run-in with the outlaws and says to them, 'I wouldn't give you the combination to the gates of hell.' After the whole town is painted red and the outlaws are dispatched, flames hellishly engulf Lago. The next day the stranger gallops off and vanishes into the horizon from whence he came, but not before implying to the dwarf that he is the ghost of Jim Duncan, or some kind of demon, or quite possibly the devil himself.

As in *Django* and *High Plains Drifter*, the central protagonist in Jim Jarmusch's 1995 Western, *Dead Man*, represents a symbol of death. Additionally, like *High Plains Drifter*, *Dead Man* depicts the town in which the action takes place as a veritable hell on earth. When William Blake, a young accountant, travels on a train from Cleveland to the Western town of Machine, the coal stoker tells Blake that his reason for moving west 'doesn't explain why you came all the way out here to hell.' The stoker further admonishes Blake that in the town of Machine, Blake is 'just as likely to find [his] own grave' as he is to obtain gainful employment.

As with the *Django* films and *High Plains Drifter*, images of skulls and coffins litter Jarmusch's Western landscape, as do vestiges of terrific violence and decay. Also reminiscent of the *Django* films, the credits to *Dead Man* signify death by virtue of their bone-shaped lettering.

Jarmusch further ramps up the film's Gothic motifs when the tenderfoot William Blake meets a former prostitute and stays the night with her. When her well-heeled ex-boyfriend walks in on them and shoots her, Blake shoots him, but not before suffering a wound himself. From then on he becomes an outlaw and is hunted by bounty hunters eager to collect the bounty on his head.

Blake escapes the town on the dead boyfriend's horse, at some point passes out and is awakened by a Native American named Nobody who ushers him not only into the world of non-white Native American culture, but also into the spiritual world beyond the grave. Nobody's presence, and Blake's transformation from a white man from Cleveland to a non-white 'killer of white men', references the atrocities enacted on Native American populations as Americans moved westward to achieve their so-called 'manifest destiny' of occupying all lands west of the Mississippi regardless of Native American claims or deals struck. In the minds of western expansionists, the Native Americans were neglecting the land by refusing to develop it. As Patricia Nelson Limerick relates:

> Indians held 138 million acres in 1887. In the next forty-seven years, 60 million acres were declared, after allotment, to be surplus land and 'sold to white men'. Also, in the next forty-seven years, 27 million acres left the Indians' possession through allotment to individuals and then sales to whites . . . a process that took nearly two-thirds of tribal land away. (1987: 198–9)

As a result, as Dee Brown explains:

> Between 1860 and 1890 . . . the culture and civilisation of the American Indian was destroyed, and out of that time came virtually all the great myths of the American West – tales of fur traders, mountain men, steamboat pilots, goldseekers, gamblers, gunmen, cavalry-men, cowboys, harlots, missionaries, schoolmarms, and homesteaders. (1970: xxiii)

Brown further argues:

> To justify these breaches of the 'permanent Indian frontier,' the policy makers in Washington invented Manifest Destiny, a term which lifted land hunger to a lofty plane. The Europeans and their descendants were ordained by destiny to rule all of America. They were the dominant race and therefore responsible for the Indians – along with their lands, their forests, and their mineral wealth. (1970: 8)

Most of the white men in the film are Gothicised, symbolising their role in Native American genocide. After Nobody takes peyote, he sees an image of a skull overlaid on Blake's face. Cole Wilson, one of the bounty hunters hired to hunt Blake, is a cannibal who 'fucked his parents'.

Another bounty hunter further amplifies Wilson's grisly legacy when he offers: 'After he killed them, he cooked them up and ate them.' Indeed, we later see Wilson eat the cooked arm of this fellow outlaw, ostensibly for talking too much.

Out on the frontier, Blake and Nobody happen upon three white men who have entered into an alternatively gendered 'family' structure, wherein one of them wears a dress and cooks while the other two vie for masculine supremacy. When they initially happen upon the trio, Blake and Nobody overhear a fragment of a conversation. Sally, wearing a dress and bonnet, describes to the other men how 'Nero would illuminate his whole garden with bodies of live Christians covered in burning oil strung up on flaming crosses crucified. At dinner he would have the Christians rubbed by his guards with aromatic herbs and garlic and sown up into sacks. Then they would throw these sacks to the wild dogs'. This conversation fragment directly references European Gothic history, situating the film squarely within that style. The two men eventually fight and kill each other over who gets to 'have' Blake, allowing Blake and Nobody to narrowly escape. Later, when Cole Wilson finds one of the marshals Blake has killed, Wilson squashes his face with his boot and the head explodes like a piece of fruit.

High on peyote, Nobody paints Blake's face and removes Blake's glasses, marking his transition from white man to 'a killer of white men'. Blake's new membership into non-whiteness highlights his fate as another non-white mowed down during American's march westward and, in this sense, de-Gothicises him. Underscoring this transition, Blake comes upon white men who have been inexplicably shot by arrows. This image seems to suggest that Blake is not killed by similar arrows because he is no longer white. After recognising Blake, a trading post clerk tells him, 'God damn your soul to the fires of hell,' to which Blake replies: 'He already has.' In this sense, America signifies a Gothic hell for the barbaric other driven by monstrous white supremacy and its construct of manifest destiny.

Lastly, Stewart Scott's Gothic Western vampire tale, *Priest* (2011), contains all the elements of a fusion between European Gothic elements, such as vampires and crucifixions and American Gothic elements like racial subjugation. In this case, the vampires represent Native Americans that exist on 'protected lands' called 'reservations'. The film's mythology rests on an ancient conflict between the priests and the vampires. Although the priests, or whites, have subjugated the barbaric vampires, herding them into protected spaces, there exists evidence that the vampires have been secretly proliferating and planning another war with the 'civilised' whites.

In addition to Gothic elements from both continents, *Priest* clearly intends to be a Western and harbours many of the visual markers endemic to the genre. For example, a powerful locomotive-style train figures in the plot as the primary transport between the 'wastelands' and the cities, and there are outposts and small towns in the wastelands run by sheriffs who carry guns and wear bandanas around their necks. Perhaps the most telling aspect of the film, and the one that situates it firmly in the pantheon of racist, if not Gothic, Westerns, is its obvious debt to John Ford's *The Searchers* (1956). The parallels begin when the priest/central protagonist, who looks eerily similar to a skinhead, finds his brother's family killed by vampires. Similarly, in *The Searchers*, Ethan Edwards (John Wayne), a former confederate soldier, finds his brother's family massacred by Native Americans. The Priest, like Ethan, discovers that his niece (who in both films turns out to be their daughter) has been kidnapped. The fear in both films is that the niece will be racially infected beyond all hope or repair. In the case of *The Searchers*, her white purity might be compromised by Chief Scar's Native American seed, and in *Priest*, the girl might become a vampire. *The Searchers*, considered one of the best westerns of all time, echoes both America's history of racial slavery and Native American genocide, but it never emerges as a Gothic Western because of its complete lack of European Gothic influences, as well as its relatively low-grade depictions of graphic violence compared to other films in this study.

The American Gothic tradition combines the European Gothic elements of violence, death and spirituality, linking the original 'other', the barbarians, with America's own history of otherness and violence predicated on its legacy of racial slavery and Native American genocide. The American Western is particularly suited to this aesthetic fusion since as a genre it inherently contains aspects of violence linked to a history of racial slavery and Native American genocide. The Gothic is a style not a genre, and the criteria by which I would characterise an American film as Gothic depends on how it portrays violence, how it deploys Gothic symbols and how it references America's history of slavery and genocide. Like *The Wild Bunch*, the two *Django*s, *High Plains Drifter*, *Dead Man* and *Priest* aestheticise violence, incorporating symbols of the European Gothic and highlighting America's legacy of racial slavery and Native American genocide.

Note

1. The employment of a dwarf or little person within a contemporary American Gothic Western film evokes the traditional Euro-Gothic imagery of the sympathetic monster in classic European Gothic novels such as Mary Shelley's *Frankenstein* (1820) and Bram Stoker's *Dracula* (1897). This evocation also highlights the American Gothic tradition as essentially drawn from its long history of demonising otherness.

References

Bandy, M. L. and Stoehr, K. 2012. *Ride Boldly Ride: The Evolution of the American Western*. Berkeley, CA: University of California Press.

Brown, D. 1970. *Bury My Heart at Wounded Knee: An Indian History to the American West*. New York: Picador.

Carpio, G. R. 2013. 'I Like the Way You Die, Boy', *Transition*, 112, pp. 1–12.

Groom, N. 2012. *The Gothic: A Very Short Introduction*. Oxford: Oxford University Press.

Hutcheon, L. 1994. *Irony's Edge: The Theory and Politics of Irony*. New York: Routledge.

Limerick, P. N. 1987. *The Legacy of Conquest: The Unbroken Past of the American West*. New York: Norton.

Slotnik, R. 1992. *Gunfighter Nation: The Myth of the Frontier in Twentieth-Century America*. New York: Harper.

Chapter 14

This Is America: Race, Gender and the Gothic in *Get Out* (2017)

Elaine Roth

When Eve Kosofsky Sedgwick asserted in 1975 how 'distinct and useable the Gothic is as a literary tradition' (7), she might have been presciently predicting the success of the film *Get Out* (Jordan Peele, 2017), over forty years later. The directorial debut by established television comedy writer and actor Jordan Peele, *Get Out* draws heavily on the Gothic in its indictment of predatory white culture.

The low-budget film was wildly successful, receiving positive feedback from critics and audiences alike and garnering unprecedented Academy Award nominations and wins. Jordan Peele became the first black writer awarded an Academy Award for Best Screenplay (only four have ever been nominated) and just the fifth black director nominated for an Academy Award (none have won). It was further unusual that *Get Out* was nominated for Best Picture: not since *The Exorcist* (William Friedkin, 1973) had a horror film received such acclaim.

Peele, who himself labelled the film a 'social thriller' in the vein of *Night of the Living Dead* (George Romero, 1968), invokes the conventions of the Gothic. These conventions include the phenomenological, such as a 'terrible house', the term Carol Clover (1992) uses for the dangerous settings of horror films, houses in which time and space are undermined, which occurs in the basement torture chamber the protagonist of *Get Out* discovers. The film also features the thematic anxieties of the Gothic, including the dangers of sexuality and the terror of states of voiceless paralysis (Clover, 1992). However, the film extends the Gothic by foregrounding race and reversing a familiar US narrative of eroticised white female victimisation at the hands of dangerous black men; by contrast, *Get Out* features sympathetic black men preyed upon by white female sexuality.

The film begins with several incidents of violence: first, the unexplained kidnapping of a black man in the film's opening scene sets a threatening, genre-specific tone. The narrative then shifts to follow an interracial couple: Rose, a young white woman selecting doughnuts at a bakery, and Chris, a young black man who is a skilled photographer. Although the *mise-en-scène* and mood adjust accordingly, from low-key to high-key lighting, from menacing music to a more generic soundtrack, the couple are haunted by the violence of the first scene, even before the young man draws blood cutting himself shaving. Ominousness continues: the couple head out for a weekend get-away to meet Rose's parents, but they are quickly involved in a shocking and lethal collision, when the car Rose is driving hits a deer. Chris follows the wounded animal into the woods and returns without the audience knowing what has transpired there; he is both the tracked and vulnerable prey in this encounter, as well as a possible representative of violence in that he may have put the animal out of its misery. A white police officer arrives and Rose performs a white liberal defence of Chris's rights as the officer appears to scrutinise him. The threat of violence, both natural and institutional, is quickly invoked. The couple then arrive at the terrible house and meet Rose's parents, as well as two African American servants who behave strangely.

In many ways, Sedgwick's theories of the Gothic map well onto *Get Out*. In the 1986 introduction to her 1975 book, *The Coherence of Gothic Conventions*, Sedgwick divides the Gothic's approach between feminine hysteria and masculine paranoia; masculine paranoia, Sedgwick suggests, is characterised by a male subject pursuing his monstrous mirror. The slogan for this dynamic, Sedgwick suggests, might be, 'It takes one to know one.' Sedgwick was identifying manifestations of homosexual repression in her inquiries into nineteenth-century literature, but her analysis extends into twenty-first-century cinema. In *Get Out*, Chris navigates the film in Sedgwick's 'masculine' mode, searching for ones to know, trying to find a mirror among the creepiness that permeates the white family that both fetishises and seeks to destroy him. He seeks African American allies, but instead encounters subjugated prisoners. Chris repeatedly approaches African American characters, hoping for a point of identification among the increasingly strange behaviour he encounters. Instead, the characters rebuff and alienate him, refusing him intra-cultural identification. By the end of the first act, he has been captured by the cult run by Rose's family and is bound for destruction, like the other African Americans he has met in that house. 'It takes one to know one' indeed. In an echo of Alfred Hitchcock's *Psycho* (1960), it appears that the film's protagonist may have been permanently incapacitated. The film now approaches unfamiliar territory. If audiences are used to a plucky white girl, or in Carol Clover's terms, a 'final girl', rewarded for her chastity and emerging from terrible houses at the end of horror films, it is unclear what will happen to Chris at this point, since his adversary seems to be exactly one of those girls.

Typically in the Gothic tradition, white women have served as victims, not perpetrators, of violence; often their demises function as harbingers that something is awry. In Bram Stoker's *Dracula* (1897) and Mary Shelley's *Frankenstein* (1818), the victimisation of young virginal white women reveals the horror of the monster. Even in films peripheral to the genre, the spectre of the dead white wife haunts the narrative, such as *Shutter Island* (Martin Scorsese, 2010) or *Inception* (Christopher Nolan, 2010); conveniently, she can often serve both as victim and as irritant to the white male protagonist. Occasionally, white women play survivors, from the young Mrs DeWinter in *Rebecca* (Alfred Hitchcock, 1938) to the 'final girls' who manage to escape in films such as *Halloween* (John Carpenter, 1978). The horror cycle of the *Scream* films (1996–) extended that persona, so that the protagonist no longer needed to be virginal.[1]

Rarely, however, do white women participate in violence as aggressors, and when they do, their behaviour must be justified in some way. In *Carrie* (Brian De Palma, 1976), Carrie herself is a victim of first a bad mother and then of bullying. *Single White Female* (John Lutz, 1992) and *Basic Instinct* (Paul Verhoeven, 1992) both demonise lesbianism to explain a white woman's violence, while *Fatal Attraction* (Adrian Lyne, 1987) and *The Crush* (Alan Shapiro, 1993) function as cautionary tales for heterosexual men, warning against the perils of aggressive female heterosexuality.

Generally, however, white women serve as the very locus of innocence; protecting against or revenging their violation is what motivates violence. *Get Out* reverses this dynamic by positing Rose as the primary source of deception. According to the logic of the film, she has deliberately seduced Chris and lured him to her family home, as she has many black men before him, in order to harvest his body. Rose's first scene in the film, in which she peruses and then selects donuts from a large display, foreshadow her as a careful connoisseur of objects that will be consumed.[2] Significantly, her brother has similarly been charged by their family cult with collecting black men for sacrifice, but he does not do so via a sexual lure. Instead, the first scene of the film depicts him overpowering a young black man. Although the actor who plays the brother is not particularly imposing, he effects a sneak attack. Rose, by contrast, engages in a long con that involves pretending to be Chris's girlfriend and then eventually inviting him to meet her parents. Rather than anesthetising him after an initial drink, Rose masquerades as his girlfriend for months. It is a time-consuming endeavour that relies on

Rose's attractiveness and willingness to prostitute herself for the cult. No such demands are made of her brother; his contribution to the cult does not rely on his sexuality.

The film thus works in keeping with Gothic horror's fixation on monstrous sexuality. Rose's feral nature is revealed by her family at the dinner table, when they tell a supposedly embarrassing story about her biting the tongue of the first boy who tried to kiss her, a vagina dentata invocation that indicates how dangerous she is. Although Chris increasingly recognises that something is awry in both the house and his relationship with Rose, despite her performance of a liberal awakening in regard to racial dynamics, he nonetheless continues to hope that she is removed from the situation. During the second act, as he mobilises to leave the house (or 'get out'), he continues to rely on her for help, even after discovering her history of accruing black victims, the proof of which comes in the form of photographic evidence tucked away in a closet. (Chris's talent, photography, also functions to generate trophies.) Regardless, however, he asks her for the car keys in order to escape, still hoping somehow that she is on his side; like the audience, Chris suffers from an inability to tell who is on his side and who is sabotaging him. Not until she dangles the car keys in front of him does he recognise that he is trapped.

It comes as a surprise when it is revealed that Rose is an active participant in the threat Chris has sensed throughout the film; the audience and Chris have increasingly identified other uncanny moments as threatening but are unclear about Rose's relationship to them. Rose is further played by a familiar actress, Allison Williams, who made her name in the HBO series *Girls* (Lena Dunham, 1912–), and who is also the daughter of MSNBS newscaster Brian Williams. By contrast, Chris is played by a relative newcomer to Hollywood, British actor Daniel Kaluuya.

Sedgwick focuses her discussion of the Gothic on literature, but the Gothic's usability allows it to extend to the cinematic, as Judith Halberstam demonstrates twenty years later in *Skin Shows: Gothic Horror and the Technology of Monsters* (1995), and as exemplified more than twenty years after that in *Get Out*. Halberstam runs up against the notion of race in his early investigation of the Gothic, commenting that the prevalence of US racism has effectively rendered most representations of the black body as always already monstrous. Halberstam suggests that:

> The gothicization of certain 'races' over the last century, one might say, has been all too successful. This does not mean that Gothic race is not readable in the contemporary horror text, but it is clear that, within Gothic, the

difference between representing racism and representing race is extremely tricky to negotiate' (1995: 4)

Get Out navigates this dilemma by presenting an African American protagonist for the audience to identify with, the sacrificial but ultimately powerful Chris, pitted against an unusual antagonist, his conventionally attractive white girlfriend, the beautiful but deadly Rose. By the end of the film, she becomes the film's monster, as well as the primary site of racist forces threatening our protagonist, which the film can then eliminate, at least superficially, for the purposes of closure. Ultimately, however, the film posits the danger of white usurpation of blackness as more problematic and widespread than a single character.

Building upon Halberstam, but before the release of *Get Out*, critics had posited the Gothic as in fact exactly a site where race plays out in the US. Ellen Weinauer credits Teresa Goddu with firmly establishing that 'the Gothic must be understood as a historically responsive genre that tells a complex and often vexed story of the nation's failures to deliver on its political and social promises' (2017: 96). *Get Out* invokes this failure in several ways. First, it suggests a long history that predates the protagonist's discovery of the savagery he encounters; the terrible house he approaches is an established house, drawing upon a historical understanding of land and property rights and whiteness. While the film seems to situate itself in perhaps upstate New York, the foliage reflects the location where it was actually filmed, in Alabama, thus invoking the institutions of both southern slavery and northern racism. In addition, the film targets white liberals, or at least the performance of white liberalism, with a patriarch thrilled with himself for having voted for a black president, and his awkward appropriation of 'street' lingo to describe his daughter's interracial relationship. Although it is revealed that the family is actually playing roles in order to lure Chris to his demise, their act is surely informed by the fact that probably not even they – the murderous cult members – believe they are racist.

In the wake of a long history of savagery associated with black and brown bodies in the US, the film usefully reveals and indicts the violence that underwrites racial categorisation. As Goddu has noted, 'African American authors' appropriation and revision of gothic conventions shows that the gothic is not a transhistorical, static category but a dynamic mode that undergoes historical change when specific agents adopt and transform its conventions' (1997: 153). The intervention that Peele makes by using the Gothic in *Get Out* specifically locates savagery in white liberalism, among white characters whose admiration of people of colour is underwritten by the blood thirst and butchery associated with not only the Gothic, but also the realm of horror. Despite the narrative power of the film's reveal, Rose's complicity is entirely in keeping with a long, bloody but quiet history in the US by white women perpetuating and benefitting from crimes against black bodies.

In identifying Rose as a daughter and beneficiary of a family whose power depends upon the exploitation of African Americans, as well as a primary perpetrator of violence against black bodies, *Get Out* both breaks new ground as a Gothic film, but also references a long history of US narratives, including the nineteenth-century slave narrative. In those stories, white women repeatedly serve as primary instigators of brutal violence against black victims. The film, then, uses the Gothic to unearth the Gothic history specific to the US.

For instance, in *Incidents in the Life of a Slave Girl* (1861) by Harriet Jacobs, the protagonist, Linda, based on Jacobs's own history, explicitly identifies the brutality she and other slaves suffer at the hands of white women. With intense irony, Jacobs notes, 'Mrs. Flint, like many southern women, was totally deficient in energy. She had not strength to superintend her household affairs; but her nerves were so strong, that she could sit in her easy chair and see a woman whipped, till the blood trickled from every stroke of the lash' (22). Jacobs notes that these are women who have become comfortable not only with the rapacious nature of the white men in their lives (Rose works in tandem with her father and brother), but who also view African American bodies as disposable commodities. Jacobs comments, 'Southern women often marry a man knowing that he is the father of many little slaves. They do not trouble themselves about it. They regard such children as property, as marketable as the pigs on the plantation; and it is seldom that they do not make them aware of this by passing them into the slave-trader's hands as soon as possible, and thus getting them out of their sight' (57). In order to escape Mrs Flint's assaults and the incessant rape threat from Mrs Flint's husband, yet also remain near her two children, born with a white man who passively fails to affect her freedom, Linda hides in the attic of her grandmother's house for seven years, a historical parallel to the 'Sunken Place' that contains Chris in the film.

Sedgwick asserts that 'unspeakable' is a favourite Gothic word, while the fear of live burial and the horror of unintelligibility are the central sources of terror. Peele's version of live burial and unintelligibility is characterised as the 'Sunken Place' and is delivered by Rose's mother, a sinister therapist with the ability to hypnotise people without their consent. Playing the role of a cosy maternal figure, she chimes her teaspoon in a cup of tea, rendering the slaves around her mute and trapped. In Peele's presentation of the 'Sunken Place', the paralysed subject sinks away from reality, viewing it as a receding, shimmering screen that can be seen from a distance and heard dimly, but without any agency in the physical body left above. The audience witnesses Chris screaming mutely, unable to register his outrage to those around him via his corporeal form.

When Chris is commanded to sink to the 'Sunken Place', we belatedly recognise the uncanny nature of the African American characters he has previously encountered. They have gazed at him beseechingly, viewing him, we now recognise, from the depths of the 'Sunken Place', unable to prevent him from being victimised himself and unable to intervene as he misrecognises their passivity. Instead, their bodies register their pain: the maid's nose bleeds and her eyes tear; similarly, the nose of a slave at an auction disguised as a garden party bleeds.

When Chris unwittingly snaps this male guest out of the 'Sunken Place', he charges Chris. His aggressive quest to rescue Chris registers as violent; his cry, a brief return to intelligibility, is initially misunderstood by Chris. His 'Get out!' sounds like exclusion and banishment; later, particularly after it is echoed by Chris's friend Rod, we understand that it was an effort to save Chris.

The 'Sunken Place' registers as an excavation of black power for white benefit, whereby black bodies are subsumed and consumed for white pleasure while actual black identities are silenced and sidelined. It also registers, particularly given its visual presentation in the film, as a metaphor for audiences of horror films, moved to yell to unwitting protagonists that they should not explore the basement, take a shower, swim in the ocean or go home with white girls. Masochistically, we passively, mutely watch our hapless protagonists preyed upon by patriarchal and racist violence. Peele takes the unintelligible utterance, the misunderstood rescue attempt, as his title, voicing the cries of countless horror audiences. The title also simultaneously invokes a specific racial warning, charging black protagonists with escape.

However, as Sedgwick establishes in her analysis of the Gothic, it is a realm of doubles, where sites of horror – tombs, nightmares, the 'Sunken Place' – resemble the horrors of the waking world. For Peele's film, this metaphor seems all too clear: the film's presentation of wealthy whites literally purchasing and capitalising on the life force of black bodies reveals the shallow liberalism that voted for President Obama and then delivered President Trump and his consistent public racism. Like the Gothic itself, the film's metaphor is flexible, invoking a long history of white profit off of the sacrifice of black bodies, from the outrages of slavery to contemporary mass incarceration, the war against drugs, police violence against black civilians and the commodification of black bodies in entertainments that take a physical toll, such as major league football. From Fanny Hurst employing Zora Neale Hurston as her secretary while writing *Imitation of Life* (1933), a novel adapted into several films about a white woman's success underwritten by the uncredited talent of her black maid, to Melania Trump repeatedly using the words of former first lady Michelle Obama without citation in her speeches and initiatives, white imitation and appropriation of black voices and bodies has a long and aggressive history in US culture and politics.

As Sedgwick notes, one of the horrors unearthed by the Gothic is the parallel between the waking world and the nightmare, or between being alive and being buried alive. Audiences cheer when Chris escapes from the terrible house, but how he can get out of a US culture that consistently privileges whiteness at the expense of the black body? His bloodied, exhausted visage at the end of the film speaks to that dilemma and to the physical cost of that struggle.

If *Get Out* extends the Gothic in many ways, in other ways, it departs from Sedgwick's understanding of the Gothic. The film resolutely disavows the queerness upon which Sedgwick's original reading relies; Chris and Rose are punished for sex, but for heterosexual sex, and the film upholds strict gender binaries: male bodies are swapped for male bodies and female for female, despite the fact that these are brain transplants that presumably could transcend specifically gendered embodiment.

Another departure from Gothic conventions is raised by Halberstam's efforts in 1995 to claim horror for feminist and queer readings. *Get Out* poses a compelling challenge to this mission. The monsters that populate the examples of Gothic horror that Halberstam peruses – in *The Birds* (Alfred Hitchcock, 1963), *The Texas Chainsaw Massacre* (Tobe Hooper, 1974, and Tobe Hooper, 1986) and *The Silence of the Lambs* (Jonathan Demme, 1991) – are all monstrous outsiders who underwrite Halberstam's theory that monstrosity is used to shore up the boundaries of normalcy. Early on, he explains that the Gothic functions to produce normal humans against the monstrosity of the monster, who is figured as other, black, Jewish, foreign or disabled. By contrast, the normal, the human, thereby emerges as white, male, heterosexual.

Get Out usefully complicates these terms by situating the site of horror and monstrosity in the white nuclear family, and simultaneously invoking a long history of horror associated with that family. Halberstam ends the Introduction to *Skin Shows* by noting that monsters represent impurity, miscegenation, mixing, and that, as a result, 'we need monsters and we need to recognize and celebrate our own monstrosities' (1995: 27). However, if the heterosexual wealthy white woman is the monster, it is hard for feminist and queer theory to need her, hard to celebrate her. Peele turning the tables and situating monstrosity at the heart of the

familiar and in the face of conventional innocence destabilises the rehabilitation of the monster that Halberstam advocates.

The film thus justifies, at both the level of narrative as well as the
level of analysis, the brutalisation of the white female body, for she
has become the monster that must be destroyed. A reviewer of *Get
Out* notes that he saw the film with a black audience; he connects the
specificity of that audience with their vocal glee at the demise of Rose
at the end of the film (Benjamin, *Get Out*). Yet I viewed the film with
an all-white audience that was similarly vocal and appreciative at the
execution of the white female monster. The film functions to mobilise
animosity for the white female regardless of viewing audience (although
the response will, of course, vary).

Meanwhile, Rose's father, the brain surgeon, performs the operations,
stages the slave auctions and maintains the cult his own father developed. Rose's father is played by Bradley Whitford, drawing cunningly
on his star persona as a liberal thinker established by *The West Wing*
(1999–2008). The conspiracy her father now helms, in addition to brain
surgery, presumably also involves disposing of the white bodies that
have been discarded in their quest to inhabit and absorb black bodies.
As part of that process, the father has raised his son and daughter,
viewed several times as children in the cult's propaganda material, to
participate. His son violently apprehends and kidnaps black men on the
street, while his daughter has been taught to prostitute herself to a series
of black men (and occasionally women). Although she is neither the
architect nor the mastermind of this agenda, she nonetheless serves as
the film's primary monster. Her father is dispatched quickly, penetrated
by a deer's antlers, a symbol of his violently acquisitive nature, so that
he is brought down doubly by his own trophy (Chris and the deer, an
echo from the beginning of the film). Similarly, the white mother, who
has played a central role in hypnotising and immobilising Chris, is
eliminated efficiently. After she stabs him in the hand, he stabs her to
death, a moment that occurs offscreen, as film critic Kelli Weston notes.
Weston believes the discretion given this death suggests the power white
femininity – or perhaps maternity – continues to wield in the film.

By contrast, Rose's death is protracted, as she figures as Chris's
primary adversary. First, she is rendered into a bloody hole in the
abdomen, shot by the captive who had been used to house her grandfather, the original leader of the cult. Presumably targeted because of his
talent as a runner (her grandfather had also been a competitive runner),
he first works together with Rose to attack Chris. However, Chris is able
to use his talent as a photographer as a weapon against his opponents.
Having earlier noted that the flash of his cell phone camera seemed to

suddenly release from the 'Sunken Place' the captive who then exhorted him to 'Get out!, Chris photographs the man housing the grandfather, similarly releasing him from the 'Sunken Place'. The captive quickly convinces Rose, who has not registered his transformation, to give him the shotgun, only to shoot her instead and then immediately afterwards himself. His suicide raises the ominous suggestion that it might be too difficult to inhabit a world that wants to cannibalise him. Chris, who by contrast has managed to escape brain surgery, continues to resist.

Rose, in classic horror monster mode, survives being shot and reaches again for the gun, so that Chris is compelled to dispatch her another way, by strangling her. (Did he similarly break the neck of the deer, earlier?) However, he cannot complete his assault because of her apparent pleasure in his act. Grinning through bloody teeth, the suggestion that sex and violence are inherently linked for her overcomes Chris and he turns away in disgust, presumably to let her bleed to death in the road.

Nonetheless, Rose's status as a victim is powerful, and when a police car pulls up, Peele invokes the pessimistic ending of *Night of the Living Dead*, in which the sole survivor of zombies, a black male, is gunned down by a white militia and the police. Chris is once again rendered paralysed, this time by the optics of the scene, which play dangerously into familiar and racist US archetypes: the white female body as victim; the black male body as aggressor. In the version of the ending that Peele decided to circulate after the election of Donald Trump in 2016, the car turns out not to be driven by the police, but instead by his black saviour friend, Rod. In his work, Halberstam asserted the 'plurality of locations of resistance' (1995: 23) in Gothic films, which apparently include, in this moment, the Transportation Security Administration, Rod's employer and the source of his vehicle, along with a nod to the conspiracy theories that Rod has fostered and which the film ultimately corroborates.

Previously, however, in 2016, Peele had filmed a different finale – a far more extensive ending than the one he ultimately decided to deliver to audiences. In the original ending, Chris is in fact arrested by white policemen and eventually charged with the murder of Rose and her family. In an extremely downbeat final scene, Rod visits Chris in prison; the final shot is of Chris, in an orange jumpsuit and handcuffs, walking away down a long prison hallway accompanied by a guard. The film thus invokes the mass incarceration of African American men and unjust charges from white police officers against the black community. It's a depressing ending; it's further hard to imagine that the film would have been as successful with this final scene. Having identified with Chris, the audience desperately wants him to emerge from that terrible house. After the election of Donald Trump, Peele felt that audiences had received a jolt and now needed a hero (Peele, Alternate ending).

This theatrical release's ending, however, while saving Chris, directs all the rage at Rose, not the penal system, not the lethal police and not the white male patriarchs who have set this dynamic in motion. Instead, audience members cheer as Rose is shot, choked and left to die in the road. Perhaps these are the lengths cinema must go to in order to claim a black male heterosexual subject as human, as normal. It's also possible that this dynamic had recently played itself out in the larger political arena, with President Barack Obama normalised and presidential candidate Hillary Rodham Clinton demonised. An important response to the film, then, might be to locate guilt and power with the white patriarchs who founded the cult that preys on black bodies and who trained their white daughters to participate in its bloody rites. Through this lens, it is possible to view Rose as a brainwashed victim reduced to a sexual commodity; perhaps by considering her as a #MeToo representative, it might be possible to return to Halberstam's claim that we need our monsters and reclaim Rose. Furthermore, if the film crystalises white liberal racism in the figure of Rose, it also suggests that racism is an endemic phenomenon, ultimately larger than her, including not only the members of her family's cult, but also random New York state police officers.

Meanwhile, Chris's survival delivers great satisfaction and relief. He rises from the lethal grasp of the white monster as the landscape registers the sacrifice of black bodies that came before him. Nonetheless, as Kyna Morgan notes, he is 'only safe for now' (2018: 30). Significantly, Morgan's work, 'Woke Horror: Sociopolitics, Genre and Blackness in *Get Out*' (2018), poses Chris as a photographer on its cover. In contrast to the film's poster, which figures Chris trapped in the basement of the terrible house, or one of the widely circulated images of the film, a close-up of Chris's horrified tear-streaked face, Morgan asserts Chris as an active, viewing subject. In fact, this is why Chris has been targeted by the cult in the first place; he is desired for his 'eye' in both a literal but also artistic sense. As an active spectator, Chris's camera – the extension of his eye – ultimately also saves him, as his flash frees the captives trapped in the 'Sunken Place'. His ability to see, to navigate the Gothic confusion that makes it difficult to 'tell' who is an ally, who is a captive and who is an adversary, allows him to survive the film.

In this and many other ways, the film usefully expands the elastic boundaries of the Gothic horror genre. Peele extends the range of the Gothic's monstrosity to include racial categorisation, as well as the white nuclear family's resemblance to a cult. The film further reveals that the innocence claimed by white female privilege is a fantasy underwritten by violence and predicated on the physical repression of others. In breathing life back into the Gothic, Peele demonstrates the efficacy of the genre and its ability to convey a range of social and political messages.

Notes

1. Kathleen Rowe Karlyn noted this significant shift in her article, '*Scream*, Popular Culture, and Feminism's Third Wave' (2003).
2. Thanks to IUSB Film Studies minor David Pugh for pointing this out.

References

Benjamin, R. 2017. '*Get Out* and the Death of White Racial Innocence', *New Yorker*, 27 March. www.newyorker.com/culture/culture-desk/get-out-and-the-death-of-white-racial-innocence

Clover, C. J. 1992. *Men, Women, and Chain Saws: Gender in the Modern Horror Film*. Princeton, NJ: Princeton University Press.

Goddu, T. A. 1997. *Gothic America: Narrative, History, and Nation*. New York: Columbia University Press.

Halberstam, J. 1995. *Skin Shows: Gothic Horror and the Technology of Monsters*. Durham, NC: Duke University Press.

Jacobs, H. A. 1990. *Incidents in the Life of a Slave Girl*. New York: Oxford University Press.

Karlyn, K. R. 2003. '*Scream*, Popular Culture, and Feminism's Third Wave: "I'm Not My Mother"', *Genders*, 38, p. 6.

Morgan, K. B. 2018. *Woke Horror: Sociopolitics, Genre, and Blackness in* Get Out. Bristol, IN: MacBain & Boyd.

Peele, J. 2017. Alternate ending on DVD with director Jordan Peele commentary. *Get Out*. Universal City, CA: Universal Pictures Home Entertainment.

Sedgwick, E. K. [1986] 1975. *The Coherence of Gothic Conventions*. New York: Methuen.

Weinauer, E. 2017. 'Race and the American Gothic', in Weinstock, J. A. (ed.), *Cambridge Companion to the American Gothic*. Cambridge University Press, pp. 85–98.

Weston, K. 2018. '1) *Get Out*: Jordan Peele. That Sinking Feeling', *Sight and Sound*, January, pp. 37–9.

Chapter 15

'Part of my soul did die when making this film': Gothic Corporeality, Extreme Cinema and Hardcore Horror in the Twenty-First Century

Thomas Joseph Watson

> Gothic texts are, overtly but ambiguously, not rational, depicting disturbances of sanity and security ... displays of uncontrolled passion, violent emotion or flights of fancy to portrayals of perversion and obsession ... Gothic texts are not good in moral, aesthetic or social terms. Their concern is with vice: protagonists are selfish or evil ... their effects, aesthetically and socially, are also replete with a range of negative features: not beautiful, they display no harmony or proportion ... gothic texts register revulsion, abhorrence, fear, disgust and terror. (Botting 2014: 2)

Introduction

In his work on historical iterations of Gothic horror cinema, Xavier Aldana Reyes argues the following:

> Gothic horror is interstitial ... Gothic horror is hard to define precisely because it is neither a genre, in the strict sense in which horror is a genre, nor a distinct subgenre. Instead, Gothic horror's distinctiveness lies in its reliance on specific Gothic atmospheres, settings, music, tropes or figures, yet always with the intention of scaring, disturbing or 'grossing out'. (2013: 388)

These latter three elements point to the affective resonance of Gothic horror and explicit associations with the corporeal (chiming with the epigraph opening the present chapter). Focusing on relatively recent developments in the horror genre, key films within the millennial cycle of 'torture porn' (namely *Saw* (James Wan, 2004) and *Hostel* (Eli Roth, 2005)) are explicitly framed by Aldana Reyes in terms of the Gothic.

These films also act as extensions of earlier films, marking a 'Gothic turn to corporeality'. The distinctive characteristics of torture porn are described as extending certain Gothic sensibilities:

> The Gothic settings, trappings, mood and tone, together with the villainous quality of the horror that followed these two films, need to be acknowledged as distinctly and eminently Gothic. Films such as *A Serbian Film* (Spasojevic, 2010) or *The Human Centipede II: Full Sequence* (Six, 2011) have once again pushed the boundaries of decorum, instituting the Gothic as the thoroughly excessive genre it is often understood to be. (2014: 398)

It is these latter concerns of excess that will be explicated in the present chapter, specifically how hardcore horror as a Gothic manifestation pushes these boundaries of decorum even further. Aldana Reyes has gone on to suggest how 'torture porn deals openly with the mutilation and annihilation of the human body' but does so in a way that is 'inherently Gothic'. As such, the Gothic is somatic and corporeal' (2014: 2). This chapter aims to chart the development of hardcore horror cinema from the turn of the century, specifically the symbolic and physically violent mutilation and annihilation of the cinematic body on screen, as a contemporary manifestation of the Gothic. However, the semantics of a term like somatic, offered by Aldana Reyes above, would suggest that there is a separation between embodied trauma and psychological ramifications (factors that remain central to the ordeal logic of torture that permeates the narratives of hardcore horror films). The separation of the body from the mind is drawn into question when examining discourses of pain and the Gothic body, and it is the body in pain that remains central to my analysis. Hardcore horror cinema is able to reconcile the somatic and corporeal representation of violent torture with the performative, embodied and psychological experiences of those involved in such films. An examination of hardcore horror cinema, as a form of extreme performance art, allows for a nuanced examination of these tensions and allows for a sustained analysis of the Gothic themes and tropes inherent in this type of horror.

Although not necessarily as ubiquitous as the cycles of torture porn from 2003 onwards, hardcore horror in its contemporary state is in fact framed in the same discourse that surrounds that other perhaps more 'legitimate' and visible example of horror cinema. Hardcore horror, like its name suggests, places the films associated with such a moniker at the boundaries of violent representation and explicit depictions of transgressive sex and bodily abjection. It is hard to move beyond the implications that the prefix 'hardcore' suggests, as a great slew of these films focus on what Steve Jones has noted as 'abduction and torture motifs' which are distinguished from examples of torture porn through 'a combination of vérité, first person camerawork and humiliation themes' (2013: 175). Although that is not to say that torture porn narratives do not focus on this ordeal logic themselves, it is the formal differences permeating examples of hardcore horror that are of concern (in addition to the inclusion of thematic taboos and instances of physical mutilation and self-harm). In relation to the Gothic, instances of corporeal transgression have been examined in terms of 'a fictional representation of the body exceeding itself or falling apart, either opening up or being altered past the point where it would be recognized by normative understandings of human corporeality' (Aldana Reyes, 2014: 11).

The films discussed in this chapter (*Scrapbook* (Eric Stanze, 2000) and *The Bunny Game* (Adam Rehmeier, 2011)) test the boundaries between 'extreme pornography' and 'torture porn', and it is this transgressive confluence of ordeal logic and explicit, genuine violence that has presented significant problems when hardcore horror has faced official censure. Representations of genuine violence that lead to an apparent corporeal fracture are largely absent from a discourse largely focused on strictly fictional representations. *The Bunny Game* will be discussed in detail as it is a film that remains largely absent from contemporary scholarship. The film expertly confuses and conflates the distinctions between both real violence and sexual contact as 'performance' and aesthetic violence in the contexts of a fictional narrative. As this chapter aims to reconcile the corporeal and somatic aspects of the Gothic with the visceral psychological horror that permeates the ordeal narrative of hardcore horror, *The Bunny Game* is an apt film that represents monstrosity, extreme violence and transformation through 'mediatized performance' (Auslander, 1999: 10).

Hardcore Horror and the Discourse of Extremity

Over the last decade, a wide range of film scholarship has responded to an influx of what may be identified as 'extreme' cinema (Frey, 2016). Ranging from contemporary cycles of 'torture porn', descriptors such as 'torture horror', the emergence of the 'New French Extremity' and its later expansion encompassing films from wider Europe and global art cinemas, 'pseudo-snuff' fiction and found-footage horror films, representations of violence occupy a prominent position within wider horror film culture in the twenty-first century. However, when examples of so-called torture porn have been discussed, there has been a sustained tendency to group this cycle of films in terms of allegorical and socio-political readings. As such, the aesthetic and thematic complexities of these films is often negated. As Steve Jones contends:

> Although the allegorical reading is not inappropriate per se, its proliferation impedes debate. The cumulative effect of this interpretation's reiteration is that allegory becomes the rationalisation for torture porn's significance rather than an answer. The allegorical reading has thereby become a stopping point that has inadvertently hindered discussion. (2013: 63)

Additionally, discussions concerning the more 'extreme' examples of 'realist' horror cinema, typically pseudo-snuff fiction and faux-snuff, have largely fallen within ontological debates concerning realism and affect. This chapter aims to elucidate the Gothic tropes and themes evident within examples of hardcore horror cinema (perhaps best defined as a more 'extreme' precursor to the mainstream torture porn cycle), specifically focusing on the captivity narratives and aspects of torture and ordeal in the films *Scrapbook* and *The Bunny Game*.

Aaron Michael Kerner and Jonathan L. Knapp astutely connect certain examples of 'extreme cinema' with the assumed 'visceral experience of the viewer'. In support of the apparent affective resonance(s) (termed 'affective charge') offered by 'extreme cinema', it is asserted how 'these films are accused of disregarding narrative conventions in favour of grandiose spectacles of gore and violence that play to the spectator's baser senses'. As such, 'extreme cinema . . . is frequently associated with expressive brands of horror . . . featuring elements of brutal violence sometimes coupled with graphic sexual imagery' (2016: 1). Kerner and Knapp suggest that the violence inherent in extreme cinema is a product of film form just as much as representational content (if not more so). In examples of hardcore horror, it is the symbiotic relationship between these aspects that has proven to be of great concern when these films face official censure. Film form and instances of experimentation exacerbate the representational violence onscreen, especially when instances of physical violence are experienced as real. Although alluding to 'extreme cinema' more broadly, the following analysis is applicable to the films discussed in the present chapter:

> Violence manifests itself in a variety of ways: through jagged editing, through unnaturally vibrant colour, through disorientating camera work. It is through form, above all, that extreme cinema gains its power. It is not simply *what* the films represent that is extreme; it is *how* they do it. (159)

Contemporary examples of 'transgressive' realist horror cinema provide a useful way of exploring the relationship between image-form, the physically violent act (image-content) and affective resonance(s). This is especially pertinent in 'pseudo-snuff' films and examples of hardcore horror and the way these films replicate a violent reality onscreen. In the limited discourse that surrounds hardcore horror cinema, it is worth pointing out the pervasiveness of snuff and its influence on those horror texts classed as 'hardcore'. It should also be noted that Fred Vogel's *August Underground* series is something of a cult or critical benchmark in the examination of hardcore horror and that the aesthetics of snuff permeate these hardcore narratives. Regarding issues of authenticity and verisimilitude, Steve Jones contends the following in his examination of Vogel's films:

> In order that the pseudo-Snuff film can have any impact, it must conform enough to a realistic depiction that there can be a possibility that it could be real . . . a common response to extreme material that seems authentic would be to probe the image for signs of fakery. This may be especially true if the viewer is seeking assurance that what they are watching is a fabrication rather than 'real' Snuff. (2011: 14)

In these examples of pseudo-snuff, aspects of realism and authenticity associated with the violent act of murder hinge on more than what is represented onscreen. Although the violent acts depicted in these films are themselves important, it is the formal elements of these films that augment the representation of the 'extreme' violence shown. More specifically, it is the audio-visual medium itself (home video equipment and digital video) that is used to evince the authenticity of the films. In order to seem 'real', there is a requirement for the formal properties of the medium (and its errors) to remain visible. In these examples of pseudo-snuff, 'form draws attention to itself, making it difficult to forget the process of mediation'. Yet it is also the response to these 'signs of fakery' that re-codifies the text as fiction (for the comfort and 'assurance' of the viewer). As such, 'this aesthetic is not conductive to suspending disbelief as it foregrounds formal properties, yet those markers are required to pass the film off as reality' (14).

Issues of authenticity therefore hinge on notions of realism, yet, as Joel Black discerns, 'documenting actual objects, characters, and events (referential realism), or even making objects, characters, and events *seem* real (perceptual realism), is altogether different from making them explicit' (2002: 8). Black draws on the work of Stephen Prince who argued that 'unreal images can be referentially fictional but perceptually realistic' (1996: 32). Certain images may not have a material basis, yet they may seem real; they may look like something else that serves as a frame of reference. If instances of violence are thought to have some material basis via an aesthetic replication of reality (pointing towards conventionalised structures of what 'reality' is), this is complicated further by films that include genuine violence as a part of their diegesis. The boundary between referential realism and perceptual realism is therefore clouded, an issue dominant in a film like *Cannibal Holocaust* (Ruggero Deodato, 1980) in which real images of animal slaughter are juxtaposed with staged images of violence, and in which real instances of violence are also staged as fiction.

With reference to the film, Neil Jackson argues that instances of 'actual and simulated mutilation of the body are presented through identical stylistic modes in order to equalize their perceptual effect' (2002: 42). The same is true of hardcore horror films like *Scrapbook*, *August Underground's Mordum* (Fred Vogel, 2003), Lucifer Valentine's *Vomit Gore* quadrilogy (2006–12) and *The Bunny Game* that present scenes of genuine violence, self-mutilation and regurgitation as a source of horror within a wider diegesis of staged violent fiction. The aesthetics of snuff are replicated in two of these hardcore horror films that were submitted to the BBFC (British Board of Film Classification), *Scrapbook* facing 15 minutes 24 seconds of compulsory cuts when the film was submitted for classification in 2003. It is notable that this act of interventionist censorship constituted the most substantial number of cuts afforded to a non-sex work that year, and that those extensive cuts were made 'to remove scenes of sadistic sexual violence and humiliation' in addition to 'terrorization and rape' (BBFC, 2004: 77). Furthermore, the cuts were made to an entire sequence in which the film's antagonist records the sustained humiliation of his victim and replays this degraded videotape footage as a means of torture (see Figure 15.1).

Transgression in these films is not just about physical violence. It is amplified by abjection and instances of abject realism. In noted examples of hardcore horror, acts of self-mutilation, hardcore sex and genitally explicit sexual activity and the ability to vomit over a victim on demand grant a heightened sense of abject realism in addition to their fabricated violence and depravity. These transgressive acts are conflated with violent image-content and are therefore coded as being horrific. The reality of these transgressive acts thereby offsets the pseudo reality of the violent fiction. As these authentic, graphic depictions are placed alongside fictional representations of abuse, incest and paedophilia, it is perhaps the reality of such transgression that creates a jarring effect between violent reality and its representation. Themes of rape, incest and child abuse are offensive and transgressive. The violent content of these pseudo-snuff films and examples of hardcore horror is contextualised by these transgressive themes and is therefore amplified. Snuff fiction

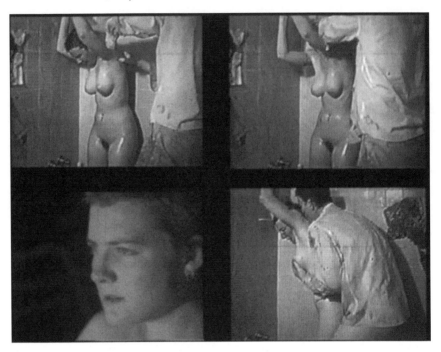

Filmed degradation and abuse as torture device in Scrapbook (Eric Stanze, 2000). © 2011 Wicked Pixel Cinema.

(and elements from these examples of hardcore horror) are constructed as forms of hyperreality in the sense that they 'threaten the difference between the "true" and the "false," the "real" and the "imaginary"' (Baudrillard, 1983: 5).

Gothic Extremities: The Case of *The Bunny Game*

One question that is perhaps worth retreading is the contention between art and exploitation, whereby films such as *The Bunny Game* face the most restrictive forms of censorial intervention (in the context of the UK) and other examples of 'extreme art' are applauded and accredited. The established Art-Trash/Exploitation binary is determined by representational content and formal qualities, distinctions that have been applied to an array of cultural texts. Scholars have argued that these distinctions are in a state of flux and are permeable and are indeed temporally and culturally specific. Films that would be considered 'art' and therefore traverse censorial restrictions contain similar content to films that have faced official censure and controversy.

As Tina Kendall argues, 'the art house credentials' (2016: 258) of the former 'lends cultural legitimacy to, and opens transnational channels of dissemination for, their sensational subject matter' (258). In a continuation of such arguments, Kendall contends that 'when a snuff element is imported into extreme art cinema, it tends to amplify questions of spectatorial complicity, making ethical reflexivity a strong component of the intensely affective and problematic experience of watching' (258). As such, because what constitutes 'worthy' extreme art cinema is something of an inconsistency, interesting readings which may be applied to films such as *The Bunny Game* and other examples of hardcore horror are denied as they are not judged to be met by the same audiences as those consuming extreme art cinemas. This is a double-edged sword so to speak, as the 'performance' of real violence and 'real' torture in the contexts of hardcore horror is not without its ethical problems. To better frame *The Bunny Game* within such arguments, I will turn to Joan Hawkins as she lists the 'three prevailing features of twentieth-century avant-garde aesthetics' as follows: '[t]he breaking of taboos surrounding the depiction (and performance) of sex and violence, the desire to shock (*épater*) the bourgeoisie, and the wilful blurring of the boundary lines traditionally separating life and art' (2000: 117). Although this commentary relates to experimental film art on a broader level, Hawkins alludes to 'the avant-garde's apparent willingness to hurt real people for the sake of art' and how this has in turn created 'ethical dilemmas for both the practitioners and consumers of experimental work' (117). If we extend these arguments into discussions of twenty-first century hardcore horror, the desire to shock the bourgeoisie and the blurring of boundaries between reality, realism and representation is also evidenced in the reception and subsequent rejection of *The Bunny Game* when submitted to the BBFC.

When submitted to the BBFC in 2011, *The Bunny Game* was immediately refused classification, effectively banning the film and thus making it illegal to distribute the film in the UK (although, at the time of writing, the film is available on YouTube in its entirety). For Steve Jones, 'banning denotes that films are hardcore, inasmuch as they are officially outlawed' (2013: 173). The film encompasses a narrative not unfamiliar with conceptions of hardcore horror in that a female victim is abducted and subsequently tortured both psychologically and physically by a male aggressor. Here, aspects of location are also central to Gothic horror, and this is something that is also explored in both *Scrapbook* and *The Bunny Game*. With reference to the work of Bernice M. Murphy on 'the rural gothic' (2013), it should be noted that *The Bunny Game* is not quite set in the rural environment characteristic of 'cabin in the woods' inflected horror cinema, but there is a distinctive movement away from the urban setting in these films into an isolated rural environment. This movement is explicit in *Scrapbook*, where sustained torture and abuse occurs in an isolated homestead. *The Bunny Game* is different in that the torture and violence permeating the film's narrative occurs in the articulated lorry of Hog (Jeff Renfro) on an isolated piece of disused freeway. The torture in the film is therefore enacted in a liminal space between the rural and the urban, a non-place to use the phrase afforded to Marc Augé (2009). The space within Hog's vehicle therefore acts as a torture chamber in which a large portion of the film's violence is contained. Kerner and Knapp argue that this motif is central to 'extreme' cinema:

> Space specifically designed for the execution of pain is also present in many extreme films. The cinematic torture chamber – like the spaces used for scared rituals – is frequently associated with the transformation of a character. The torture chamber tends to be a hermetic space, and more than this a non-place, sequestered from the day-to-day civilized world. (2016: 45)

The narrative of the film goes on to echo some of the broader thematic tropes of Gothic narratives. As Fred Botting suggests:

> The sense of power and persecution beyond reason or morality is played out in the two central figures of the narratives: a young female heroine and an older male villain. The latter, beyond law, reason or social restraint gives free reign to cruel, selfish desires and ambitions and violent moods and intentions. His object, the body or wealth of the heroine, registers danger in a series of frights and flights . . . Her vulnerability and his violence play out the lawlessness and insecurity manifested in settings and landscapes. Their distance from social and familial bonds is simultaneously the locus of adventurous, romantic independence and physical danger: she may be active but is alone, with nowhere to turn, without protection and security: he, outside social scrutiny, is able to act out all manner of unacceptable wishes unchecked. (2014: 4–5)

The press statement released by the BBFC stated the following, problematising these narrative concerns to a further degree:

> The principal focus of *The Bunny Game* is the unremitting sexual and physical abuse of a helpless woman, as well as the sadistic and sexual pleasure the man derives from this. The emphasis on the woman's nudity tends to eroticize what is shown, while aspects of the work such as the lack of explanation of the events depicted, and the stylistic treatment, may encourage some viewers to enjoy and share in the man's callousness and the pleasure he takes in the woman's pain and humiliation. (BBFC, 2011: 57)

The BBFC Annual Report from 2011 advances the notions of pleasure afforded to the film's antagonist Hog (Jeff Renfro) and states that the viewer is invited 'to share the sadistic and sexual pleasure which the man derives from his assault' (2012: 57). The rejection of the film and the reflection on this decision emphasise the principal focus of sexual and physical abuse in addition to the sexual and sadistic pleasure that is gained from these acts. Film scholar Jenny Barrett (2013) argues that the content of *The Bunny Game* 'is comparable to some of the most intense of European SM pornographic video material' in addition to the film's status as a 'very particular hybrid of drama and documentary'. Issues of realism and performance are therefore central to an examination *The Bunny Game*. Although violent content is addressed by the BBFC in the censorial decisions they make, form (read as tone) is the resounding problem. The problem is not that the *violence* is too real but rather that the violence is *too real*. If the focus were on isolated instances of violence, image-content would be excised to make the film less objectionable. The issue with the film is the combination of violent image-content and image-form. The violence is *too real* not because of what is shown, but rather how it is shown, i.e. the unremitting aestheticisation of sexual abuse and the 'stylistic treatment' of graphic, genuine violence.

The Bunny Game is an example of hardcore horror that confuses and conflates the distinctions between real violence and sexual contact as 'performance', and the aesthetic violence in the context of a fictional narrative. Linda Williams discusses similar distinctions when differentiating examples of sadomasochistic pornography. For Williams, there is a distinction between '"real" violence in the Bazanian sense' as 'it appears neither acted nor faked in editing' and aesthetic violence whereby the 'hard-core "evidence" of violence remains beneath the surface' (1999 [1989]: 199). Witnessing potentially abusive acts (regardless of their degree of performativity) is construed as harmful if those acts are deemed entertaining or pleasurable, thus normalising behaviour that is otherwise deemed objectionable. Williams suggests that 'two primary concerns animate these discussions of extreme and violent content in pornography. The first centers on the possible harm done to individuals whose bodies are used to create these images. The second centers on the possible harm done to viewers' (186). It is the latter concern that remains the focus of regulatory systems of film censorship in the UK. *The Bunny Game* combines these representational modes. The 'hardcore' violence is both real and visible, exemplified in the physical brands Getsic receives in the later stages of the film and the visible pain she experiences. Although genuine acts of physical harm have been defended as 'bold performance art', it is film form that brings the immediacy of the violent act into the frame of the fiction itself.

The nature of transgressive performance art is worth unpicking here as the 'abuse' and suffering experienced by Rodleen Getsic resonates with recent scholarship concerning the Gothic body. Tracy Fahey alludes to a complex relationship between audience and performer when addressing the 'autobiographical function' of transgressive performance art. For Fahey:

> As the artist's body becomes ever more manipulated and pushed beyond boundaries of taste and pain, it forces artist and audience alike to ask what lies beyond the parameters of the body. Experimentation with torture methods, with cutting, with abject materials, seems to lead back inevitably to the notion of the Gothic, othered body, and a desire to pass beyond the boundaries of the repeatedly invaded and wracked body. (2014: 1)

In referencing the work of Elaine Scarry (1985) *The Body in Pain: The Making and Unmaking of the World*, it becomes apparent that torture, which contains specific acts of inflicting pain, is also itself a demonstration and magnification of the felt-experience of pain. In the very processes it uses to produce pain within the body of the prisoner, it bestows visibility on the structure and enormity of what is usually private and incommunicable, contained within the boundaries of the sufferer's body (see Aldana Reyes, 2014: 27). This visibility is compounded when the torture motifs of hardcore horror extend beyond fictive representations. This also speaks to the affective resonance(s) of the film. As Ruth McPhee notes:

> Visceral responses to self-mutilation could not take place without a subjective identification with the body of the other as similar to our own. This process of identification contains the seeds of an ethical encounter, and yet this potential is too often shut down by attendant feelings of revulsion towards the alterity of the wounded body. (2014: 77)

The work of Getsic as a performance artist within *The Bunny Game* illustrates the felt responses to genuine instances of violence and successive psychological and physical trauma.

The Bunny Game is far more formally complex in that the film's narrative is composed of fragmented editing signatures and abrasive non-diegetic music, factors which amplify the genuine physical violence and torture Getsic herself has responded to: 'I was in and out of being present because I was being literally tortured ... hanging by chains, locked ... it sounds crazy in retrospect that I was being tortured, but I was, I really had to endure all of those games.'[1] These claims support some of the wider scholarship examining the aesthetic, formal dimensions of extreme cinema:

> It is not simply that extreme cinema includes highly graphic scenes of sex and violence, but rather that in certain instances these films render excessive elements in highly stylized manners . . . extreme cinema operates according to the 'violence of sensation' . . . extreme cinema might host abrupt ruptures in the diegetic narrative – experiments in form and/or composition (editing, extreme close-ups, visual disorientation, sounds that straddle the boundary between non-diegetic and diegetic registers), the exhibition of intense violence. (Kerner and Knapp, 2016: 4–5)

This scene has since been disputed by Getsic herself who refers to the film as a 'living shockumentary' in which 'no processes caused any harm to our actors'. Elaborating on the branding scene (see Figure 15.2) and the veracity it lends to the actions depicted onscreen, Getsic argues the following:

> Brands are like getting a tattoo. Receiving the brand onscreen in *The Bunny Game* did not cause me pain . . . I have a high threshold for what most

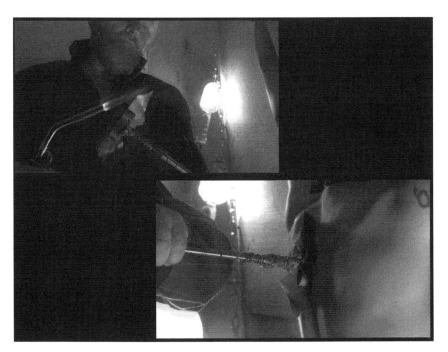

Composite of the fragmented depiction of Rodleen Getsic's genuine branding as performance art in *The Bunny Game* (Adam Rehmeier, 2011). © 2011 Death Mountain Productions.

consider pain . . . the reaction to the 'pain' was a theatric consummation . . .
No one was hurt in *The Bunny Game*, nor was anyone sexually aroused . . . I
did not suffer emotionally nor physically for the film. In fact, although impro-
visational, I was aware of everything as it happened. (2013)

Such statements also seem to contradict her previous comments when
making the film but can also be read in response to the BBFC decision to
reject the film (although no specific scenes are picked up on by the BBFC
in the justifications for the film's rejection). There have also been dis-
putes and conflicting arguments to whether all the acts in the film were
consensual and if Getsic was willing to be branded onscreen, evoking
some of the more problematic arguments offered by Joan Hawkins
(2000) previously with respect to issues of ethics and complicitness in the
avant-garde. Getsic can only speak for herself regarding sexual arousal
and emotional and physical suffering. Nevertheless, the inclusion of this
act in the narrative of the film is problematic regarding violent image-
content. The images of the female victims Bunny (Rodleen Getsic) and
Martyr (Drettie Page) being branded by Hog are visual representations
of genuine acts. In this sense, *The Bunny Game* is a document of violence (although how that violence is defined depends on which side of
the discourse is voicing their opinion).

Depictions of unsimulated sexual and violent acts are juxtaposed with
the problematic sexual and sadistic pleasure of the film's antagonist
(a point outlined by the BBFC). The BBFC make no reference to the
genitally explicit acts of fellatio or the physical violence of the branding sequence yet the sexual and sadistic pleasure of Hog is connected
to the potential pleasure a viewer might take in the pain inflicted by the
character. Adam Rehmeier has also addressed the 'sadistic pleasures'
of Hog in the film. The director alluded to the following question as
inspiring the narrative of the film and Hog's actions: 'What if he had a
living, breathing fuck doll that he drove around with?' This comment,
presented to a *Fangoria* journalist no less, perhaps diminishes some of
Rehmeier's artistic credibility, perhaps favouring shock and exploitation in this instance (see Slater, 2012: 54). Nevertheless, the distinctions
between fiction, reality and sadistic pleasure are purposefully confused
in the film through the manipulation of form in relation to image-
content (i.e. the performance of physical violence). Although films such
as *Scrapbook* and *The Bunny Game* share similarities under the auspices
of hardcore horror, they have all suffered either extensive cuts or rejection due to depictions of image-content viewed as sexually violent and
sadistic by the BBFC. Furthermore, the BBFC have levelled these films
by grouping them in such a way with reference to their subject matter

and have limited any further critical engagement with their content (a criticism that could also be directed at hardcore horror if used as a generic descriptor). The fact that these films have all faced rejection (and are still without legal UK certification, except for a heavily truncated *Scrapbook*) evinces that they have tested the thresholds of regulation and the excesses of decorum promised by the Gothic.

As a means of conclusion and taking *The Bunny Game* as a principal case study, in this example of hardcore horror aspects of realism and authenticity associated with violent acts of torture and possibly murder hinge on more than what is represented onscreen (and therefore present a challenge to contemporary regimes of UK censorship). It is the formal qualities of the violent image-content that are problematic in the contexts of censorship. It is the formal elements of this film that augment the representation of 'extreme' violence and, for all intents and purposes, *The Bunny Game* is far more complex than the rejection from the BBFC would imply. Examples of hardcore horror are therefore important as it is 'their taboo-flouting sex-violence combinations' that 'repoliticise' porn, horror and the nature of the Gothic. As such, 'repoliticising entails rethinking how these genres operate as sites of contestation against which acceptability standards are formed and disputed' (Jones, 2013: 185). It is perhaps in this light that examples of hardcore horror can be considered an extreme form of Gothic adaptation, *The Bunny Game* existing as a conflation of both Gothic and 'extreme' sensibilities.

Note

1. Getsic made these claims when interviewed on the Nutja Films DVD release of the film.

References

Aldana Reyes, X. 2013. 'Gothic Horror Film (1960 – Present)', in Byron, G. and Townsend, D. (eds), *The Gothic World*. London: Routledge, pp. 388–98.

Aldana Reyes, X. 2014. *Body Gothic: Corporeal Transgression in Contemporary Literature and Horror Film*. Cardiff: University of Wales Press.

Augé, M. 2009. *Non-places: Introduction to an Anthropology of Supermodernity*. London: Verso.

Auslander, P. 1999. *Liveness: Performance in a Mediatized Culture*. London: Routledge.

Barrett, J. 2013. 'More than Just a Game: Breaking the Rules in *The Bunny Game*', *Cine-Excess eJournal: Subverting the Senses: The Politics and*

Aesthetics of Excess [Online]. Available at: http://www.cine-excess.co.uk/more-than-just-a-game.html (accessed December 2013).

Baudrillard, J. 1983. *Simulations*. New York: Semiotext[e].

BBFC, 2004. 'British Board of Film Classification Annual Report and Accounts 2003' [Online]. Available at: http://bbfc.co.uk/sites/default/files/attachments/BBFC_AnnualReport_2003_0.pdf (accessed January 2013).

BBFC, 2011. *The Bunny Game* [Online]. Available at: http://www.bbfc.co.uk/releases/bunny-game-1970 (accessed December 2014).

BBFC, 2012. 'British Board of Film Classification Annual Report and Accounts 2011' [Online]. Available at: http://www.bbfc.co.uk/sites/default/files/attachments/BBFC_AnnualReport_2011.pdf (accessed June 2012).

Black, J. 2002. *The Reality Effect: Film Culture and the Graphic Imperative*. Routledge: New York.

Botting, F. 2014. *Gothic: The New Critical Idiom*. Abingdon: Routledge.

Fahey, T. 2014. 'A Taste for the Transgressive: Pushing Body Limits in Contemporary Performance Art', *M/C Journal*, 17: 1.

Frey, M. 2016. *Extreme Cinema: The Transgressive Rhetoric of Today's Art Film Culture*. New Brunswick, NJ: Rutgers University Press.

Getsic, R. 2013. 'My Monster Piece: An Art Film by Rodleen Getsic', *Cine-Excess eJournal: Subverting the Senses: The Politics and Aesthetics of Excess* [Online]. Available at: http://www.cine-excess.co.uk/my-monsterpiece.html (accessed December 2013).

Hawkins, J. 2000. *Cutting Edge: Art Horror and the Horrific Avant-garde*. Minneapolis, MN: University of Minnesota Press.

Jackson, N. 2002. '*Cannibal Holocaust*, Realist Horror, and Reflexivity', *Post Script: Essays in Film and the Humanities*, 21: 3, pp. 32–45.

Jones, S. 2011. 'Dying to Be Seen: Snuff-Fiction's Problematic Fantasises of "Reality"', *Scope*, 19.

Jones, S. 2013. *Torture Porn: Popular Horror in the Era of Saw*. London: Palgrave.

Kendall, T. 2016. 'Affect and the Ethics of Snuff in Extreme Art Cinema', in Jackson, N., Kimber, S., Walker, J. and Watson, T. J. (eds), *Snuff: Real Death and Screen Media*. New York: Bloomsbury.

Kerner, A. M. and Knapp, J. L. 2016. *Extreme Cinema: Affective Strategies in Transnational Media*. Edinburgh: Edinburgh University Press.

McPhee, R. 2014. *Female Masochism in Film: Sexuality, Ethics and Aesthetics*. Surrey: Ashgate.

Murphy, B. M. 2013. *The Rural Gothic in American Popular Culture: Backwoods Horror and Terror in the Wilderness*. London: Palgrave.

Prince, S. 1996. 'True Lies: Perceptual Realism, Digital Images, and Film Theory', *Film Quarterly*, 49: 3, pp. 27–37.

Scarry, E. 1985. *The Body in Pain: The Making and Unmaking of the World*. Oxford: Oxford University Press.

Slater, J. 2012. 'Rabbit, Run: Adam Rehmeier Interview', *The Darkside*, 145, pp. 53–7.

Williams, L. 1999 [1989]. *Hardcore: Power, Pleasure, and the Frenzy of the Visible*. Berkeley, CA: University of California Press.

Filmography and Other Media

2001: A Space Odyssey, film, directed by Stanley Kubrick. UK: MGM, 1968.

Abbott and Costello Meet Frankenstein, film, directed by Charles Barton, 1948.

Airplane!, film, directed by Jim Abrahams, David Zucker. USA: Paramount, 1980.

Alice/Něco z Alenky, film, directed by Jan Švankmajer. Czechoslovakia, 1988.

Alien 3, film, directed by David Fincher. USA: 20th Century Fox, 1992.

Alien Resurrection, film, directed by Jean-Pierre Jeunet. USA: 20th Century Fox, 1997.

Alien, film, directed by Ridley Scott. USA: 20th Century Fox, 1979.

Aliens, film, directed by James Cameron USA: 20th Century Fox, 1986.

All About Eve, film, directed by Joseph L. Mankiewicz. USA: 20th Century Fox, 1950.

'Ballin' the Jack', song. Music by Chris Smith. Lyrics by Jim Burris, 1913. Song.

Black Sunday, film, directed by Mario Bava. Italy: Galatea Film, 1961.

Blade Runner, film, directed by Ridley Scott. USA: Warner Bros, 1982

Blazing Saddles, film, directed by Mel Brooks. USA: Crossbow Productions, 1974.

Bram Stoker's Dracula, film, directed by Francis Ford Coppola 1992.

Bride of Frankenstein, film, directed by James Whale, 1931.

Brief Encounter, film, directed by David Lean. USA: Cineguild, 1945.

Cabaret, film, directed by Bob Fosse. USA: Allied Artists, 1972.

Castle of Blood, film, directed by Sergio Corbucci. Italy: Giovanni Addessi Produzione Cinematografica, 1965.

'Chattanooga Choo Choo', song. Music by Harry Warren. Lyrics by Mark Watson, 1941.

Creature from the Black Lagoon, film, directed by Jack Arnold, 1954.

Dark Star, film, directed by John Carpenter, USA: Jack H. Harris Enterprises, 1974.

Dead Man, film, directed by Jim Jarmusch, USA: Miramax Films, 1995.

Destination Moon, film, directed by Irving Pichel. USA: George Pal Productions, 1950.

Django Unchained, film, directed by Quentin Tarantino, USA: Weinstein Company Columbia Pictures, 2013.

Django, film, directed by Sergio Corbucci. Italy: B. R. C. Produzione S. r. l. Tecisa, 1966.

Down to the Cellar/Do Pivnice, film, directed by Jan Švankmajer. Czechoslovakia: 1983.

Dr. Strangelove: Or, How I Stopped Worrying and Love the Bomb, film, directed by Stanley Kubrick. USA: Columbia, 1964.

Drácula, film, directed by George Melford, USA: Universal Studios, 1931.

Dracula, film, directed by Terence Fisher. UK: Hammer Films, 1958.

Dracula, film, directed by Tod Browning. USA: Universal Studios, 1931.

Dracula: Dead and Loving It, film, directed by Mel Brooks. USA: Gaumont, 1996.

Event Horizon, film, directed by Paul W. S. Anderson, USA: Paramount, 1997.

Ex Machina, film, directed by Alex Garland, UK: Film4, 2015

Faust/Lekce Faust, film, directed by Jan Švankmajer. Czechoslovakia: 1994.

Fight Club, film, directed by David Fincher. USA: 20th Century Fox, 1999.

Frankenstein, film, directed by J. Searle Dawley, 1910.

Frankenstein, film, directed by James Whale. USA: Universal Studios, 1931.

Galaxy of Terror, film, directed by Roger Corman. USA: New World Pictures, 1981.

Get Out, film, directed by Jordan Peele. USA: Universal Pictures, 2017.

Get Out: Alternate ending with director Jordan Peele commentary, DVD. USA: Universal City, CA: Universal Pictures Home Entertainment, 2017.

Haunted Honeymoon, film, directed by Gene Wilder. USA: Orion, 1986.

High Plains Drifter, film directed by Clint Eastwood. USA: Malpaso Company, 1973.

Hotel Transylvania, film, directed by Genndy Tartakovsky. USA: Columbia, 2012.

Jekyll and Hyde, film, directed by John S. Robertson. USA: Paramount/Artcraft, 1920.

Jekyll and Hyde, film, directed by Lucius Henderson. USA: Thanhouser Company, 1912.

Jekyll and Hyde, film, directed by Rouben Mamoulian. USA: Paramount Pictures, 1931.

Jekyll and Hyde, film, directed by Victor Fleming. USA: Metro-Goldwyn-Mayer, 1941.

Journey's End, film, directed by James Whale. USA: Gainsborough Pictures, 1929.

King Kong, film, directed by Merian C. Cooper, Ernest B. Schoedsack. USA: RKO, 1933.

Little Otik/Otesánek, film, directed by Jan Švankmajer. Czechoslovakia: 2000.

Love at First Bite, film, directed by Stan Dragoti. USA: Melvin Simon Productions, 1979.

Lunacy/Šílení, film, directed by Jan Švankmajer. Czechoslovakia: 2005.

Mary Reilly, film, directed by Stephen Frears. USA: Tri Star Pictures, 1996.

Metropolis, film, directed by Fritz Lang. Germany: Universum Film (UFA), 1927.

Moon, film, directed by Duncan Jones. USA: Stage 6 Films, 2009.

Moon, DVD commentary with Jones, D., Shaw, G., Rothery, G., Noble, T. USA: Sony Pictures, 2009.

Mr Vampire (Jiangshi Xian Sheng), film series, directed by Ricky Lau. Hong Kong: Bo Ho Film Co., 1985–92.

Never Let Me Go, film, directed by Mark Romanek. UK: DNA Films, 2010.

Nosferatu, Eine Symphonie des Graunes/Nosferatu, A Symphony of Horror, film, directed by F. W. Murnau. Germany: Prana, 1922.

Oblivion, film, directed by Joseph Kosinski. USA: Realtivity Media, 2013.

Orphan Black, television. UK: BBC America, 2013–17.

Pandora's Box, film, directed by Georg Wilhelm Pabst. Germany: 1929.

Penny Dreadful, television, directed by Damon Thomas, James Hawes et al. Desert Wolf Productions, 2014–16.

Pontianak, film, directed by B. Narayan Rao. Singapore: Cathay-Keris Film Productions, 1975.

Priest, film, directed by Scott Stewart, USA: Tokyopop DMG Entertainment, 2011.

'Puttin' on the Ritz', song. Words and music by Irving Berlin, 1929.

Ready Player One, film, directed by Steven Spielberg. USA: Warner Bros, 2018

Rebecca, film, directed by Alfred Hitchcock. USA: Selznick International, 1940.

Saturday Night Fever, film, directed by John Badham. USA: Robert Stigwood Organization, 1977.

Scrapbook, August Underground's Mordum, film, directed by Fred Vogel. USA: Toe Tag Pictures, 2003.

Shadow of a Doubt, film, directed by Alfred Hitchcock. Universal Pictures, 1943.

Son of Frankenstein, film, directed by Rowland V. Lee. USA: Universal Studios, 1939.

'Springtime for Hitler', song. Music and Lyrics by Mel Brooks, 1967.

Star Trek, television, produced by Gene Roddenberry. USA: Paramount Television, 1966–9.

Star Trek: First Contact, film, directed by Jonathan Frakes. USA: Paramount, 1996

Star Wars: The Force Awakens, film, directed by J. J. Abrams. USA: Walt Disney Studios, 2015.

Stoker, film, directed by Park Chan-wook. USA: Fox Searchlight Pictures, 2013.

Suspense!, radio, Ted Bliss, Anton Leader et al. USA: CBS, 1940–62.

Taxi Driver, film, directed by Martin Scorsese. USA: Columbia, 1976.

The Art of Gothic: Britain's Midnight Hour, television, directed by Paul Tickell. USA: BBC, 2016.

The Blood of Dracula, film, directed by Herbert L. Stock. USA: Carmel Productions, 1957.

The Bunny Game, film, directed by Adam Rehmeier. USA: Death Mountain Productions, 2012.

The Castle of Otrant/Otrantský Zámek, film, directed by Jan Švankmajer. Czechoslovakia: 1979.

The Chronicles of Riddick, film, directed by David Twohy. USA: Radar Pictures, 2004.

The Closed Door (Bandy Darwaza), film, directed by Shyam Ramsey and Tulsi Ramsey, 1990.

The Criminal Code, film, directed by Howard Hawks. USA, 1931.

The Demon Lover: Frayling on Dracula, film, directed by Marcus Hearn. 2012.

The Fall of the House of Usher/Zánik domu Usher, film, directed by Jan Švankmajer. Czechoslovakia: 1980.

The Flat/Byt, film, directed by Jan Švankmajer. Czechoslovakia: 1968.

The Golem, film, directed by Karl Boese and Paul Wegener. Germany: Projektions-AG Union, 1920.

The Horrible Dr. Hitchcock, film, directed by Riccardo Freda (as Robert Hampton), Italy: 1962.

The Hunchback of Notre Dame, film, directed by William Dieterle. USA: RKO Radio, 1939.

The Invisible Man, film, directed by James Whale, 1933.

The Island, film, directed by Michael Bay, USA: Parkes/MacDonald, 2005.

The Lady from Shanghai, film, directed by Orson Welles. USA: Columbia, 1947.

The Little Stranger, film, directed by Lenny Abrahamson, Ireland/UK/France: 20th Century Fox, 2018

The Mummy, film, directed by Karl Freund. 1932.

The Naked Gun 2½: The Smell of Fear, film, directed by David Zucker. USA: Paramount, 1991.

The Naked Gun 33⅓: The Final Insult, film, directed by Peter Segal. USA: Paramount, 1994.

The Naked Gun: From the Files of the Police Squad!, film, directed by David Zucker. USA: Paramount, 1988.

The Old Dark House, film, directed by James Whale. USA: Universal, 1932.

The Ossuary/Kostnice, film, directed by Jan Švankmajer. Czechoslovakia: 1970.

The Pendulum, the Pit, and Hope/Kyvadlo, Jáma a Nadeje, film, directed by Jan Švankmajer. Czechoslovakia: 1983.

The Producers, film, directed by Mel Brooks. USA: Crossbow Productions, 1967.

The Searchers, film, directed by John Ford, USA: C. V. Whitney Pictures, 1956.

The Shining, film, directed by Stanley Kubrick. USA: Warner Bros, 1980.

The Student of Prague, film, directed by H. H. Ewer, Germany: Deutsche Bioscop, 1913.

The Thing from Another World, film, directed by Christian Nyby. USA: Winchester Pictures, 1951.

The Whip and the Body, film, directed by Mario Bava. Italy: Vox Films, 1965.

The Wild Bunch, film, directed by Sam Peckinpah. USA: Warner Brothers, 1997.

The Wolf Man, film, directed by George Waggner. 1941.

'These Foolish Things', song. Music by Jack Strachey. Lyrics by Eric Maschwitz, 1936.

Universal Monsters: The Essential Collection, film, directed by Universal Studios. 2012.

Waterloo Bridge, film, directed by James Whale. USA: Universal Studios, 1930.

Young Frankenstein, film, directed by Mel Brooks. USA: 20th Century-Fox, 1974.

Young Justice, television. USA: Warner Brothers Television, 2010–.

Notes on Contributors

Xavier Aldana Reyes is Reader in English Literature and Film at Manchester Metropolitan University and a founder member of the Manchester Centre for Gothic Studies. He is the author of *Gothic Cinema* (2020), *Spanish Gothic* (2017), *Horror Film and Affect* (2016) and *Body Gothic* (2014), and the editor of *Twenty-First-Century Gothic: An Edinburgh Companion* (with Maisha Wester, 2019) and *Horror: A Literary History* (2016). He is chief editor of the Horror Studies book series published by the University of Wales Press.

Josef Benson is an Associate Professor of Literatures and Languages at the University of Wisconsin Parkside. He is the author of *J. D. Salinger's the Catcher in the Rye: A Cultural History* (Rowman & Littlefield, 2018) and *Hypermasculinities in the Contemporary Novel: Cormac McCarthy, Toni Morrison, and James Baldwin* (Rowman & Littlefield, 2014). He is currently working on three books under contract: *The Invisible Costume: Whiteness and the Construction of Race in American Comics and Graphic Novels* (University of Mississippi Press, 2020), *The Triumph of Nerd Culture: George Lucas and Star Wars Fandom* (Rowman & Littlefield, 2020) and *The Sniper: A Cultural Reading of Jeffrey Dahmer* (University Press of Kentucky, 2021).

Martin Danahay is Professor of English at Brock University, Canada. He is the author of *Gender at Work in Victorian Culture: Literature, Art and Masculinity* (Ashgate, 2005) and co-editor with Deborah Denenholz Morse of *Victorian Animal Dreams: Representations of Animals in Victorian Culture* (Ashgate, 2007). He is editor of the Broadview editions of Robert Louis Stevenson's *Strange Case of Dr Jekyll and Mr Hyde* and H. G. Wells's *The War of the Worlds*. He has published numerous articles on a variety of topics in Victorian culture, including the working-class body in *Jekyll and Hyde*, the Arts and Crafts movement, and H. G. Wells and eugenics. He has also published an article on steampunk in the *Journal of Neo-Victorian Studies*.

Geraint D'Arcy is a Lecturer in Theatre and Drama and teaches theory for TV and Film Set Design at the University of South Wales. He has published works on science fiction theatre, stage horror and TV, film and radio adaptations of John le Carré, as well as work on the philosophy of technology. Geraint is the author of *Critical Approaches to TV and Film Set Design* (Routledge, 2018) and has had creative works published in science-fiction short story collections and poetry zines. His next book is about *mise-en-scène* and acting in comics.

Richard J. Hand is Professor of Media Practice at the University of East Anglia, UK. He is the author of numerous studies of popular horror culture including two books on horror radio drama and is the co-author of three books on Grand Guignol horror theatre. He is the co-editor (with Jay McRoy) of *Monstrous Adaptations: Generic and Thematic Mutations in Horror Film* (Manchester University Press, 2007). He is the founding co-editor of the *Journal of Adaptation in Film and Performance*, and his interests include adaptation, translation and interdisciplinarity in performance media (with a particular interest in historical forms of popular culture, especially horror) using critical and practical research methodologies.

Adam Charles Hart is a Visiting Assistant Professor in English and Film and Media Studies at the University of Pittsburgh and has previously taught at North Carolina State University and Harvard University. He has published articles in the *New Review of Film and Television, Studies in the Fantastic, Imaginations*, the collection *The Companion to the Horror Film* (Wiley-Blackwell, 2014) and the *Journal of Cinema and Media Studies*. His monograph, *Monstrous Forms: Moving-Image Horror across Media* will be published in 2019 by Oxford University Press.

Mikel Koven is Senior Lecturer and Course Leader in Film Studies at the University of Worcester. While much of his research explores Italian horror and exploitation cinema in a variety of guises, specifically the *giallo*, he also writes on the interstices between folklore and popular cinema. He is the author of *La Dolce Morte: Vernacular Cinema and the Italian Giallo Film* (2006), *Film, Folklore, and Urban Legends* (2008) and *Blaxploitation Films* (2010).

Jay McRoy is Professor of English and Cinema Studies at the University of Wisconsin – Parkside. He is the author of *Nightmare Japan: Contemporary Japanese Horror Cinema* (Rodopi, 2008), the editor of *Japanese Horror Cinema* (Edinburgh University Press, 2005) and the co-editor (with Richard J. Hand) of *Monstrous Adaptations: Generic and Thematic Mutations in Horror Film* (Manchester University Press, 2007).

James L. Neibaur is a film historian and writer with over twenty-five published books as well as hundreds of articles including over forty essays in the *Encyclopedia Britannica*. Neibaur's books are film-by-film studies on such diverse subjects as Charlie Chaplin, Buster Keaton, Clark Gable, Jean Harlow, James Cagney, Jerry Lewis, Elvis Presley, Clint Eastwood and Jack Nicholson. He has also done books on the Charlie Chan film series and an overview of B-movie director William Beaudine. He regularly writes DVD reviews, book reviews and film essays on his website at: https://jln4151.wixsite.com/jlneibaur-writer.

Andrew Hock Soon Ng is Associate Professor of Literary Studies and Creative Writing at Monash University Malaysia. His research interests include Gothic and horror narratives, postcolonial writings and post-modern literature, and he has contributed articles to numerous peer-reviewed journals and collections of essays. His most recent monograph is *Women and Domestic Space in Contemporary Gothic Narratives: The House as Subject* (Palgrave, 2015).

Anna Powell retired from her post as Reader in English and Film at Manchester Metropolitan University to become an Honorary Research Fellow. She is the author of *Deleuze and Horror Film* and *Deleuze, Altered States and Film* and the co-author of *Teaching the Gothic*. She continues to publish articles and chapters on Deleuze and Gothic film and literature, its affects and effects. Among her recent research topics are Gothic children in *The Shining*, H. P. Lovecraft and Oc/cult film. Anna is a member of *Deleuze Studies* and *Dark Arts* editorial boards and founder of *A/V*, the online journal for Deleuze-related studies. As well as working as a visiting lecturer and running public study groups, she enjoys creative writing.

Laurence Raw was Professor of English at Baskent University, Turkey. His wide spectrum of interests as a scholar is reflected in his many publications including works on the adaptations of Henry James and Nathaniel Hawthorne, the films of Merchant Ivory and Ridley Scott, the science fiction and horror genres, radio drama and Turkish culture.

Laurence was also editor of the *Journal of American Studies of Turkey*. His final edited collection of essays is *Adapted from the Original: Essays on the Value and Values of Works Remade for a New Medium* (McFarland, 2018).

Elaine Roth is Professor of Film Studies at Indiana University South Bend where she is Co-director of the General Education programme. The co-editor of the collection *Motherhood Misconceived* (2009), she has also published articles in *Genders, Quarterly Review of Film and Literature* and *Feminist Media Studies*. Her most recent article, on active female protagonists with mothers in a range of US films, appeared in the *Journal of Popular Film and Television*. She teaches History of the Motion Picture and Film Genres, among other courses, and is currently working on two projects: one on Patricia Highsmith's novels and another on early women screenwriters.

Andy W. Smith is based in Cardiff, South Wales. He has published book chapters with Manchester University Press, Routledge and Oberon across a wide range of subject disciplines including horror cinema, postwar British Theatre and the Gothic in popular culture. He has also contributed chapters to *The Encyclopaedia of the Gothic* and the *Routledge Companion to the Gothic*. Andy is the co-editor with James Reynolds of *Howard Barker's Theatre: Wrestling with Catastrophe* (Bloomsbury, 2015), which was shortlisted for the Society for Theatre Research Book of the Year 2016. Andy works for the Quality Assurance Agency for Higher Education as the Quality and Standards Manager, responsible for the maintenance of the UK Quality Code for Higher Education.

Thomas Joseph Watson is an Associate Lecturer in Media, Film and Television at Northumbria University, specialising in representations of violence in screen media. His research focuses on aspects of horror cinema, cult film and transgressive media cultures. He is one of the co-editors of *Snuff: Real Death and Screen Media* (2016) and his forthcoming work includes chapters focusing on cinematic representations of underground music subcultures and radical politics in contemporary horror cinema ('The Kid's Are Alt-Right: Hardcore Punk and Subcultural Violence in *Green Room*') and the application of transgression as a label in cult film discourse.

Index